ON BENDED KNEES

The Night Rider Story

Bill Cunningham

McClanahan Publishing House, Incorporated,
Nashville, Tennessee

Copyright © 1983

McClanahan Publishing House, Inc.
Library of Congress Catalog Card No. 83 060651

ISBN — Hard: 0 913383 00 7 $15.95

All book order correspondence should be addressed to:
McClanahan Publishing House, Inc.
Rt. 2, Box 32, Kuttawa, Kentucky 42055

Dedicated to
PAULA

Hereditary bondsmen! Know ye not that by your own hands ye must be freed? Your own hands must strike the blow.

Lord Byron

Chapter 1

The shapely brunette withered in the dust on this warm spring night, bleeding profusely from the gunshot wound to her neck. She was lying in her own front yard underneath a towering oak.

Shouts and curses of hooded men brandishing rifles, shotguns and buggy whips completely overwhelmed the tranquil and bucolic sounds of katydids and crickets.

Also enveloping the evening air were the wailing groans of her husband. He was being held to a nearby tree by three men, the back of his nightgown shredded and matted with blood. Two other masked assailants applied their lashes to the suffering victim under the flickering fire brand.

But most prolonged and poignant were screams of a thirteen-year-old boy standing nearby in the shadows watching his parents being beaten and kicked by this heinous group of masqueraders.

After a dreadful time, the beatings ceased and one of the attackers stepped forward and placed a last resounding kick to the posterior of the weeping beauty.

With that the mob slowly moved out of the tiny enclosure which surrounded the small farmhouse. In an orderly fashion they filed through the gate out onto the road and silently disappeared into the night.

Only then did the natural sounds of a peaceful spring night come back and mingle with the sobbing and painful cries of the vanquished family.

**

It is a beautiful plant — dark tobacco.

Perhaps the most beautiful plant in America.

In full bloom, it stands in the warm summer earth about four and one-half feet high. The full deep green leaves fold out from the thick stalk, curling slightly at their ends, back toward the ground. The breadth of the leaves may reach fifteen inches. Rising at the top is the bloom, a flower which must be "topped" before harvesting.

But it is the color which provides a character of its own. Its deep olive green complexion fixed against the background of bleached August soil and hazy blue sky frames it like a huge shadow — like a dark cloud upon the land. It is a parent tobacco of the lighter colored burley and, to a great degree, shares the same controversial history.

"Tobacco is a nasty weed," so spoke King James I of England in 1604 while in a rather lyrical mood. "Right from the hell they brought the seed. It fouls the mouth and soils the clothes and makes a chimney of the nose."

This such maligned "nasty weed" is a relative newcomer as far as agricultural crops are concerned. We are sure that it was unknown to those first tillers who began to scrape the earth for a living in the Tigris Euphrates Valley in 9,000 B.C. Wheat, barley, rye and even corn have taken most of the attention of the world farmer.

Those prehistoric pipes and smoking devices excavated from ancient sites bordering the Mediterranean Sea are thought to have been used for smoking marijuana and other types of plants — not tobacco. There is no evidence that tobacco was used anywhere in the world prior to the discovery and exploration of the Americas. In fact, it is likely that the natives of the Western Hemisphere were the ones who developed the growth and use of this green narcotic plant with the assistance of the Spanish Conquistadors. Many varieties of the herb grew wild. The American Indian — like the early explorers — was expert in extracting the medicinal or narcotic benefits from all plants.

Tobacco was to be American long before apple pie, if not motherhood. In fact it was reported that, in 1492, the voyagers with Columbus were greeted with gifts of this spirited leaf as a sign of friendship on behalf of the native Americans.

After the first visitors to the Western Hemisphere became "contaminated" by the craze for tobacco, its appeal spread around the globe. By 1565 traders and sailors had taken back so much of the dark leaf that its use was the fashion of the day throughout Europe.

The growth and export of tobacco became an early occupation

of Virginia farmers when John Roth acquired from Cuba seed for a milder type than that which the natives were smoking. It was established as Jamestown's primary export. By 1664, the colonies were exporting 24,000,000 pounds per year. Thus, the plant was no longer just a fashionable plaything — it was serious business.

And a serious business it was ever to remain.

In America, a few states quickly took an early lead in the growing and processing of tobacco. Out of the leading tobacco growing colonies, Virginia and North Carolina were equally proficient in the production of tobacco as were the newer states of Kentucky and Tennessee. This crop was especially accommodating to the vast woodlands of the South since it required much smaller patches of land to be hacked out of the forests. A large yield per acre as well as the close care and supervision required has always confined tobacco to a relatively small plot of farming land.

Even the pre-Revolutionary War tobacco boom did not escape the revenue raising eyes of government. King James I, the same monarch who wrote so harshly against the intrinsic evils of this product, nevertheless found tobacco lucrative to the English treasury when he imposed an excise tax upon it, which, by the mid-1700's, reached two shillings a hogshead on all leaf shipped from the colonies.

This was the first movement of government into the tobacco trade. It would not, however, be the last or even the most important.

Soon there evolved in America different strains of tobacco bearing varying colors, textures and uses — all of which depended upon general geographical locations. The tobacco plant of the growing trade was not measurably different in color or texture from that of the Aboriginal culture, except for a larger leaf and a slightly smaller stalk. That is, not until 1864 when there appeared a revolutionary strain of tobacco.

It is not known exactly how this lighter golden leaf of tobacco first evolved upon the agricultural scene. In all likelihood, it developed by accident and spontaneously in different locations throughout the country. We do know that in Brown County, Ohio, on the farm of Captain Fred Kaute in the spring of 1864, two of Kaute's tenants were seeding tobacco beds when they ran out of seeds. They quickly crossed the Ohio River into Kentucky to purchase enough seed to round out their planting. But the added seed seemed to produce strange looking plants — fine, textured leaves dirty yellow in color and somewhat fragile. As the plants matured to full growth in the field, they possessed a creamy stalk and pale green leaves marked by a white vein of superlatively fine light texture that cured out to a handsome, almost golden light tan.

At first it was thought to be an inferior mutation undesirable for marketing. But it didn't take long for growers and buyers alike to discover that this "white" burley had advantages over the dark tobacco.

During the Civil War, the Yankee troops invading the South had acquired a great taste for the sweet flavor of twist or plug tobacco. In fact, it may have been one of the few good things to come out of that grim, devastating era of the South. Southern boys, long on chewing tobacco but short on coffee, would often trade Confederate "plugs" to the Yankee soldiers under a truce for "camp luxuries."

In this way — unknowingly and certainly unintended — these homesick, war-tattered youngsters were opening up new markets for future generations of Southern farmers. After the war, there was a great demand in the North for plug tobacco. As it turned out, however, the light burley was much preferred because of its milder, sweeter chew and the ability of this variety of leaf to absorb more quantity of the sweetening and flavoring agents. The manufacturers of plug tobacco could mix it well with the darker tobaccos to meet the public's fancy.

It was also preferred for smoking tobacco for similar reasons. The success of this strain of tobacco was thus assured, and its cultivation and consumption quickly spread throughout the country. By 1867 the white burley had won both first and second place prizes at the St. Louis Fair and Exposition and sold for the unbelievable price of 58¢ per pound.

The new leaf was also much easier for the farmers to grow and process. The curing did not require smoking the tobacco over smoldering hickory coals as did dark tobacco, and it got to the market much quicker — usually before Christmas. This, needless to say, was an important advantage to the impoverished, cash starved farmers of the South.

With the exploding effect that the white burley had on an already expanding market, the tobacco trade simply leaped by gigantic bounds after the Civil War. The leaf became one of Kentucky's economic mainstays. By 1870, factories in the Bluegrass state were turning out over 2 million dollars worth of tobacco products. This was mostly in the form of chewing tobacco and snuff. Nationwide, the cigarette — now machine made and mass produced — was beginning to dominate the tobacco boom. Name brands were cascading upon the American public at a dazzling rate.

The year of 1890 marked the high water mark to date for tobacco in this country. It was then that the nation enjoyed a state of prosperity. It was also at that time that everyone — growers, buyers, merchants, and manufacturers — were making money on King James' "nasty weed."

As that last decade of the century began, Kentucky had a bountiful year, increasing its production from over 50 million pounds to 221 million pounds making it by far the leading tobacco producing state in this country.

There were 38 factories in Kentucky making chewing and smoking tobacco by 1890. The giant among them was the National Tobacco Works of Louisville which accounted for a whopping 15 percent of the nation's plug.

For the farmer in the field, prices were settling in at a very comfortable 8 to 12¢ per pound for both light and dark tobaccos. This provided a solid profit for his hard labor and established this crop firmly as the main cash crop — excepting cotton — throughout the South, especially in Kentucky and Tennessee. Good prices encouraged greater production in the 1890's, and consumption was still keeping pace.

Until that crested date of 1890, competition had been fierce in the marketplace. The number of buyers and manufacturers were great and the advertising war ferocious, as evidenced by the fact that there were more than 12,000 different brands in the hands of the American consumer. The plug named "Battleax" seemed an appropriate label for the stiff competition of those times.

But, by the mid 1890's, the capitalistic laws of survival began to take their toll and most of the competing businesses fell more and more into the hands of fewer and larger companies.

The small manufacturer and seller of tobacco products — including chewing, plug, cigarettes, cigars and bagged pipe tobacco — had all but disappeared toward the end of the century. Ten large manufacturers now controlled 60 percent of the plug trade in America. Americans of the waning years of the 19th century were watching something happen to the tobacco business similar to that which succeeding generations would witness in the second half of the 20th century to the beer industry. It was a fond farewell to the

Ma and Pa ventures and an ushering in of the monolithic business powers.

One of the surviving and prosperous companies was that of W. Duke & Sons of Durham, North Carolina.

James Buchanan Duke, by any measure, is one of the most formidable men in the history of American commerce.

Born December 23, 1856, Buck, as he was early called, lost his mother to typhoid fever when he was only 20 months old. It was the second time that his father, Washington Duke, had been widowed and was now left with two sons by each wife.

Before Buck reached the age of 5 years, the booming guns of Fort Sumter erupted some 300 miles southeast of his Durham North Carolina home. Neither his 43 years nor his stout disagreement with the cause kept Washington Duke from being conscripted into the Confederate forces.

Washington Duke's farm had grown to 300 acres and was well stocked when he turned it over to a neighbor. He left the three youngest children with his late wife's parents, John and Mary Roney, in Almance, North Carolina. His oldest son, Brodie, then seventeen, also marched off to war with the Gray.

Buck, the most prodigious and energetic of the group, was pretty much incubated from the horrors and tragedies of that bloody war as he whiled away those turbulent years on the quiet and elegant grounds of his Roney grandparents.

But, as soon as it was over in the spring of 1865, Buck was to learn quickly the brutal economic consequences of that conflict. His ragged and impoverished father strolled back from the war and up to the door of Granddaddy Roney's home on a warm April afternoon to reclaim his offspring and to take them back to what was left of the family farm.

What was left was not much.

As it turned out, however, it was enough to ultimately affect the far-flung markets of the world.

As twice-widowed Washington Duke stood with his young children and surveyed the wreckage brought about by the merciless Union forces, all must have seemed hopeless. The cropland was barren and the farm depleted of any food or livestock. Most of the buildings left, including the house, had been stripped of their contents.

But Washington Duke's Yankee enemies had left behind one valuable prize — a barn full of the previous year's yield of tobacco. It had apparently not seemed worth either taking or destroying by the marauding troops from the North.

Wash pondered the situation. He discovered two blind mules grazing in a nearby field. He seized upon an idea for survival. He immediately put his family and hands to work together, flailing out the tobacco in the barn. Then Buck began a peddling tour of eastern North Carolina at a time when the region was still reeling in economic shock and devastation.

It was a romantic, if arduous, time for young Buck Duke. He and his father traveled with their tobacco on a wagon pulled by the old team of mules. In the back of the wagon, along with their produce, they also carried their blankets, a water barrel, and a wooden box containing cooking utensils along with their daily diet of bacon, cornmeal, and sweet potatoes. These vagabonds slept out under the stars around a campfire much like gypsies as they made their way across the red clay of North Carolina.

But this excursion was a financial success and was followed by many others. Out on the rutted Carolina backroads, bumping along from town to town, young Buck Duke had plenty of time to think and to plan. There was a bright future for light tobacco, he thought. Washington Duke agreed. They made a formidable combination — the experience and wisdom of the elder mingled with the dynamic energy and daring of the son.

Both Dukes knew the capricious and fickled nature of growing tobacco. It was a lengthy process, starting in early spring and ending in late fall. The profit depended upon quality, and quality depended upon skill, expertise and a good share of luck as well. A mid-summer drought, too much spring rain, or an irregular curing season could turn a year's work into ruin.

The Dukes decided early on to let the other farmers grow the leaf. They would sell it.

And sell it they did.

It wasn't long before the old tobacco barn from which they started became much too small and inadequate for the ballooning stock of purchased tobacco. The Dukes then bought a log "factory" where their newly named "Probono Publico" tobacco — later called "Duke's Mixture" — could be granulated and packed.

But that facility too was soon outgrown by the Dukes' success and was replaced by a larger frame structure equipped with an old styled screw press where the tobacco could either be squeezed into plugs or ground into smoking tobacco.

In 1866, Wash Duke and his sons — including Brodie and Ben — turned out 15,000 pounds of tobacco from that little factory in Durham. By 1872, the business was growing like the teenage Buck Duke. But he still traveled on his sales trips throughout the state with great thrift — sometimes sleeping on trains to save the cost of lodging.

Buck Duke was tireless. Every waking hour, every thinking moment, he poured into the tobacco venture. Even though still a boy physically, his concept of business and the world around him was racing far ahead of his years. He bossed the help of the factory, assisted in labeling the bags, and delivered the goods to country stores where he acquired new orders.

But, as valuable to the business as he was, it was still a family effort. Wash Duke grew through the middle years of life toughened by his war experiences and with a lasting memory of want etched across his mind. He, like the classic father, set the example, policy and goals for their frantic pace. Most importantly, he possessed the wisdom that tempered the occasional rashness of young Buck's energy. Brother Brodie brought to the effort the vision and imagination which set the aim for a much larger enterprise than any of them had ever imagined. He would not be a part of that venture much longer as he set out on his own and, in later years, his cavalier ways placed him in an estranged relationship with his family. Benjamin Duke, however, with his sound judgment and managerial skills, would become a solid member of the family partnership. Still, young Buck remained the most intense, looking upon sleep and leisure as enemies of man.

By 1880, Durham, North Carolina, had become the tobacco capital of the world. The leading firm there was the Bull Durham Company, processing 20,000 pounds of tobacco each day. But W. Duke & Sons Company, as this family business was now known, was picking up steam. It was expanding its facilities frequently and taking in new and experienced partners from other companies. Serious, rough and aggressive, young Buck was beginning to lead the charge.

Now a peculiar thing began happening to the industry.

Cigarettes.

Granular tobacco has been rolled in thin paper and smoked for a long time. Up until the Civil War, tobacco was primarily smoked in the traditional pipe. The discovery of the milder, lighter type of tobacco caused cigarette smoking to catch on. Northern soldiers returning home had acquired a taste for this Southern product, and a growing demand for cigarette tobacco began to rival that of cigars, pipe leaf, snuff and chewing tobacco.

Of even lesser number in those antebellum days were the "factory made" cigarettes. Most were handrolled by the smoker himself from fine slips of rice paper and filled from small drawstring bags which contained granular tobacco. Less than 2 million cigarettes were factory-made in the United States in 1869. But, within ten years, the cigarette boom had already begun.

Buck Duke caught a bracing whiff of the cigarette trend and quickly seized the initiative. He hired some of the best cigarette rollers in the country for the Duke Company and began to manufacture cigarettes on a large scale. Markets were expanded westward to Atlanta, St. Louis, and beyond.

Cigarette packaging and promotion was a new concept to late 19th century America. Buck Duke became a master — initiating many of the tricks of the trade we know so well today. Free samples, billboard advertising, personal endorsements by stage stars and — believe it or not — athletes were all part of the Duke cigarette push.

It caught on like wildfire.

Assisted significantly by a crackerjack salesman named Edward Small, the Duke Company's "Pinhead," "Cameo," and "Crosscut" cigarettes began to sell by the millions.

In the spring of 1884, the business of the Duke clan had begun to take on the semblance of an economic empire. Cigarette machines, up until that time thought to be a faulty and undependable substitute for the hired hand, were perfected and in operation at the Dukes' factory. This substantially increased their production.

Representatives of the company were sent overseas to set up international markets around the globe. Young Buck Duke, now 24 years old, surprised his old father and everyone concerned by taking his rough and tumble ways to the big city of New York, the bustling hub of a young country now stretching its muscles. There, from his seedy $10 a week room on Gramercy Park, he prepared to take over the leading markets of the world.

In New York, through sheer determination, perseverance and hard work, Buck Duke steadily broke into big city business by personally visiting the many jobbers and retail tobacconists. From that booming city, Duke directed the mass advertisement drive that promoted their product which was now being turned out at an enormous rate.

He overwhelmed people with his confidence, his salty language, Southern drawl, and occasional breach of manners. This robust youngster with a wad of dark tobacco swellings in his cheek was more than a match for the stiff moguls of Wall Street. Within two years, this city of chaos and yearning immigrants sported one of the Duke plants. The competitors were feeling the sting of this country upstart.

Socially, Buck Duke was rebuffed by his business peers. The city men of starched collars and Derby hats did not include him in their social circles. Never mind. "While they eat and drink and talk, I work," was Buck's gruff response.

James Buchanan Duke, now a full-grown man in all respects, was the recognized leader of the family business even though the venerable father back in Durham was still respected as a solid patriarch. This youngest and brightest of the Dukes was a man obsessed with business. "I hated to close my desk at night," he later revealed, "and was eager to get back into it early the next morning. I need no vacation or time off. No fellow does who is really interested in work. There ain't a thrill in the world to compare with building of the business and watching it grow before your eyes."

Of course, Buck Duke possessed the qualities of all great businessmen — brillance, energy, ambition and an uncluttered and ruthless mind. But probably the greatest talent he had was his ability to attract, develop and retain greater talents than his own. From far and wide came men who were tops in their respective fields to join the Duke forces. Manufacturing, promoting, marketing, advertising, selling, and financing were all fields of expertise in a firm which was becoming amply stocked by first rate personnel.

Duke was fully aware of their value, smugly satisfying himself as he watched them become wealthy men in their own right. He astutely recognized their being paid well for their efforts would in return benefit him and his family.

By 1890, there were over 2.1 billion cigarettes consumed in the United States. W. Duke & Sons Company of New York and Durham, North Carolina, produced 940 million of that total. Over a period of five years, Buck Duke had driven the company past its competitors and into a large and comfortable lead.

But the enterprising men of W. Duke & Sons Company had much more than cigarettes on their minds. At last, Buck Duke wanted their world dominion over all tobacco markets to include the cigar and plug tobacco trade. Although his father, Wash, now quite old yet still active, expressed strong concern about the mounting complexities of the company's almost unbelievable growth, Buck set out not merely to compete against, but to eliminate, the competition.

What followed was one of the most spectacular epics of corporate monopolization in the history of this country.

Tailoring his scheme after John D. Rockefeller's Standard Oil phenomenon, Buck began at first to simply buy out the leading competitors. In 1889, he put together the American Tobacco Company, astonishing the business world by consolidating into it some of the leading firms of the day with the Duke family firmly in control. Companies such as the powerful Allen & Ginter Company and the prestigious William S. Kimball Company and Kinney Tobacco Company all fell into line. Duke did this by his hard nosed and convincing bargaining techniques with the leading men of the respective companies. Though not personally popular, he had nevertheless gained their respect as evidenced by being elected President of the new firm. He was at the young age of 32 the acknowledged leader of the industry.

Buck Duke, if not greedy, held an insatiable appetite for more power, business, profits — more everything. Like a kid on the roll at the playboard of monopoly, James B. Duke was piling up the stakes with every move. His creativity, like his ambition, knew no bounds.

The American Tobacco Company bought up the rights for the exclusive use of the most successful cigarette making machines. The company began brutal "cut rate" tactics to stagger what competition was left. In some areas thousands of dollars would be lost simply to underprice and freeze out the opposition.

And while cigarettes were the raging vice in vogue, Duke did not overlook other branches of the business — namely, the plug and chewing tobacco fields.

The people of this country were still predominantly a tobacco chewing, not smoking, congregation. In Louisville, Kentucky, for instance, the longtime successful firm of Pfingst, Doerhoefer & Company which dealt exclusively with manufacturing plug tobacco caught the eye of Buck Duke. In January of 1891, it too was swallowed up by the American Tobacco Company due to Duke's mixture of conjoling and intimidation of the firm's leading people. In that same year, numerous other smaller companies were pyramided under the American Tobacco Company. This was all accomplished through high finance manipulation whereby the interests of their respective businesses would be transferred to a parent company while members of their respective boards would join the larger conglomerate with either non-existent or minimal influence.

This trickery and deceit was oftentimes used to avoid the restriction of state anti-trust laws. Many times the company would own the interests or subsidiaries, yet allow them to operate ostensibly independently while maintaining their name and personnel and keeping the ownership a close secret. In addition to the cigarette monolopy, the American Tobacco Company now held an entangling and exclusive stranglehold on cigar, snuff and plug tobacco markets in this country.

In 1894, in spite of the national economic panic of '93, the American Tobacco Company netted over 5 million dollars. While most of these profits came from cigarettes, Uncle Buck — as the master was already being called — turned his attention more and more to the plug tobacco trade.

As the 19th century faded away into history, the powerful trust of the American Tobacco Company ruled the entire tobacco industry in this country. It produced 92.7 percent of the cigarettes, 80.2 percent of the snuff, 62 percent of the plug tobacco and 59.2 percent of smoking tobacco.

But Buck Duke was still not satisfied. From his office on Fifth Avenue in New York, he began to seriously think about controlling all of the world markets by monopolizing international tobacco trades. The Duke interest was being represented already in such far places as Australia, New Zealand, India, China and Japan. Buck himself initiated an invasion of the tobacco markets of Great Britain. He caused the American Tobacco Company to buy up numerous foreign companies and finally, after a long and bitter price war with the companies of England, he entered into an agreement with their firms, thus enhancing his position on the international markets.

World dominion — it was the last frontier for this mighty conglomerate to conquer.

By 1900, the Duke Trust, as it was now referred to by most people, had sales representatives around the globe. The tobacco products of the American Tobacco Company were being consumed by everyone from proper British gentlemen of Picadilly to the ancient and remote herdsmen of Tibet.

Selling and making money overseas was not enough for James B. Duke. That was competing with other companies. As much as he loved to compete, there was one thing he loved more — to win. According to his own unique Duke philosophy, the way to ultimately win in business was to eliminate or at least neutralize — monopolize — the opposition.

Through his own strong persistence, price wars, and a mixture of intimidation and Southern charm, Duke led the American Tobacco Company into a merger with international firms which was favorable and gave this American firm a considerably better position in the world markets. In 1904, a reorganization plan by the American Tobacco Company allowed it to continue its aggressive policy of absorption and domination which had placed it at the top of the tobacco world.

The Trust now sold 82 percent of this country's cigarettes and chewing tobacco. In the process, the Trust used 400 million pounds of leaf tobacco.

It was a phenomenal power.

This company, through its consolidations, was manufacturing literally hundreds of different brands of both cigarettes and chewing tobacco — all, of course, under the same control. Profits were skyrocketing, averaging in 1903 around 32 million dollars annually. The bulk of the earnings went to the Dukes and a few other lesser men who assisted them in controlling the business.

On May 8, 1905, shortly after falling and breaking his hip, the old founding father, Wash Duke, died at the age of 85 at his Durham home. In the latter years of his life, he had become not only awed but somewhat frightened by the startling size of the Duke Trust. He had become sensitive to the growing criticism leveled at the Duke family by the increasing number of farmers who were receiving less and less for their tobacco because of the diminishing competition between buyers. The North Carolina Press was blaming the Trust for cutting the price of tobacco in half and robbing the farmers of more than 5 million dollars on their 1904 crop alone. In the tobacco patches of the Southeast, the Duke name was increasingly becoming associated with falling prices and rising poverty among the farmers.

Although there remained to the end a special fondness in old Wash Duke's heart for his youngest son, he was nevertheless overwhelmed by Buck's unbelievable drive for power. He supposedly remarked in his latter years that, "There are three things that I could never understand: electricity, the Holy Ghost, and my son Buck."

Perhaps as he reflected and mused during those last months of his life, Wash Duke returned in spirit to the red clay, one mule tobacco farm of his father. Perhaps that was where his heart had been all along. In any case, he died and his son, Buck Duke, undaunted by either his father's demise or the farmers' complaints, continued to march.

Chapter 2

In history, East always marries West.

It has been so since the descendants of the Garden of Eden left Mesopotamia to go westward to the land of Ur, and Father Abraham moved westward to the Land of God — Canaan. From the ancient Pyramids to the medieval castles of Europe to the settlement at Jamestown, civilization has moved westward. And so it was simply another small step in the grand historical scheme of things for many of the early settlers of the Carolinas to move westward into what is now Tennessee and beyond.

The movement which began almost as soon as the first white man grew tired of his neighbor's chimney smoke continued for many years. Not until the grand Pacific Ocean blocked the stream of humanity did going west lose some of its momentum.

There was no easy way of traveling across the virgin territory of this continent in the days of old. On foot at first, then by horseback and later by wagon train, the trips took a tremendous toll on those brave travelers. One method of trangressing that proved easier than all the rest was by water, following the currents of rivers and streams to their mouths. Flatboats and crude wooden rafts were built and steered out into the mainstream of the current where these vessels would simply move along sluggishly but constantly, laden with their passengers and meager belongings. It was not only an easier way to travel, but also provided better protection from violent ambush by hostile Redskins.

Unfortunately, few rivers ran downstream from east to west, at least not for a measurable distance. When the high spirited and determined frontiersmen from North Carolina moved westward into Tennessee, however, they found not one, but two such resourceful streams moving the way they were going.

Immediately northwest of the North Carolina Smokey Mountain Range along the Virginia border, small streams from the mountains flow together to form the head of the Tennessee River.

From there it ambles southwesterly. It was, in frontier days, a meandering lengthy cruise for those brave wanderers. But it was scenic, easy and relatively safe; equally important, its shoreline provided bountiful game. Most crucially to those starry-eyed dreamers, it headed west, if in its own good time.

If determined travelers of yesteryear did not wish to catch that particular river, they could cross it and stroll a thousand blocks or so to another transit.

The smaller, faster Cumberland River was the express route. Out of Kentucky it runs from the area of the Cumberland Gap, circling through the tip of Tennessee. While more narrow, it was also a swifter stream. It heads westward in a much more direct route through similar terrain as its sister waters at the southern part of the state. Then it too, like the head of a huge snake, points upward and moves into the western end of Kentucky, paralleling the Tennessee River so closely at places that their flood waters mingled. This smaller but most scenic waterway joined the mighty Ohio just eight miles north of where the Tennessee emptied out into that same river. Perhaps no other place in the world do two such resourceful rivers run so closely together for such distance and end their streaming so near to one another.

All of this river talk is a way of saying, historically and geo-graphically, that many Carolinians from early time on not only moved westward into Tennessee but were also funneled in great numbers by these two convenient streams into what is now the extreme western part of Tennessee and Kentucky.

This movement was further enhanced by the setting aside of large portions of land in Kentucky and Tennessee by the fledgling new United States of America as land grants to persons who had served in the Revolutionary cause and had not been adequately paid because of the depleted treasury. Many Revolutionary War veterans from the Carolinas, especially veterans of the famous battle of King's Mountain, were compensated for their services with land in this Western frontier. A great number of them moved to make their own claim, while others sold their interests and allowed others to move in their stead.

In any case, many North Carolinians, including Daniel Boone, came to Kentucky through the famed Cumberland Gap in the eastern part of the state. Many others came to the western part of the state directly through the use of the two river routes. Although separated by the length of Tennessee, there is a very strong histori-cal and cultural tie between the people of western Kentucky and

Tennessee with their ancestral land of North Carolina.

Western Kentucky is a soft and pleasant land. Watered by faithful yearly rainfall with a moderate climate and, in spite of sweltering humidity during the summer months, it was during those early days, as it is today, an attractive place to live. Hardwoods of hickory, ash and oak were abundant upon the rolling hills and bottom lands. It is delta country — the Mississippi bordering to the west, the Ohio on the north, and the Tennessee and Cumberland cutting through the middle. Yet it lacks the low, flat desolateness that is normally associated with river country.

It was, before the days of asphalt and concrete, a land reminiscent of the old country. With rolling hills and small streams, dark woods and sunlit meadows, it smacked of home to many who had been natives to Scotland, Ireland and Wales. Even today, when riding along the backroads of Kentucky, a motorist can still be impressed with its ancient scenery.

Tobacco became a regular crop with that earthy stock of settlers who first began to scratch small plots for planting out of the wilderness. At first a few plants would be mingled with their corn or wheat, just enough for their own personal use. Rapidly it became a cash crop as market towns and transportation developed. By this time in American expansion, white farmers were not learning tobacco from the Indians but bringing it overland from the hands of their own ancestors whom they had left in the East in Virginia, Maryland and the Carolinas.

The "dark tobacco" of frontier western Kentucky, as distinguished from the lighter burley which has since come upon the scene, has always been a crop requiring special care. Through the years, the growing of dark tobacco has pretty much settled into a certain section in western Kentucky and western Tennessee called the Black Patch. This name has derived from the deep olive, almost ebony, color of the leaf.

The rolling land with an abundance of hardwood gave rise very early to the delicate and fine art of fire-curing the dark leaf. Since this type of tobacco is used primarily for chewing and for snuff, it was discovered quite by accident that applying smoke to the leaf while it was housed in the barn gave it not only a more malleable and varnished texture, but also a distinct and desirable flavor.

It became a tiresome and involved task — this growing and firing of dark tobacco. Those men who would learn to grow it and pass their knowledge down to following generations were dedicated to the art from necessity since, for many small farmers, it was their only cash crop. So they stayed with it, even though it worked them every month of the year.

The ordeal would begin — if one could tell the beginning from the end — in late winter, preferably on an unseasonably warm day. A long rectangular patch of earth would be cleared on the slope of some hill and burned off with old logs and dead limbs. The purpose of the burning was not only to adequately clear the spot but also to create much needed potash in the soil from the wooden ashes. Burning was also the most efficient way of assuring that weeds would have a late start. With the clearing of the plantbed finished, long poles were placed alongside the cleared area and the soil was worked into a fine texture whereupon tobacco seeds would be broadcast. To protect the early growing plants against the cold, a cotton canvas covering was staked out over the plantbed and left in place until after the last frost. This time worn procedure, with very little margin for error, was perhaps the most crucial. A bad plantbed meant retarded — or worse yet — nonexisting plants, upon which all future fortunes would rest.

Of course, while the young seeds nestled under the canvas and then began to sprout, the field had to be prepared on which the young tobacco plants would be transferred and eventually grow to maturity. Sometimes it was new ground, cleared by chopping down trees and cutting away underbrush. Stumps would then have to be burned and, in many cases, hooked to log chains and pulled out by mules. Only then could the ground be broken and harrowed several times. It was torturous, time-consuming work.

The spring rains would come, and the days would grow long and warm. Plants grew to above the ankles, then the canvas was removed. It was then time for "drawing" and setting. The plants were taken up by hand from the plantbed and replanted in the open field. It was best to begin this phase after a slow, steady rain with the ground soft and even muddy when the burning sun reappeared. Then all family hands were called into service — men, women and children. Rows were staked out three feet apart, and the plants were set at the same intervals up and down the lines in hills. One person dropped the plant, another followed with a sharp stick known as a tobacco peg, punching a hole in the spongy ground and dropping in a plant. Another hand close behind packed the mud in over the roots.

The tobacco plants, for a while at least, were on their own. It would oftentimes take even these toughened and conditioned people of the earth days to get over the aching pains that settled in their backs from the constant stooping.

Once the plant was in the field, hard work became mixed with agonizing worry about the weather. A prolonged drought would mean disaster. Too much rain would mean the same. And, if the weather was just right, the work would be even harder for then the weeds would grow with the plants and have to be hoed out so that the young tobacco crop would have a fighting chance of survival. Tobacco worms appeared and had to be plucked off the plants by the hands of farmers who moved slowly and painstakingly up and down the rows examining every part of each plant. Usually they flung them into cans of kerosene. Children simply squeezed them and dropped the remains. Late in the growing season, flower buds grew upon the plant and had to be "topped" in order to give the plants a fuller body. Small suckers growing in between the stems and stalks also had to be removed or "suckered" by hand.

As the tobacco plants finally reached their full height and their broad dark leaves unfolded, there would usually be one late summer hurdle yet to overcome — the hailstorm. For in this land of western Kentucky and Tennessee, hail came ripping down out of the August skies in fearsome and destructive sizes. It was not unusual for such a storm to rip the leaves and pound the plants down into the dirt.

Finally, at the end of the growing season when all the risks of nature had been bested, it came time for the cutting. In late August or early September, after the plant had reached its rich dark color, the farmers moved in under skies of blue with their cutting tools.

The stalks were split from the top down to about eight inches above the ground. The plants were then cut down and hung on wooden racks upside down to wilt. Then six to eight plants were placed on a tobacco stick through the slit in the stalk and allowed to be scaffolded in the field for several days for open air curing. Next, these sticks of tobacco were "housed" in the tobacco barns which were normally composed of one huge lofty square room with wooden tiers running across at different levels. At least four men would form a passing line going from the ground up into the barn at the very top, and the sticks of tobacco weighing from 15 to 30 pounds would be passed hand over head up to the top and hung across the tier. All day long this backbreaking work would continue until the barn was full.

With the tobacco housed, the hardest work came to an end and the most delicate art of "firing tobacco" began.

This is a most peculiar and demanding process, unique to the region and dependent upon the use of hardwood — mostly hickory. It was done then, as it is today, to attract the interest of manufacturers of snuff and plug tobacco who have traditionally given a higher price for leaf which has a smoked flavor.

The "firing" was accomplished by first digging ditches into the earthen floors of the barns. Hardwood sticks, preferably hickory, were then set afire in these trenches and immediately smothered to a slow burn by sawdust, quantities of which were kept piled high just outside the barn door. The thick smoke from this continuous smoldering would rise in the tight barn to envelop the tobacco hanging over the coals. Finally, it would seep out through the cracks and roofline, giving the surrounding bucolic air a mixed aroma of tobacco and hickory smoke. At this point, the tobacco's future can not be left to anyone but an experienced hand. Vigilant hands must be at the ready, and the firing process must be closely and adeptly watched. While temperatures in the barn should not exceed 100 degrees, it is not unusual for the heat to reach such intensity as to make the outside planking uncomfortable to the touch. The disastrous kindling point must be avoided by all means as one small spark at the wrong place can send the entire barn up into flames and the farmer's entire year's work with it.

The sight of smoke billowing out of old unpainted tobacco barns sitting serenely in the autumn sun has caused many a stranger to the region — city slickers, of course, — to stop at the nearest house to report the fire to bemused residents.

The fires were kept smoldering until the tobacco obtained a good finish of even color, malleable texture and a thin glaze. At that time the barn would be opened and the moist air allowed to circulate until the leaf "came in order," normally two to three weeks. By this time, usually in the late fall, the leaf is stripped from the stalk and tied in "hands" composed of six to ten leaves each. This task was normally reserved for rainy days since it was performed indoors, usually within the barn itself.

This procedure of stripping and bulking and arranging for shipment was the last step of the farmer's year long labor. After the final step, normally in late December or early January, the finished crop of dark fired tobacco was taken to market. It was one of the few enjoyable times of this demanding ordeal. Usually, late in the evening, these stripped leaves would be loaded into wagons pulled by mules. Through the night the farmer, along with his excited children, would travel to the nearest market town arriving there in the early morning hours. There, as the "floors" would open, the tobacco would be unloaded, graded, and packed in hogsheads which were large, wooden barrels or casks used for storing the tobacco. The successful farmer would then get his cash, pay off numerous bills, some as much as a year old, and then, if the crop had been good enough, treat his wife and children to some new clothes and maybe even a toy and some sweets for the youngsters.

It was a gala time for all if the crops were good and the prices right.

But even while one crop was being finished and hauled to market, work had already begun preparing the plantbeds for the following season as the rigorous cycle went on and on.

There were good years and bad years and, like almost everything else, fluctuation in the prices for tobacco. But, since there was always a great demand for the crop, prime leaf was kept at around 8 to 12¢ per pound. Western Kentucky and Tennessee dark-fired tobacco went to the four corners of the world. The product came about only through life-ebbing toil and trouble.

The men and women who pursued this way of life in Kentucky and Tennessee were like farmers everywhere in days of old, a unique blend of human being. Tough, compassionate, stoic, and perservering, they passed the art of growing tobacco down through the generations.

Families rose long before dawn and quickly consumed their hog meat, eggs and black coffee. By lamplight they plodded through the cold winter or the humid vapor of summer dawns to feed their stock and milk their cows.

The menfolk and able-bodied boys would hitch up the mules and move to the summer fields or winter woodlots just as the gray lines of dawn were streaking the eastern horizon. It was not unusual for tobacco farmers to arrive in the fields before it was light enough to see. There they would stand in the dew-drenched weeds silently watching and listening to nature come alive. As the sky to the east turned red and grew light, they could at last see the green worm on the tobacco leaf and begin the day of labor.

The women, normally blessed with smaller children or burdened with elderly kin at home, were in constant motion. The repeated, mind-numbing chores are too numerous to list. Whether cooking over wood stoves in the heat of summer or washing clothes in the outside winter air with numbing hands, it made no difference.

Theirs was a dreary plight.

Nighttime meant early bed and hopefully uninterrupted sleep. But sick children were the rule, and the crackling cough and feverish cry of a baby most often mingled with the midnight sound of a wooden rocker bumping rhythmatically against the floor.

This weary routine lasted from Monday to Saturday at noon. At that time, the menfolk would usually take off and go to town or to a crossroad's grocery store. There, in the farflung hamlets, villages, and gathering places across this rugged land, they would visit and discuss the main topics of the day, usually weather and crops mixed with a little politics. Young boys would tag along and meet a girlfriend if they were of the age, or simply run and frolic with other boys if they were younger. Meanwhile, the women would normally continue to slave away at the house taking care of the chores of cleaning, washing, cooking and making soap.

Only on Sunday was there some respite for all. Then the entire family visited the House of the Lord. The men would take their weekly baths, dress in clean work shirts and their freshly washed pair of overalls. The women wore their best dresses, and the children were scrubbed and combed. At the small crossroads church, their hard life would be relieved only by the promise of a better one to come if they lived the straight and narrow. But, even then, the emphasis was most times placed on the dreary prospects of hell, brimstone, and deathbed horror stories.

The Sabbath was not without its work, however. The women still had large meals to prepare and the men livestock to tend. Large families and many children were necessary to work the farm, but they also took their toll when feet of all sizes slid under the supper table. Infant mortality rates were high. Mothers often died in childbirth and widowers were left with hordes to raise. Visits to old cemeteries even today give a sad and graphic history of how the younger population was decimated through natural causes. Weather conditions were harsh. Bitter cold in the winter bunched families around hearths and dangerously hot stoves. Summer heat beat down making toil of land by day agonizing and the suffocating nights almost unbearable. Education of one's children in hopes of a better life was limited to local one-room plank schoolhouses and eight grades — the last being repeated continuously by most students simply for the learning, until their size made it an embarrassment to return.

There were of course occasionally good times — Christmas visits, a wedding, dance, or barn raising. But, by and large, their lives were hard and monotonous. When tobacco prices were normal these tireless workers could meet their yearly payments and, on one memorable Saturday out of the year, at least, take Mama to town and buy her a new calico dress, fit the youngin's out in shoes and even buy a new pair of overalls for themselves.

Such was the life of the typical dark tobacco farmer of west Kentucky and Tennessee.

It was in the heart of dark tobacco country that David Amoss was born in Cobb, Kentucky, on October 17, 1857, at about the same time that James B. Duke was learning to walk.

Two men, born ten months and a thousand miles apart, destined never to meet. Yet both lives would be tied to tobacco and enmeshed in a turbulent conflict with each other. One, a man of money, power and greed. The other, a man of medicine, mercy and violence.

Mixed in his blood of Virginia stock, David Amoss felt the family call to medicine. He came from a line of distinguished physicians, including his maternal grandfather and his father, E.N. Amoss.

The community of Cobb, Kentucky, was merely a congregation of a few farm houses and a store during Amoss' early years — without even a name until he was practically grown. It was situated in the southeast corner of Caldwell County in western Kentucky near the county line of both Lyon and Trigg counties. Amoss grew up there during the disturbing years of the Civil War and Reconstruction.

As a young lad, he was a keen observer of social changes occurring within his own community. The numerous blacks in that part of the country made the transformation from slave to tenant farmer with an almost imperceptible change — their docile and impoverished ways and even their places of abode hardly changing at all. Whites still acted as their protectors and benefactors and, if not their physical masters, still maintained economic dominion over them. Amoss also watched his father continue to serve the blacks affectionately and, in most instances, without charge.

Little David Amoss idolized and mimicked his father, growing quickly to admire the easy giving and caring of this healing profession. Yet, he also dreamed of other things during those early years — mainly horses and soldiers.

As a bright and curious youngster, he would hear the exciting reports of battles and famous generals clashing in a war between the states which by and large remained romantically distant to him. Far away places such as Antietam, Shiloh, Vicksburg, and Chancellorsville became familiar to him as sketchy accounts of crucial battles discussed at the store on Saturday afternoons and at church meetings on Sundays.

The names of such military giants as Stonewall Jackson, Bedford Forrest and Robert E. Lee arrested this youngster's mind with heroic fantasies. And, although he knew or cared little about the Confederate cause so staunchly supported by this Southern community, he loved to read and hear of military leaders and their masterful conquests.

David was becoming, in short, obsessed with military tactics and history. Though loathe to mention it to his father, he even dared dream of becoming an Army officer.

He became enrolled in the Wallonia Institute, an elongated, simply built wooden frame schoolhouse in the small hamlet of Wallonia in Trigg County, Kentucky, which was in walking distance from his home. This country schoolhouse was built, sponsored, and maintained by the more prominent men in the community for the instruction of their sons. During his early school years, little David was imbued deeply with an appreciation for that farming community's reliance upon dark fired tobacco. Although his father did not grow it, those friends he associated with during those formative years in most instances relied body and soul on that cash crop. David became more aware of this as he followed his father on his rounds throughout the community, observing closely the farmers tending to their tobacco and hearing the repeated stories to his father that payment for his services would be forthcoming as soon as the "baccer is taken to the floor."

In the warm confines of his own home late at night, David Amoss overheard his father and mother discussing the books as his father made notations in the ledger under the pale glow of the coal oil lamp. He knew that those farmers' accounts would be paid only if and when a suitable price was obtained for their tobacco. In short, he learned that the practice of medicine depended upon the energy, dedication, and compassion of the physician. The payment for it depended upon the farmers' only cash crop at that time — dark fired tobacco. Later he would learn that it was the same for all the people in that community who depended upon the farming business for their livelihoods.

By all accounts, David Amoss was from the very beginning an exceptionally bright youngster — quick to pick up on subtleties of human nature and one who understood adult problems much better than his young years would imply. Although he was very small in stature for his age and did not participate in many athletic activities, he possessed and developed a tremendous love for horses as he grew older. Among the many things that attracted him to follow his father on his rounds was the opportunity to drive the buggy and care for the faithful family horse.

It was within this very positive environment of medicine, tobacco and horses that David Amoss grew steadily into his early teens. This growth was further nurtured and strengthened by his family's close association with and devotion to the nearby Christian church. As he matured, David grew comfortably with the belief that divine guidance would direct him either to the position of commanding troops in the midst of battle or to following his father's and grandfather's footsteps serving unselfishly in the field of medicine. He viewed both possibilities with a sense of acceptance and his personality took on the bearing of a young man fully in command of himself, worthy of respect.

Hopkinsville, Kentucky, lay only 20 miles to the southeast of the little town of Cobb. It was the big town — a bustling center of commerce, trade and excitement for this rural community. The town had wooden sidewalks and gravel streets and a periodic trip to this city of 5,000 people was looked forward to with happy expectations by people of all age groups in the Cobb community.

It was there that David Amoss was sent by his father to attend high school at the James O. Ferrell Military Institute.

Ferrell had been a Confederate Army major of some local military repute and had returned to Hopkinsville after the war to establish and maintain a military school for boys.

This fell right in line with David's liking.

Living in Hopkinsville with friends and away from home gave him a feeling of independence. The strict discipline and martial arts of the school's program sharpened his already growing interest in military history, strategy, and tactics. He perfected his own inclinations by becoming a drill master for the students.

Equally important, the school offered a very solid field of academic instruction in all other subjects. David Amoss excelled as a leading student. He matriculated at this institution from 1875 to 1879 at which time he graduated, some twenty years before that same school would be transformed into the Hopkinsville High

School.

It was now time for David Amoss to make a decision: whether to pursue the medical profession or to seek some other endeavor such as the military. It was a difficult choice for him to make. No doubt the times played a great part in influencing his selection.

The romance of the uniform and the fantasies of soldiers marching heroically off to do battle for mothers, girlfriends, and homeland had dissipated in that long bloody struggle between the states. The glamour and prestige that soldiering may have once possessed in the public's eye had turned to bitter disillusionment with the terrible carnage at Gettysburg, Shiloh, and Missionary Ridge. In short, the historic rebellion had soured this country's affection for anything military and had brought to every family hearth the grim, frowning visage of war.

The losing Confederate Army no longer existed. The Union Army was still considered by many Western Kentuckians as an occupying enemy force. The land was at peace yet undergoing the awful throes of reconstruction. All bugle calls to gallantry had been silenced at Appomattox thus making the consideration of a military career of little social redeeming value. Besides, encouragement by the Amoss family for David to enter the field of medicine and carry on the tradition was very strong.

So David Amoss fell in cadence with family history and pursued the healing science instead of the call to arms.

With his worn and tattered suitcase, he loaded into the buggy beside his father and made the familiar trip to Hopkinsville, this time to the railroad station to catch a train. He was off to Cleveland, Ohio, where he enrolled in the Homeopathic Hospital College. There he was an outstanding student and was educated, not only in the healing science, but also in the worldly ways of the big city. Cleveland, in that day a bustling port city of Lake Erie, was just beginning to flex its industrial muscles. David Amoss enjoyed the camaraderie of keen-minded classmates and the many cultural and social activities of that metropolis. Time went by quickly and David Amoss soon received his medical degree, graduating with honors.

In 1880, Dr. David Amoss proudly returned to Cobb, Kentucky, to pick up the practice of medicine with his aging but still energetic father. At the young age of 23, David Amoss enthusiastically moved into the demanding life of the country practitioner. He stood only 5' 6" tall, weighing around 170 pounds, but his stocky build and erect military bearing gave him the appearance of being much larger. This was due in part also to a very large head which was covered with a shock of thick, brown hair. His piercing blue eyes, strong chin, and sporty handlebar mustache made him — even at that young age — a picture of masculinity. There was no doubt that he was the object of attention for all the unattached young ladies in the community.

Amoss' amiable and self-assured personality, combined with his handsome looks, made him popular with not only women but with men as well. In fact, there was in his demeanor and movement a certain self-confidence. His strong intellect and well chosen words garnered him a tremendous amount of respect among his peers. If the country practice of medicine was his aim, David Amoss had the world in his pocket in the summer of 1880.

Across the river valleys and Appalachian Mountain chain, over 1,000 miles away to the east of Cobb, Kentucky, young Buck Duke was also in charge of his destiny that same summer. He had just imported a handful of skilled foreign laborers to commence the mass production of a new, popular smoke that everyone predicted was a passing vogue — cigarettes.

Not far from Cobb, Kentucky — a good long walk or a short gallop on horseback — is another small hamlet called Cerulean. At the time David Amoss was beginning his professional career, this Trigg County village was known as Cerulean Springs.

It was a bustling little health resort town, set down in the middle of this Protestant farming community. The attraction was the resourceful and medicinal mineral springs which blessed this community. In 1870, a large two story hotel with a veranda running across its entire length was built, and it quickly became a social mecca for the area. For many years, people from far and wide would come to "take the water" and to enjoy dancing, skating, bowling, fishing and feasting on fried chicken and ice cream. All of this was squeezed into a hectic social calendar that included numerous balls and a season orchestra.

In 1887, the completion of the L & N Railroad which passed through both Cobb and Cerulean ushered in a new era of popularity to the Cerulean Springs Resort. Daily trains brought hundreds of guests to the hotel as its reputation spread throughout the country.

Among the activities of this splendid center of entertainment was the "upstairs room," where men congregated for a game of pool or poker and drank whiskey.

It was there at this elegant and manly attraction of the Cerulean

Springs Resort Hotel that the young Dr. David Amoss recreated during his leisure hours. At the poker table, the conviviality that came from the warm glow of good bourbon whiskey brought Amoss in close personal association with prominent men from all over west Kentucky and parts of Tennessee. Wealthy farmers, planters, tobacco buyers, bankers, and merchants enjoyed his companionship.

Sometimes these friendly and gentlemanly gatherings would become quite serious as the stakes at the poker table became high and the winner's take rode heavily in the saddlebags on the dark trips homeward. The Cobb sawbones found it comfortable to begin carrying a pistol under his coat. One night the doctor's winnings at the table especially aggravated a burley and intoxicated railroad construction foreman who was taking a licking. The railroader threatened to tear the little family physician apart limb by limb. Amoss remained unmoved as the boisterous drunk continued his loud and belligerent threats. The onlookers became concerned; but, before they could intervene, the outsized and seemingly outmatched doctor calmly made his adversary aware that he was armed with Smith and Wesson's great equalizer. The heated aggressor cooled off instantly and amiable play was resumed.

Thereafter, Amoss became an expert pistol shot — dazzling friends with his unerring target practice. It was pretty much assumed in the Cobb, Wallonia, Cerulean Spring community that Doc Amoss — the young one — could do just about anything he put his mind to.

One of the things he soon turned his mind toward was marrying. As it was quite common in those days, David Amoss married a close relative, Carrie Lindsay, on August 19, 1885. She was the daughter of a Christian County teacher and scholar, Charles Alfred Lindsay, half brother to David's father. The newlyweds were "half cousins."

He wore married life well, giving up his wandering single life as easily as shedding an old coat and settled into the responsibilities of a devoted husband. Soon Amoss became a doting father as Harold Lindsay, a boy, was born in 1886. Their second child, a daughter with the unusual name of Harvey, arrived 3 years later. They all lived in the old home in Cobb.

Their lifestyle was casual, consisting of his growing medical practice, the rearing of their two small children, and regular attendance at the Wallonia Christian Church. He became such a stalwart at that place of worship that he was often called upon to fill the pulpit in the absence of the regular preacher. He also became quite proficient at giving moving soliloquies at the funerals of friends.

Amoss' love for horses continued, and, like most men of the community, he kept hunting hounds for frequent fox hunts that graced his leisure time. Mixed into it all, he was certainly not opposed to a frequent drink of whiskey — either bonded store bought bourbon or preferably, the clear, smooth taste of moonshine liquor peddled in from "between the rivers".

As for his popularity within the community, married life only served to stabilize and enhance it.

As the 19th century moved through its final decade, David Amoss was a man thoroughly enjoying life. He was happily married with two bright and healthy children. His work was totally satisfactory, falling into the family tradition of providing healing comfort to those in need. His income was more than adequate and he enjoyed the good times with neighbors and friends, especially in their frequent hunts and occasional trips to Cerulean Springs Resort Hotel.

In January of 1896, David Amoss became a Master Mason at the little Masonic lodge at Wallonia. It was a monumental step in his life. For although he had been thoroughly educated and was well traveled for a man of that community, Masonry quickly became a new and meaningful experience for him. He enthusiastically embraced its code of truth, honor and fair dealing. The beautiful ritual of that ancient order enthralled him and the eloquence of the secret creeds appealed to his love of moving orations. The symbols, signs, passwords — all of it obsessed him.

"When is a man a Mason?" he would read from Joseph Fort Newton's Masonic classic.

"When he can look out over the rivers, the hills, and the far horizon with a profound sense of his own littleness in the vast scheme of things, and yet have faith, hope and courage. When he knows how to sympathize with men in their sorrows, yea, even in their sins ... Knowing that each man fights a hard fight against many odds."

Masonry became a burning passion in the heart of David Amoss. Indeed, within his heart of hearts.

In those years, Dr. Amoss also took a special liking to a young farmer from nearby Wallonia.

Guy Dunning was a man right out of a picture show. Only in his early 20's, he was already a stout, handsome, six-footer, erect as a post. His suntanned face gave evidence of his farming livelihood and this broadshouldered, flatbellied youngster cut an impressive figure wherever he went.

Unlike most other people in this rural setting, Dunning was an educated man. He, too, had graduated from the Wallonia Institute and had gone on to Centre College in Danville, Kentucky, one of the top schools in the country. Thus, this agrarian Adonis was able to combine the rustic demeanor of a country boy with the poise and dignity of an erudite scholar.

Dunning was a tobacco farmer working his mother's 1500 acres. In a short time, he would be in control of 1000 more acres of his own land to include a dozen tenant farmers. He not only knew how to grow tobacco — dark fired tobacco — but he produced it with an obvious attachment that bordered on reverance.

Perhaps it was Guy's intellect and learned manner that attracted David Amoss. He had known the Dunning family, including his father Levi, all of his life. It was a distinguished and respected farming family whose lineage came from the very first settlers in this west Kentucky country and a family — who at one time it was reported — owned over 10,000 acres.

In visiting the Dunning home place and treating the family in times of sickness, not to mention the frequent social calls, Dr. Amoss found that he and Guy — despite the latter being 15 years his junior — possessed a great deal in common.

They both liked to read, discuss current events and talk about deeper meanings of life than were normally kicked around at the crossroads country store on Saturday afternoons. Each had a dry and subtle sense of humor and a knack for overlooking the ignorance of some of their more narrow-minded neighbors. Both Amoss and Dunning were quite modest, firmly attached to their families and their hunting hounds.

And both enjoyed this earthen culture tied to the toiling of the soil and the brotherhood of the common people. From Guy Dunning, David Amoss added to his already ample knowledge of tobacco. Oftentimes Amoss would stop to visit his young friend on his way home from late sick calls. There, sitting together on the front porch steps on a warm summer night, Amoss would listen intently as Dunning's soft, low voice competed with the orchestration of crickets and katydids in discussing not only the growing of dark tobacco but the economics of it as well.

As happy as David Amoss was in Cobb, Kentucky — the land of his birth — there was something that bothered him a great deal.

He was not satisfied with the education his children were receiving there in the backwoods of Caldwell County. Harold, now ten years of age, was bright, perhaps precocious. And Amoss, to his own amusement, found himself doing the same thing his father had done; he wanted his son to become a physician. His daughter, Harvey, was blossoming into a real beauty. Her attractive looks were matched with a quick wit and a growing talent and inclination for music. As one would expect, there was no formal training in Cobb available for music aspirants.

Dr. David Amoss and wife Carrie worried that their children might be stymied. Already they seemed to be losing interest and becoming bored with school. As the children moved toward their high school years, this country doctor made a difficult decision. He would leave his practice and the tranquil way of life in Cobb and take his family to live in Paducah, Kentucky, the metropolis of west Kentucky which was some fifty miles north on the Ohio River. Paducah offered Amoss what his family needed. An energetic and thriving river city, it possessed a fine school system with music instruction. Socially, it was also to the doctor's liking with an opera house and a sizeable population of learned and educated people.

Professionally, it offered him stimulation as well. The city boasted two fine hospitals, and a distinguished list of practicing physicians, inspired by the legacy of the late Dr. Reuben Saunders of Paducah, one of the leading doctors in the United States during the latter part of the 19th century. Amoss was also encouraged to make the move by many of his friends in Paducah whom he had met at the Cerulean Springs Resort Hotel and other social gatherings in west Kentucky.

The move would be temporary, he assured friends and relatives in Cobb as they packed their furnishings and belongings and bid farewell in the fall of 1898. Their plan was to remain in Paducah only long enough for the children to finish high school and then return to the village of Dr. Amoss' birth for the remainder of their days.

The Amoss four moved into a comfortable frame house at 6th and Clark Streets right across the street from the McCracken County Courthouse. There David Amoss set up his practice of medicine. The Amoss family quickly adapted to city life with Carrie and Harvey enjoying the social activities which the doctor's practice was sufficient to maintain. Harold found time enough away from his studies to take a job as a paper carrier with the

Paducah News at the same time Irvin S. Cobb was editor.

The years passed quickly in Paducah and soon Harold graduated from high school at the young age of 15 as valedictorian of his class. At that time, Amoss made plans to bring his family back to the rustic life of Caldwell County.

His practice in Paducah had been successful enough to afford him to build the family a new home in Cobb for their promised return. So, in 1902, to the excitement of his many friends and relatives, Doc Amoss and family returned to Caldwell County, moving into their brand new bungalow on a spacious and beautifully landscaped lot in "downtown" Cobb, Kentucky.

As if the Paducah interlude were only a dream, Dr. Amoss quickly fell into his former way of life.

Eagerly, the returning doctor caught up on the latest happenings of that rural corner of the world. Happily, he renewed his friendship with Guy Dunning who was now in his early 30's and one of the most respected and prosperous tobacco farmers in the area.

Almost immediately, however, Dr. Amoss was able to discern a subtle sense of dread hovering over the countryside. He could sense it in the troubled sun creased face and worried words of Guy Dunning. The inate merriment of country folk and springy steps of farmers had disappeared.

Tobacco wasn't bringing anything these days.

Chapter 3

As the new century broke over this country, two economic groups of people were moving rapidly in opposite directions . . . the buyers of tobacco and the growers of tobacco.

The buying market belonged almost exclusively to the former Duke & Sons Company, now the American Tobacco Company, better known by farmers as the Duke Trust.

By 1904, the Trust had reshaped its mammoth tobacco organization and completely dominated the world markets. It made its influence felt in every climate of the world. The North Carolina family controlled all facets of the market from buying to transporting to converting the leaf into all uses, including cigarettes, cigars, chewing tobacco and snuff. The Trust also controlled the sale of tobacco.

As far as tobacco went, the Duke family had at long last destroyed all competition. The corporation's enormous chewing tobacco business — 138 million pounds of plug and 6 million pounds of twist annually — had quickly become one of its most lucrative ventures, especially in foreign markets. One of the largest plants in the Duke holdings was the National firm in Louisville, Kentucky. Of chewing tobacco, there were literally hundreds of popular brands — Brown's Mule, Sweepstakes, Early Bird, Applejack — just to name a few.

The dark fired tobacco of west Kentucky was prime produce for this bulging consumer use of plug tobacco. The Trust — virtually the only buyer in town — was getting richer and richer. On the other hand, the farmer who grew the green leaf that fed the unanswerable appetite of the Dukes was getting poorer and poorer.

Buck Duke, by that time cavorting between New York and London and raking in tremendous profits, apparently could care less about this widening gulf between the "haves" and the "have nots." Wash Duke, his more sensitive and aged father, had been much more conscious during his lifetime to the plight of the farmer and, along with Buck's brother Ben, had taken great pains to make sure that large contributions from the family fortune were made to worthy causes, one of which included Trinity College in Durham, North Carolina.

But the youngest son and head of the company was too preoccupied with profit and loss statements to either be diverted by the growing clamor in the tobacco fields or by the increasing amount of criticism now being launched by the news media.

Leading newspapers in the East, even those in the Dukes' home state of North Carolina, became critical of this monopoly which was driving the prices for tobacco growers downward to a perilously low price. Josephus Daniels of the **RALEIGH NEWS AND OBSERVER** printed various auction market quotations in North Carolina to prove his assertion that the Trust had gradually cut the price of leaf tobacco in half. The farmers, he claimed, had been robbed of more than five million dollars during the crop year of 1904 alone. Dissatisfied and restless farming groups assembled in Rocky Mount, North Carolina, where they leveled blasts at the Trust and discussed plans for a permanent organization to protect their rights. One spokesman of that movement compared the Trust to war and famine and stated that the "sleeping lion will be aroused and the American people will yet be delivered from their present slavery to the men whose dishonest dollars now dominate."

The problem was even more serious in Kentucky. The farmers rightfully charged that the Trust had abolished the competitive system of bidding for leaf tobacco. The Trust representatives quoted any price they pleased, and the farmer had to accept it or let his tobacco rot. This caused tobacco, which had brought 6 to 8 cents a pound at the turn of the century, to drop to 3 cents and lower. Land which had formerly produced from $75 to $200 an acre was now yielding barely half that amount. The average Kentucky and Tennessee farmer was receiving less than 20 cents a day for his work.

In 1904, it cost the toughened and experienced Kentucky farmer roughly $42 to grow an acre of tobacco. The average yield of an acre of tobacco was approximately 700 pounds. Simple arithmetic clearly reveals that 6 cents a pound was necessary for the grower to simply break even. As prices dropped to 3 cents and 2 cents a pound, the farmer was watching his cash crop quickly become a deficit.

In west Kentucky — the best place in the world to grow dark

tobacco — the darkening clouds of want were beginning to settle in over the Black Patch. The tobacco crop — be it burley or dark — was the west Kentucky farmer's primary cash crop. From what meager profits he would wrestle away from the land in raising the leaf, the farmer would buy those necessities not produced on his land. These included such things as machinery and equipment and clothes for his family. His cash crop would also have to pay the doctor bills and, if he was lucky, make a payment on the farm.

From 1900 to 1906, many west Kentucky farmers, like their brothers throughout the South, lost their farms as they were unable to pay off their mortgages. Since tobacco was the cash crop — farm income used to purchase needed items — the merchants who provided the goods and services likewise suffered. Store owners and bankers who had advanced credit to the tobacco growers also began to go broke as the harvest profits failed to come in. In fact, the townspeople may well have suffered the worse. When the store went under and the bank closed down, that was it. At least the farmer had other crops to grow if he had managed to hang onto his farm or had survived as a tenant. Actually, many astute farmers, watching the devastating avalanche of falling prices, simply quit growing tobacco and diversified into other cash crops such as wheat. Some turned to their dense woodlands for the sale of timber. But it was a poor choice and most tillers of the earth were not blessed with such resourceful alternatives.

James Buchanan Duke's American Tobacco Company was ruining them. While Trust executives dressed splendidly, ate lavishly, and figured their millions in the mahogany paneled board rooms of New York, the men and women upon whom they depended — the tobacco farmers — were bending under the weight of their economic burdens.

In retrospect, we know the farmers' plight was not entirely the fault of the Duke Trust. In June, 1898, the United States Congress had passed an oppressive new tax of $1.50 per thousand on all cigarettes and 12¢ a pound on all other manufactured tobacco products. This, of course, added costs to the consumer and cut back demand. The doubling of production by the American farmer between 1889 and 1900 had not helped matters either.

But there was no doubt about it . . . the strangling monopoly of the Duke empire provided the most ruinous blow of all to the farmers of the Black Patch. By the summer months of 1904, the Duke Trust was a vile curse upon the lips of all tobacco growers in America and especially those impoverished areas of west Kentucky and Tennessee.

Upon this economic landscape came Felix Ewing of Adams, Tennessee. Formerly of Nashville, he was a man of considerable experience in business and had managed two factories which manufactured carriages and plows. Although they were not particularly large enterprises, he was still a very respected financial and business figure within that southern city. In 1903 at the age of 44, Ewing had turned his efforts toward fulfilling a long time dream and moved to the rolling hill country of Robertson County, Tennessee, which nudged in close to the Kentucky line. There he became a fulltime tobacco planter on his plantation of 3,000 acres. He settled in his large, palatial white mansion, Glenraven, and began to live in grand style.

It was, at first, the storybook life which he had hoped for — a large farming estate where he lived as a country gentleman farmer with a quality of life which would match the most elegant plantations anywhere in the South. Tobacco filled the great barns upon that land, and the winding tree-lined driveway to his impressive home led many important visitors to his door. The fine carriages of richly adorned guests filed in for the grand parties which he sponsored.

But Ewing's great wealth and style of living suddenly became threatened by another man of affluence, James B. Duke. Just as it made the poor farmer poorer, plummeting tobacco prices made the rich less rich. Ewing shared hurt with the poorest tobacco grower in the region. The big difference was that he knew what to do about it and commenced to do it.

Felix Ewing had conceived the plan some years before, in 1893, as he had curiously observed the rising Duke Trust and the worsening condition of the tobacco farmer from his home in Nashville.

Like all ingenious schemes, simplicity was its selling point.

Since the Duke Trust monopolized the buying market through consolidation, why couldn't farmers monopolize the supply?

If the farmers — he soundly opined — congregated universally to pool their tobacco and hold it off the market, then the tobacco conglomerate would be forced to raise its prices in order to purchase the much needed product. When Ewing became a tobacco planter himself, he gave the idea even more thought. His highly respected position in the farming community made him the likely leader for the people to rally around. As this considerable man grew even larger in the public's esteem, he felt more and more compelled to come to the aid of his fellow growers. In spite of

failing health, Ewing began to meet with farmers in the area —
both large and small, rich and poor. His idea of a common association was warmly received by all.

At last, as the crops were laid by in the summer of 1904, this
"Moses" of the Black Patch put out the call to arms — a meeting
of all interested persons, farmers and non-farmers alike, to be held
on a warm, dusty September Saturday in a small town on the
Tennessee line in Todd County, Kentucky. The town was called
Guthrie.

Today Guthrie is a quiet, slumbering burg of a few hundred
people quietly watching traffic ease by on the backroad to Nashville. On Saturday, September 24, 1904, it was a different story.
The town teemed with people and excitement as tobacco growers
from all parts of west Kentucky and Tennessee overran its corporate limits.

Riding along in empty wagons, in buggies, on horseback and
many even on foot, over 5,000 farmers faithfully arrived in force
by mid-morning. The more distant travelers poured in by train.
They gathered at the fairgrounds in Guthrie, representing a varied
assortment of stations in life — wealthy planters, large landown-
ers, tenant farmers, both black and white. They were there because of the woefully low money they were receiving for their
tobacco. Their common interest drew together both the impoverished sharecropper and the gentleman farmer of the landed gen-
try.

Although it was an embittered group of citizens, this was a
rather festive occasion. They seemed reassured and even euphoric
by their association with each other and the sharing of their
common problem. Spirits were high, some of it confined within the
many jugs that were being passed around that day. Barbeque of all
sorts was prepared in huge proportions and large black cauldrons
did their work over open fires to supply other foods such as beans
and burgoo. This was one day of plenty — a gluttonous respite in a
period of want.

True to form, Ewing had planned the large meeting well. While
thousands came together to picnic, socialize and have a good time,
he and his close associates seriously channeled the activities toward a constructive end.

Other prominent men in the area, along with Ewing, had done
their homework long before the throng of farmers arrived in
Guthrie. Charles Fort, also of Robertson County, Tennessee, and
former president of the Clarksville Tobacco Growers Association,

was an important part of this brain trust and served as Ewing's chief assistant. Guthrie would be the headquarters for the proposed Association with sales headquarters at Clarksville where the Association's tobacco would be sold. That town was chosen because of its key river and railroad connections. No doubt, the convenient distance from Ewing's home was an important consideration as well. Through membership dues, bank loans, and other forms of financing, the Association would construct their own warehouses in which to store the fruits of their labor. There it would be held until their own salesmen, who would be employed by the Association, could obtain a favorable price.

The written outline of this grand project was put together by perhaps the most prominent friend of the tobacco farmers, A.O. Stanley, who had just recently been elected to the United States Congress from western Kentucky. This charter spoke in dry and legalistic terms which very few of this uneducated gathering could even read, let alone understand. But it would make them legal — or so they thought — and, if Mr. Ewing was behind it, that would be good enough for them. Buried within its wordy context was an ominous provision, Article 7, which was a subtle call to action. It stated: "Each member of the Association also obligates himself to use his influence and strong endeavor with those tobacco planters who are not members of the Association to become members."

After much eating, drinking and visiting, this lively but orderly Guthrie crowd settled in quietly that afternoon under the large oaks to hear Felix Ewing call the meeting to order.

Their "Moses" was masterful. Introducing those upon whom he intended to rely in formulating his organization, Ewing was visibly pleased with the rounding applause given each. Adeptly and with full command, he moved into the meeting. Next followed speech after speech by spokesmen from all parts of the Black Patch — some talks long and boring, others brief and brilliant. On and on into the afternoon sun, these men of the earth viciously condemned the Duke Trust and exhorted the great need for action.

No one wandered from the mass meeting that day. Each speaker, the good and the bad, was met with approval and applause. The attention of this group never wavered as they sat on the grass, on the backs of wagons, on makeshift benches, and some even hanging from tree limbs and on the roofs of the stables located in the campground. They were the ranks of one of America's most unrepresented labor force, pondering their future. Their burning intensity glowed from their tanned and weathered faces.

Finally, as the afternoon moved toward evening, Ewing charted their future course. He briefly, but completely, explained the seven articles of their written by-laws. Quickly, and in proper parliamentary form, the plan of Felix Ewing received the full endorsement of the Guthrie gathering.

The Dark Tobacco District Planters' Protection Association of Kentucky and Tennessee came into being. Charles H. Fort was elected President and Felix Ewing was named general manager of "the Association".

Paper and pencil were passed, and lines formed to enlist names upon the rolls of what was hoped to be the final step on the way out of economic bondage.

As the meeting came to a close and the tired but satisfied mass evacuated town in the gathering twilight, the spirits of the jug were depleted but those of the soul were winging home with new confidence.

It is not known if Dr. David Amoss was in that crowd on September 24. But it is sure that he and Felix Ewing soon became friends and associates. And, there is no doubt that the country doctor was becoming more and more concerned with the prevailing economic trend of depression.

His close association with Guy Dunning and other growers in the Cobb community had influenced him greatly, not only to become a member of the newly formed Association but to be active in it as well. Amoss — much like Ewing — could not escape the role of leadership which time, circumstance and even nature had imposed upon him. He was taken in by Ewing and associates to assist in the formulation and direction of the Association's activities in the west Kentucky area.

Felix Ewing, Charles Fort, David Amoss and the rest of the Association leadership shared no delusions of the great task before them. Many of the rank and file farmers, however, anticipated instant success after the show of force and rattling of swords in Guthrie. They became disgruntled as the months rolled by and the Trust gave no indication of relenting to their pressures. Perhaps most foreboding was the number of farmers who showed little interest in the Association and, worse still, refused to join.

These non-joiners became despised by the Association membership and were labeled as "hillbillies." The only known explanation for this term was given by a farmer from Trigg County, Kentucky:

"It's this way you see. Most people that live on hills has got goats. Most of those goats is billy goats. And you know what a goat is? No matter how much grub he gets at home he is always wandering around for stuff belonging to other people than his owner. He is forever taking for his own good things he never did nothing for. For that's the way with those here men. They don't do nothing to help the Association if they takes the benefits of the prices the Association makes."

In those first few weeks and months, the Association leadership knew it would be slow sledding. It would take time before the organization could begin to flex its muscles and place tobacco into their own warehouses. These months were actually dead months as far as any possible progress in improving tobacco prices was concerned, but they were crucial months in building the infrastructure and establishing the financing of the Association. A Board of Directors had to be established, districts broken down and organized, memberships pursued, and the tedious chore that accompanies all blossoming organizations — paper work — had to be commenced.

The most demanding job was taking the message out to the country stores, crossroads, churches and schoolhouses. The Association membership extended primarily at first throughout 19 counties in Kentucky and 3 counties in Tennessee.

Association leaders went out with a religious fervor, traveling to the far reaches of the region on train and on horseback. They trekked through snow and ice and across swollen streams to proselytize the aims of their organization.

Meetings were held in plank schoolhouses, lonely crossroad churches, and at country stores in an effort to convince growers to join the Association. Some of these gatherings took on the appearance of old time camp meetings as the local chairman would open with a prayer. In an emotional and high pitched appeal, they would preach to the recalcitrant farmers until some would come to see the light only after the doubters had gone down on their bended knees in prayer.

One of the more ardent and dedicated crusaders for Association membership was Colonel Joel Fort, brother of the organization's president. He became known as the "Tennessee War Horse" of the Black Patch because of his untiring travels and cajoling throughout the rugged terrain of Kentucky and Tennessee. He cut a great figure and was difficult to deny as he mixed his vehement attack upon the Trust with bits of humor. "Everytime I make a speech, the American Tobacco Company decreases the price they offer me for my tobacco by one cent a pound," he would say with an air of levity, "and if I keep on talking, I'm going to have to pay the Trust a dollar a pound to take it off my hands."

Fort even turned poet in the process, tuning the following lines:

> "Let croakers croak and grumblers growl,
> and all the hillbillies rant and howl,
> never give up to the victories won,
> stand by your guns.
>
> Love not yourself, your neighbor hold,
> self love's a treacherous elf.
> Love God with all thy strength and soul
> and thy neighbor as thy self."

Ewing and company figured that a minimum of 70% of the growers in the Black Patch would have to belong to the Association to make the plan work. The persistence and sheer doggedness of men like Joel Fort, David Amoss and the rest brought that goal into reality. In fact, some districts reported that up to 95% of their tobacco growers were signed up with the Association. And, with each signature, a contract was issued, making the Association that farmer's agent for whatever tobacco he produced.

With the membership ranks growing, warehouses had to be built or arrangements made for them to be leased. The leaders also arranged for loans to be extended by banks to the Association by pledging future purchases as collateral, and some funds were raised by selling stock in the local associations.

In this regard, David Amoss once again took the reins of leadership by heading a local drive to construct in Cobb one of the first Association warehouses anywhere.

Through the hard and questionable first year of the Association's existence, only the persistence, prodding and guidance of such men as the Fort brothers, Ewing and Amoss kept the noble purpose alive. They did not even have funding to defer their administrative expenses and their office in Guthrie was donated. More importantly, the strength of these men's personalities was able to keep the hopes of the farmers afloat in a sea of continuing economic woes and despair. Together they still believed that, as audacious as the plan might be, the Association could still prevail.

The intellectual depth of the Association leadership can best be seen in the proposed "crop acreage allotment" plans. Recognizing that a large supply would not help in raising prices, each member of the Association was requested to cut back on his own individual production. This idea was not as enthusiastically received by the suspicious farmers as was membership in the Association. It was a devoted follower of Ewing's leadership indeed who voluntarily cut back. To some degree, however, it worked and it gave the farmers a preview of what was to come by way of government imposition years later.

While David Amoss became more and more active in the work of the Association during that winter of 1904-1905, James B. Duke was paying little attention to the distant rumblings of discontent in the hinterland.

He had personal problems of his own.

The entire Duke family and much of the curious public — especially the social elite of the Eastern seaboard — had turned their eyes and ears to a racy scandal that was affecting one of the world's most famous and prosperous tycoons.

At the age of 48 and in the midst of luxurious living that came with his unfathomable wealth, Buck Duke took to wife Lillian Fletcher McCreedy. The marriage followed a rather steamy and passionate affair. Appropriately to Duke's station in life, a nuptial ceremony took place in Philadelphia at the home of Lewis J. Steel, president of that city's consolidated stock exchange. Adding to the tantalizing nature of this gossipy event was the fact that the bride had only the night before torn herself away from the arms of another man.

The marriage took place in November. By July, 1905, the tarnished bride's affair with another man had already become common knowledge. In September of that year, Buck Duke — the proud tycoon and winner of all his economic encounters throughout the world — threw in the matrimonial towel, filing for divorce in New Jersey, the state of his palatial country estate. In his petition, he stated that Mrs. Duke had been unfaithful by a half dozen or more acts of adultery, including debauchery in Duke's own townhouse and at unspecified places on Long Island.

As one could imagine, it was a vicious and bitter divorce battle, well publicized in every sordid detail. The accused adulteress countercharged Duke of malicious wrongdoing, alleging that he drank to excess and abused her physically. Private detectives and attorneys leaped into the affray with professional relish. House servants gave exquisite and titillating testimony of infidelity. Passionate love letters were introduced in open court and in full view of the gaping world. The litigation continued in a depreciating manner throughout the closing months of 1905.

Going almost unnoticed through this sensational affair was a matter of most somber and important significance. Wash Duke, the wise and mellowed old patriarch, had died in May in Durham, North Carolina, at the age of 85. After a colorful and dynamic lifetime of sensational rise from the poverty of a one mule tobacco farm to that of one of the richest men in the world, he at last passed from this life loaded down with the worries of his son's personal problems and the growing discord in the farming land from which he came.

In those summer months of 1905, the rolling land of Kentucky and Tennessee began to bloom forth with the summer crops of corn, cotton and dark tobacco.

Felix Ewing and his band of leaders labored on.

The Moses of the Black Patch even traveled to New York City at his own expense in an attempt to find independent buyers for the Association's tobacco. As expected, all companies that he approached were tied up — either directly or indirectly — with the Duke Trust. He returned home without a single sale. His commitment to the Association's aims was even greater, however, as he became more aware of the strangle hold of the impregnable Duke enterprise. Ewing and Charles Fort also traveled to the nation's capitol to appear before the United States Senate Subcommittee on Finance and Commerce in behalf of a bill which would repeal some of the strangling tax that was imposed on the tobacco leaf. That bill was doomed from the very beginning and died in committee in the senate a year later.

Meanwhile, the buyers for the Trust seemed to be bothered very little with the rattling sabers of the Kentucky and Tennessee growers and the lower echelon executives for this monopoly began to lob their own small volleys at the upstart farmers.

First was the war of psychology. Smirkingly, they simply told the Association farmers that they did not need their tobacco, that they had a surplus built up and would simply starve them out. Within a year, they boasted, the militants would be crawling to them on their hands and knees to sell their tobacco at any price —

foreclosure and eviction papers already in hand.

But the most effective method used by the Trust and one that planted the first seeds of discord within the Black Patch was merely buying the tobacco at the high rates of 10¢ to 12¢ per pound from farmers who were not members of the Association.

An American citizen is, by political nature, independent. The farmers, especially the sort of the first years of the century, were even more so. Up and to that time, a worker of the soil depended only on his Maker. At least that was the way the average farmer perceived it at the time. Independently, but to God.

Actually, he was much more dependent than he cared to admit. In many instances he looked to the good will of the banker to keep his farm. He depended upon the town merchants to give him credit until harvest — imposing upon that business the same success or misfortunes that he might encounter in his farming ventures. Even at that early time he still leaned on the local schoolmarm to provide his children with a modicum of learning, usually eight grades. But, most importantly, he relied on his neighbor to give him help in time of need. Barn raisings were hectic but friendly occasions when farmers from miles around came together to put up a stable or a tobacco barn in a great community spirit. And, in the late summer as the toughened body gave way to the illnesses of typhoid, measles, or some mysterious malady of the day, he depended not only upon the good will, but the hard work, of his neighbors. As he laid prostrate on his bed burning with fever — his gaunt, frantic wife and bevy of barefoot children looking on desperately — his neighbors would move onto his farm before daylight, work out his crops, gather his corn or cut and house his tobacco. Neighborly women folk would bring heaps of food to the house. With all this work done and their stricken brother relieved, they would then unhitch their mules and follow them into the gathering darkness toward their own homes without expecting or receiving any approbation or praise. They were simply doing their jobs as country neighbors.

So the farmer — with his independent philosophy — lived to some degree, at least, a dependent life.

Thus, two strong rural values were converging on a collision course. First was the almost fanatical belief of the farmer that he could do damn well as he pleased with his affairs — including the sale of his tobacco — and no one could make or intimidate him to do otherwise. The second, and equally as strong, was the abiding belief, even religious conviction, that he was his brother's keeper.

The Trust appealed to the first conviction. The Association to the latter.

Greed is a common denominator among all people.

If a person can take more while his neighbor takes less and sleep well at night by rationalizing his choice as a God given right, then the higher price can be easily accepted. Twelve cents a pound is a lot easier to take with a clear conscience. And one may say, "It's not the money, it's the principle." But it's the money.

Of course greed was not all of it. To whom does a man owe his allegiance — his neighbor or his wife and children? Does he not owe that first and last ounce of devotion to those under his own roof who look to him and him only for the very sustenance of their existence? Is he not betraying that trust when he turns down a more lucrative offer in favor of none at all, making his loved ones suffer for his choice? In fact, was not his very manhood at stake?

It is also easy, however, even in retrospect, to understand the growing bitter resentment caused by this type of behavior. The Association farmer for the past few years had been receiving only about 3¢ a pound for his tobacco. In attempting to improve the lot of all, including his neighbor, he had taken steps to support the movement by withholding all the crops from the despised Trust. And he did so at great sacrifice. His wife would wear the same threadbare dress for another year. The kids would surely do without their annual new pair of shoes.

Yet, right cross the fence row was a neighbor whom he had known all his life, gone to church with every Sunday, had Masoned with and befriended, who stubbornly and independently sold to the Trust for 8¢ to 12¢ a pound. It cut deep into the pride and ego of the Association member to see his disloyal friend "showing off" new plow points and harnesses and to see his neighbor's wife and children freshly outfitted. Conversely, to the purpose of the Trust, it did not tempt him to cave in to their offers. It simply made him angry with his neighbor.

So, the question which was to bear such bitter fruit was a complex one indeed. While the Association membership enlarged steadily and significantly, the non-members — those who refused to cooperate — became the center of attention.

Bad blood was brewing which was splitting apart rural communities.

Simple, unsmiling nods had replaced handshakes and long conversations at Sunday morning worship services. Congregating Association members in town on Saturday afternoons talked in a muffled and derogatory manner of those who had not joined their group.

With Felix Ewing ailing — he reportedly suffered from a nervous condition — and giving ground in the leadership ranks of the Association, David Amoss became stronger. Although he was titled only as the Vice-Chairman of the Caldwell County Association, he was looked to with the respect which usually accompanied a much more exalted position.

Surfacing out of the character of the rural physician was a trait few people had seen before.

He was tough, a very tough, little man.

It was Amoss, asserting his own personal leadership, who advocated a boycott as a means of fighting both the hillbillies and the Trust. "Those businesses and professional men," the little doctor spoke through every dell and village, "who fail to encourage the tobacco growers in their struggle for better prices are not worthy of their patronage."

This was a tremendous idea and it spread quickly throughout the Black Patch.

Now the non-farmers in this rural area were forced to actively stake their position whereas, before, they had been satisfied simply to offer a pacific and passing gesture of support. The fearful prospects of having their livelihoods walk away from their open doors cast a sobering sense of urgency over the business people. Even school teachers in the hundreds of one room schoolhouses would find themselves without jobs unless they openly cast their lots with the Association. Ministers quickly recognized that the Lord might not be the only one to call them away from a paying pulpit and were careful not only to join the Association but, also, to use their position in behalf of the organization whenever the opportunity presented itself. An incident which reportedly occurred in a small church in a Tennessee hamlet underlines this spirit. The minister of the church had called upon a hillbilly to lead prayer meeting one night. At the end of the services, other members of that congregation approached the clergyman and sternly admonished him never to allow that particular man to lead the meeting again.

"And why not?" asked the minister.

"He is not one of us. He does not belong to the Association and we will not follow him anywhere, not even in prayer," was their reply.

In droves, non-farmers began to sign on the dotted line, joining the Association and becoming full-fledged members. Although they might not have had tobacco to pool, their dues, influence and support were a tremendous boost to the morale and ambitions of the Dark Fired Tobacco Planters' Protection Association. Bankers, merchants, lawyers, doctors, politicians, and ministers gave additional respectability to an organization already long on men of high quality.

As the first long hard year of the Association existence drew to a close, its leadership could look back upon it with proud, if exhausted, satisfaction. Although it had been an arduous struggle, full of frustrations and disappointments, they had actually done remarkably well. If tobacco prices had not climbed as the farmers had hoped, their faith in the Association nevertheless remained intact. This ringing endorsement was evidenced by the second annual meeting in Guthrie on September 23, 1905. Over three times as many people attended as did the initial gathering a year before.

But it was a much more serious group of farmers then than the year before. These men of the earth, usually long on patience, were growing hungrier and angrier. When the eating and speeches had ended, they departed to all parts of West Kentucky and Tennessee without sanguine hopes this time of instant success. In spite of the spirited activities of the day, they were in somber moods. Not a few were thinking that more drastic action was needed.

So the Association, with the same leadership but with a far more dissatisfied membership, moved on into its second year with determination and growing strength.

In some counties, membership exceeded 90% of the farmers and the entire Black Patch averaged 70% of the growers with their names proudly on the Association's rolls.

The local weekly newspapers became almost unanimously behind the efforts of the Association. Those brash and opinionated men who bought ink by the barrels spread it on thickly across newsprint, slowly molding public opinion. Henry Lawrence, publisher of the **CADIZ RECORD,** was perhaps the most eloquent, if brutal, in his scathing attacks upon both the "enslaving" Trust and the "greedy" hillbillies. His articles of partisan invective were reprinted by many other papers across the district. And, as was sure to follow, the schism between the Association members and the hillbillies widened into an irreparable division of bitter hatred.

Chapter Four

Robertson County, Tennessee, is a good Kentucky neighbor.

Not only does it share its northern boundary with the Bluegrass State but common interests in agriculture as well. Located on Tennessee's north central border, it is also ideally positioned for farm marketing outlets. Just a few miles to the west is the thriving Cumberland River port city of Clarksville, Tennessee. Of an equal distance from its southern boundary, an easy thirty minutes away, is the capital city of Tennessee, Nashville.

Even today it represents the best of all worlds. It is a land of easy country living and rural charm but within easy reach of the big city lights and air lanes to the rest of the world. Its county seat of Springfield is an elegant, picturesque Southern town mixing yesterday and tomorrow into a comfortable yet prosperous balance. At the turn of the century, the county population was just over 25,000 people. Springfield, Robertson County's largest town, was occupied by a few more than 1,700 citizens.

Tobacco was the primary crop. Only one other county in Tennessee, neighboring Montgomery, grew more tobacco, and, by 1910, Robertson County would take over the lead. The leaf most raised was "dark fired."

The reasons dark tobacco was so ingrained in this community were the same, or similiar, to those of its sister counties in Kentucky. The soil, the abundance of hardwood for firing, and the mild climate were important factors. But, perhaps, equally important was land utilization. The collapse of slavery during the Civil War left this area with a severe labor shortage. Sharecropping replaced slavery, and this system required a division of the large, antebellum farms into smaller plots of land. Tobacco was an ideal crop in that it could be produced with a good profit on limited space. Therefore, dark fired tobacco became a boom to the many Tennessee farmers of Robertson County, Tennessee.

It is no mystery why this border county played such an important role in the formation and business of the Dark Tobacco

District Planters Protection Association of Kentucky and Tennessee. It was consistent with its interests when it produced such leaders of that group as Felix Ewing, and Charles and Joel Fort, among others.

Robertson County was one of the most loyal of all counties to the Association. In the local district in which Felix Ewing lived, there were approximately one hundred farmers, less than twenty of which were suspected hillbillies.

The county seat of Springfield would in May of 1907 give birth to the **BLACK PATCH JOURNAL.** This publication, sponsored by the Association, had as its main aim to promote its membership and to build a strong Association. That journal also took a strong and even militant stand against "any man, combination of men, monopolies or trusts that seek to satisfy their greed for gold by oppression and continually strive and scheme to unjustly deprive an honest tiller of the soil of his due."

Thus, it is appropriate in light of this county's deep and abiding sympathy with the disgruntled and impoverished tobacco growers, that little Stainback Schoolhouse in the northern part of the county would play a monumental role during the gathering storm of unrest.

There, on an unusually warm October night in 1905, just a couple of weeks after the second annual Guthrie rally, a clandestine meeting of farmers was held which would ultimately prove to be of historic significance to the entire tobacco region.

Dusk was gathering when, one by one, dark shadowed figures on horseback began to silently arrive. The long, white clapboard schoolhouse was silhouetted like a huge rock in the clearing. Soon 32 horses were tethered around the outside. There was the quick but certain screech of windows being raised; then, a flicker of a match appeared through the drawn shades. The pale glow from a lantern quickly ensconced the room. There was a brief shuffling of feet and chairs, muffled voices, and then quiet. One voice at a time finally began to speak in low, almost inaudible tones. The participants of this secret and mysterious meeting had much in common.

First, they were all friends of Felix Ewing who, even though not among them, lived in his stately mansion not far away.

They were all tobacco growers of Robertson County, Tennessee with the possible exception of a stockily built country doctor from Kentucky.

They were all members of the Association.

Almost everyone had been present at the Guthrie rally a few

weeks before.

All were impatient, strong-willed and angry men. And they were all religious men — Baptists, Methodists and Church of Christ — reputable and with upstanding, untarnished positions within their community.

This was the initial meeting of the Possum Hunters. And out of it came the "Stainback Resolutions" which were unquestionably written beforehand and stamped with the almost unmistakable rhetoric of Felix Ewing and David Amoss.

There in the flickering shadows of the country schoolhouse, the men read the document out loud for the first time. Flawlessly and adeptly written, it spoke in strong terms against the Trust. It accused the empire of robbing and enslaving the tobacco growers in a nefarious and greedy manner. These words of denunciation went on to speak glowingly of the patriotism and nobility of the angered and enraged citizens of the Dark Tobacco District.

It was significant that the Stainback accords branded the Trust as criminal. But most noteworthy and foreboding were the words obviously penned for the hillbillies. The document resolved:

> "Be it further proclaimed to the world that any farmer or
> other persons who aid the Trust in any way by selling to it
> their tobacco at a higher price is an accomplice of the
> Trust and is in good morals as guilty as the Trust."

Lastly, it was established in the order of business that committees of "not less than five members nor more than two thousand" would visit the farmers outside the Association and "counsel and instruct" them as to the folly of their ways. Because of the occupation of these members, such business would have to take place at night, thus the name Possum Hunters.

A committee of not more than two thousand.

Such a nocturnal visit would hardly be interpreted by the surprised hillbilly as simply a neighborly greeting.

Yet, this small band of farmers within the Association insisted that violence was not part of their aim and would be avoided.

So the Possum Hunters went to work.

It was a convenient time for all of them to make their "visits."

The year's tobacco was in the barn, requiring occasional checking at night, and thus serving as another good excuse for them to move about after dark.

At first, the Stainback "graduates" merely scattered handbills throughout the countryside which warned in strong terms that the hillbillies were not to sell their housed tobacco to the Trust buyers who would soon be circulating.

At about the same time, Felix Ewing assured everyone through the publication the **NATIONAL AMERICAN** that the hunters were of the most amiable and lawabiding intent, only required to do their crusading at night because they were hardworking tobacco farmers by day.

Significantly enough, as if possessed by a clarivoyant intuition, the Association Board met in Guthrie in November and very conspicuously and officially, but unconvincingly, disclaimed and discouraged any acts of violence which might occur in the future.

It was clearly a matter of, in Shakespeare's terms, the "lady protesting too much."

Like an epidemic and as if invisibly guided by the heirarchy of the Association, the Possum Hunter clubs grew up throughout the Dark Tobacco District of Tennessee and Kentucky. Bands of men, unmasked at first, openly congregated at night and visited the independent hillbillies. Stern lectures and direct admonitions were given on these serious but "civil" visits. They also made a point of advising the buyers of the American Tobacco Company not to go out purchasing tobacco from the hillbilly barns.

Not all of their visits were successful, however. Ben Sory of Clarksville, Tennessee, was a buyer for the Italian Reggie, a Trust subsidiary. He didn't take kindly to such shenanigans and was not one to fool around with. The ex-sheriff of Robertson County, Tennessee, was by all accounts not one to bluff easily.

One night he was camped on the banks of the Red River when a group of 75 Possum Hunters called upon him around midnight for a little talk. Sory promptly pulled a shotgun and warned the late visitors to keep their distance. He also ordered that any talking to be done would be done from afar with them looking down the barrel of a shotgun. Needless to say, the conversation dried up and the men drifted into the darkened countryside.

There were initially no acts of violence. But the repeated nightly confrontations through the area laid tender dry kindling wherein the slightest spark could set off a mighty conflagration.

The practice of "possum hunting" unfolded almost overnight in all sections of the Black Patch. In fact, it cropped up in other locations so fast that it was as if the Stainback meeting was simply a signal for other groups already in place to begin.

Almost as quickly as the visits started, other more drastic actions broke out. In early December a group of Christian County "hunters" went looking for some buyers from the American Snuff

Company, a part of the Trust conglomerate. On horseback and in the dead of a cold winter night, approximately fifty armed and masked men gathered on a lonely stretch of railroad between Guthrie and Elkton, Kentucky. With a lantern, they flagged a large churning passenger train to a hissing halt. In the best of Wild West lore, some of the men boarded and, to the fright and panic of the sleepy occupants, searched out for the buyers.

None were found.

Typifying the audacity of these marauders, ten remained on the train simply for a free trip through the cold night to Elkton. There they peacefully disembarked and departed unmolested.

It had begun.

The Possum Hunters — the unrecognized, unclaimed but no less real militant arm of the Association — were on the move.

Meanwhile, almost simultaneously with the first meeting of the Possum Hunters, David Amoss had made an important trip to Nashville, Tennessee. There he met with leaders of the local klavern of the Ku Klux Klan. That meeting was not to solicit support of that racist organization. It was simply a learning session for the little doctor. He wanted to know more about their organization, management, rituals, and mode of operation. He listened intently as his resplendent mind soaked up the information.

Then he returned to Cobb, Kentucky, and began to put together the organization for the Kentucky branch of the Possum Hunters. It would not be a helter skelter hodgepodge assembly of irritant farmers. He intended to formalize it into a structured, disciplined, and manageable sub-group of the Association.

He combined his knowledge and long past education of military training with the experience of the Masonic ritual. To this he added his newfound knowledge of the innerworkings of the Ku Klux Klan in order to form a highly organized secret fraternity.

Swiftly and tirelessly, he accelerated his trips throughout the area of Kentucky and Tennessee revealing his grand design. At his side almost constantly now was Guy Dunning.

Meanwhile, sporadic acts of violence were already breaking out. Although the incidents were isolated in time and location, a pattern was beginning to take shape. Here and there were whippings and beatings. Warnings of physical attacks were handwritten and left on gateposts and door facings of the hillbillies.

Governor J.C.W. Beckham of Kentucky wrote a personal letter to Felix Ewing asking him to use his influence with the outlaw farmers. Ewing, true to form, responded by defending the Association and denying that his most noble and worthy organization had anything at all to do with the atrocities. His men were, as he put it, the "flower of manhood of both states."

That same year, in the midst of this bubbling cauldron, Congressman A.O. Stanley made a memorable speech in Springfield, Tennessee. The farmers' golden-tongued ally cast himself once again against the Trust, vilifying it and its purposes in degrading terms. But, then, in a rather conciliatory tone and more for the record than affect, he condemned the violence of the Association members. No one knows for sure whether his tongue was actually in his cheek when he asked that "the night riding stop."

Appropriately, if perhaps unintentionally, from the mouth of that most eloquent statesman of the day came the term that attached itself to the movement more quickly than a magnet to a ten penny nail.

The "Night Riders" were born.

The unglamorous and mundane label of "Possum Hunters" slid into historical oblivion.

Slowly but surely the persistent efforts of David Amoss were beginning to bear fruit. The intricate and masterful underground network of the clandestine order of the Night Riders moved into place throughout the region.

David Amoss was the commander or General of the entire district. Each county was broken down into several "lodges," drawn generally along school district lines. A "captain" headed each lodge and answered to the "colonel" of the county. He in turn answered to Amoss. The first lodges were established in the Kentucky counties of Todd, Logan, Christian, Caldwell, Lyon and Trigg, and the Tennessee counties of Robertson and Montgomery. Soon ten more counties in both states followed suit.

The meetings of these lodges of militant farmers were hidden, held at night in isolated schoolhouses, churches and even barns. Sometimes they simply gathered in a remote and deserted spot in the deep, dark woods. It was not unusual for squirrel hunters by day to come upon a beaten down clearing in the woods with thousands of horse and mule tracks. These signs which were left behind gave evidence of serious business being conducted by men of the earth, at night and in the middle of the wild.

What went on at these meetings?

It all depended.

Sometimes they simply met to visit, gossip and enjoy the fellowship of one another. Under the guise of a formal meeting called to order by the captain, the proceedings would break down into swapping tales about horses, crops or county elections.

Other times the business at hand was much more serious. An upcoming hillbilly visit would be discussed, including the time and method of "persuasion." The personality and character of the person to be visited would be bantered about as to what degree of punishment would be inflicted. Occasionally a hillbilly target was well liked, maybe even otherwise an amiable neighbor to many of the men there. Heavy discussions would sometimes turn into heated arguments over how much misery the poor soul deserved. Sometimes only a serious visit and lecture was opted for. Or maybe a visit and a few light lashes. On other occasions the discussions would grow low and sinister as the fate of a despised hillbilly was plotted to include a severe beating and the destruction of his barn or plantbed.

It quickly became preferable for the whippings to be conducted by "foreign" lodges — that is, those from outside the area where the hillbilly farmer lived. This laid well for two reasons. First, it was much easier personally to inflict punishment upon someone whom they did not know, and, secondly, it reduced measureably the chances of any of the attackers being identified.

The security of these meetings was always tight. Armed sentinels were posted at the entrances or, in case of an outdoor meeting, at the outer perimeter of the woods. Secret passwords were required in order to obtain admittance to the gatherings.

From out of the dark, mixed in with the mournful sounds of a whippoorwill, a long low whistle could be heard followed by two shorts. The alert sentinel would then respond with the statement, "Silent Brigade." The person seeking admission to the meeting would answer, "Silent Brigade."

The sentinel would then retort with the guarded question, "Have you been there?" The knowing member would remark, "Yes, I have been there, on bended knees."

Sometimes local lodges would also insert their own familiar passwords which would be known only by members of that local Night Rider unit. In this general manner, the Night Rider would be duly qualified to pass or repass.

The organization was replete with secret signs, handclasps and other passwords. In a similar mode of the Masonic order, phrases could be said and signs passed in a public gathering such as church or in town that would clearly send a message from one member to another.

There was also a military bearing about all the lodges, this being the mark of their leader, David Amoss. The chain of command was staunchly observed and followed. The men bore arms and, even in broad daylight, Amoss reportedly had some of his troops drilling on the streets of Cadiz, Kentucky.

Like the Association itself, the membership of this furtive group was composed of not only tobacco farmers. There were professional men such as their own leader, merchants, lawyers and bankers. Within this growing band of terrorists were also county politicians, including county judges and sheriffs.

All of these men were required to take the "blood oath" before being accepted as members. The exact wording of it might vary from lodge to lodge, but the tenor of it followed the same line. "I in the presence of Almighty God," it went, "take upon myself these solemn oaths and obligations that I never will reveal any of the secret signs or passwords of this order." This somber incantation was always with the candidate down on his knees and with his right hand on the Bible, usually in the straw colored lantern light of a one room schoolhouse. It also went on further to specify numerous commitments and concluded, "I furthermore promise and swear that I will not use this order or under cover of this order to do anything to a personal enemy for personal revenge. To all this do I most solemnly promise and swear, placing myself under no less penalty than may be put upon me by order of this lodge, including death."

Serious business no doubt.

Violent deaths and unmarked graves were planned for traitors who violated the secrets of this solemn club.

Harrison Kroll in his book "Riders in the Night" relates graphically a vivid picture of the initiation proceedings of the Night Riders as given to him by one who had actually received the secret rites:

> "I didn't want to mess up with them bastards. But things was getting hot on all sides. One of them Trust rascals come to my barn and opened his hand and showed me gold dollars. My old woman was fixing to have a fresh baby. Dr. Amoss would have a hand in the business. Hell, I couldn't make Dr. Amoss wait for his fee while I bedded up with that Trust skunk. Then I could see where if the Association got the underhold in time it would work out for the good of all us poor farmers as well as the rich. So one night when the lodge was meeting I snuck off from my

old woman and the kids, saying I thought I'd look for a stray calf, and went down to the Cumberland River where the meetings was. They'd put enough heat to me. God knows. They were separating the men from the boys, and I didn't much want to find myself a boy, with a new baby coming, and my plant bed right there to be scraped. Even Doc Amoss when he come to see my old woman pointed that out. Well, here I was at a sycamore tree at the edge of the big timber. The night was overcast and the air was close. A feller in a mask jumped out of the shadders at me. "Halt!" says he, and boy I halted. "Sam Hill." That was me. [Not his real name.] "Is this of your own free will and accord?" "More or less," I says and he says, "Yes or no." "No," says I; than I changed it. "Yes." "Give the pass word." "I don't know no pass word." "Come with me, I got the word for you." So I went down in the deep woods with him and I reckon he found the most tangled part of the woods to carry me through. I never seen so many vines and tangles, and I'd hunted these woods since I was a shaver. Then we come up on a mess of masked men away down in the jungles and all I could see was their eyes in the masks by the light of a little fire in the clearing. So they went through all the hocus-pocus again, and the password proved to be "Sinking Fork." While they had my neck chained down to a stump I heard a clap of thunder far off beyant the river, and I smelled a storm coming on. They ast me a last time, "Is this of your own free will and accord," and this time I didn't stammer. I think it was Guy Dunning that ast me, "You understand the obligations you incur?" I said I did. They were more than I liked, but this was no time to back out. As sure as the world they'd of called on me in a night or two and hollered me out and my old woman would have heard strange noises down back of the barn. So on my knees I repeated after Doc Amoss (I soon recognized his voice) ". . . in the presence of Almighty God and these witnesses . . .," and I mumbled and got through with the oath. Then they lifted me up and taken off their masks and I knowed about half of 'em, and I was a Night Rider. Then the rain busted loose and it poured like an hour, and wet that hull mess of Night Riders to the hide, and you never heard such another clapping of thunder and the lightening played so it was like day and you could've read by it."

The purpose of this secret order was well known — to compel the non-Association people by intimidation, whipping, flogging, and even destruction of property, to join up. Also, they purported to wage war directly upon the Trust, its properties and agents, whenever the opportunity arose.

Their leader, David Amoss, boldly proclaimed the philosophy of their being, "To burn or otherwise destroy the property of growers and to whip them and other persons who refuse to cooperate with you in winning your fight against the Trust is no more than they deserve. There is no reason why a few persons should continue to make the masses suffer when their cooperation would not only not be to their detriment, but would increase the earnings and thus improve the conditions of all equally."

Thus the hillbilly sat down to his supper of plenty and said his blessings to a gracious Provider while his neighbor suffered from his indifference and failure to be a brother's keeper.

The Night Riders opened their meetings with a prayer to a merciful, compassionate and loving God, then forthwith planned to do injury upon their brothers.

The soldiers of this army wore no uniforms. But, as their acts of violence and the number of hillbillies increased, discretion dictated that they not only move under the cloak of darkness, but also in disguise. They became masked riders. Some wore flour sacks pulled down over their heads with holes punched out for their eyes.

Others simply wrapped large bandannas around the greater portion of their faces and pulled the brims of their hats down low. Some more cautious men went to battle in long flowing robes which covered them and their horses for, in those days, a man was recognizable almost as readily by his mount as the features of his face. This precaution was no doubt learned by Amoss from the Klan of the burning crosses.

In any event, they were a frightening sight to behold in the dead of night, even to the most stout-hearted soul.

On horseback, most times two abreast, this group of riders moved through the back roads and woods of this rolling land, their masked faces reflected by the flickering lights of lanterns or flaming torches held out to their sides. Their movements were made even more eerie and mysterious by their hushed, almost inaudible, motions. To accomplish this effective method of cover, gunny sacks were tied to the horses' feet to muffle the sounds of their steps.

The quiet movement of this band of masked marauders through the countryside under the flickering shadows of their flaming lights gave the illusion of some floating and menacing apparition surviving on the misty vapors of night.

They were members of the Silent Brigade.

At the outset of this movement, David Amoss, like a military general, did not participate himself in the "minor skirmishes." He was too well known to attend the personal floggings of the branded outcasts where he might be recognized in some way. His role was to plan, organize and appear only when the gatherings were either legitimate or free from risk of detection.

Handsome young Guy Dunning was his right hand man, accepted and recognized throughout the Black Patch as the Lieutenant Commander of the Night Riders.

Together they penned a proclamation for the local newspaper, written in a manner which clearly revealed the learning of this educated pair.

It described the pitiful conditions of the tobacco growers who had "appealed and petitioned the tobacco captains of finance for relief, but had been spurned with contempt at the feet of the financial thrones of the country." It defended the Night Riders as simply "a band of cool, deliberate and honorable men."

This public denunciation also covered the hillbillies and finally a fearful, if slightly veiled, ultimatum that "We are in the cause to win or die, so all people take due and timely notice and govern themselves accordingly."

As indicated in the initiation report of the unknown Night Rider, the little respected doctor of Cobb held a veiled threat over the people who came under his professional care.

He made it clear that those who might need his services had better walk to the tune of the Association and, more particularly, the Night Riders. Men whose wives were laboring along in pregnancy and whose children were being attacked by all the childhood diseases of the day were reluctant to risk having their desperate call in the middle of the night go unheeded.

As it turned out, it was a bluff. All reports indicate that the doctor never discriminated in his practice of medicine or turned his back on the Hippocratic Oath. Night or day, friend or foe, when duty called Doc Amoss responded. He never confused the purpose of his healing trade with his other life of violence.

But the general unknowing populace believed the threat was real and "governed themselves accordingly."

From the cold days of late December, 1905, until the spring of the following year, things were relatively peaceful in the Black Patch. There was an occasional whipping, and the lodges met regularly and drilled often. Not until the gray and white covers of the new plant beds in the spring began to appear did the sap of the Night Riders' menace begin to rise once again.

The plant bed represented to the tobacco farmer his most prized economic possession, for it reflected his financial prospects of the upcoming year. If something happened to these young seedlings as they broke out of the cold earth under the stretch of the canvas, the farmer would have no plants to take to the field. If this happened through some misfortune of seeding or nature, he would once again turn to his neighbor for help.

Usually, if the seed bed had been properly prepared and culti-vated and if a late frost had not slipped in upon uncovered plants, there would be plants aplenty for the field. There would even be some to spare for a neighbor who had fallen upon hard luck. That is, unless that neighbor in 1905 happened to be a hillbilly. Then the destruction of a plant bed might mean total disaster.

In early April, 1906, the mass militant farmers turned their aims away from the frontsteps of the hillbillies to the unguarded plant beds which lay outside the curtilage of their homes.

All across the Black Patch, seed beds with plants just beginning to punch through the earth were destroyed.

Timing was important.

If the bed was scraped too early in the season, the hapless farmer could simply replant. So it was imperative for the malefac-tors to wait until the plants were large enough so that a second chance would be highly unlikely.

Devilishly clever means were thought of in this war of destruc-tion. One of the most lethal was to simply slip onto the victim's land under the cloak of darkness and broadcast grass seeds in with the tobacco. By the time the unfortunate victim pulled back his seed bed canvas to survey the plants, they would have been com-pletely choked out by weeds.

Salting the seed beds was another ruinous way of decimating the tobacco crop in its embryonic stage. Finally, after it was too late for most, the hillbilly farmer learned that the only sure way of escaping the spring winds and rains with their plant beds intact was to simply arm themselves and stand guard through the night.

Many men attempted to repel invaders by posting their plant beds with signs which read "I Belong to the Association."

A more drastic and foreboding measure was utilized by some of the desperate hillbillies. That was the erection of other signs which warned that their plants were mingled with sticks of dynamite. This dire possibility was intended to scare off any Night Riders who were bent on stroking the seedlings with a hard and potentially blasting thrust of the hoe.

Such was the case of that hillbilly farmer, Benjamen Hollins, who lived near Clarksville, Tennessee. It gave rise to one of the more cowardly acts of the Night Rider annals.

On Hollins' farm lived a black sharecropper named Dudley. One night the masked marauders paid a visit to the Hollins farm and were thrown into a fearful state by the dynamite menace. Not to be thwarted, they went to Dudley's house and, not finding him at home, promptly seized his terrified wife and hurried her to the supposedly infested plant bed.

Then they forced the poor female to stomp through the young seedlings as a human detonator. It was the mandate of these farmers for her to step through every inch of the patch until she either proved the veracity of the sign by being blown to pieces or disproved the proclamation by merely surviving.

It was her good fortune that the sign had been a ruse and there were no explosives present.

Chasing the reprieved and greatly relieved woman back to her shanty, they then proceeded to demolish the tobacco plants.

One may wonder how this growing group of outlaws could roam through the countryside inflicting whippings upon this group of people and destroying their property without being arrested or prosecuted. Surely their attempts at concealment of identity were many times inept, if not downright wasted.

There were many clues to make the Night Riders recognizable — the voice or a limp, physical carriage, footwear, not to mention his clothes or horse. It could even be a tool carelessly left behind or a labeled hat blown away in escape.

But, they were not arrested because there was no one left to do the arresting.

They were not prosecuted because there was no one left to do the prosecuting.

The officers of the law and the courts were either Association members and, in many instances, Night Riders; or they were so intimidated that they would go to a great extent to avoid offending them.

Sheriff Sam Cash of Lyon County, for instance, was a known and openly avowed follower of the Amoss band.

Denny Smith, the Commonwealth Attorney of the Kentucky

counties of Colloway, Christian, Trigg, and Lyon, and John Kelly, Trigg County Attorney, were Night Riders or at least avid accomplices to their actions.

The request by a hillbilly for an official investigation of wrongdoing would be met with footdragging, if not downright disregard.

And, lastly, if by some quirk of fate, a Night Rider would be actually charged and brought to court, it was impossible to obtain a jury conviction when the counties from which they were drawn were made up of over 70% Association membership.

By the autumn of 1906, the Night Riders were firmly entrenched. As best as can be ascertained, there were at least 10,000 men within its ranks. Not only did David Amoss have his troops well organized and trained, but public opinion was assuredly behind them. The independent farmer who went the way of the Trust was indeed a lonely and endangered species.

Of all the counties in the Black Patch, perhaps Caldwell County, Kentucky, was becoming the most fervent in its zeal for both the Night Riders and the Association. This was, no doubt, the work of not only David Amoss, but others as well. Guy Dunning, who had exerted tremendous influence in coaxing Amoss to become actively involved in their cause, had become the general inspector for the Association tobacco and this job carried him to far points of the region. This way he was able to gather for Amoss' thoughtful consumption the expressed concerns and ideas of the rank and file and assist him in the organization of the Association's militant arm. In their quiet but persistent manner, these two men, along with others, made their Caldwell County branch of the Association a showpiece for the rest of the District.

Under their leadership, the Association membership in Caldwell County had climbed to a great majority. The county boasted the first Association warehouse in the two state area. David Amoss himself had advanced the highly successful boycott that had contributed great numbers to their ranks. The entire governmental, political and social leadership of this county had fallen into rank behind the guidance of Amoss and Dunning.

This strong public sentiment was shown by the tobacco rally in the county seat of Princeton on September 8, 1906.

It was an impressive exhibition. Throngs of people gathered in that small town to see banners unfurl heralding the Association and to watch the main event — the parade of a thousand farmers up and down the streets.

It was indeed an impressive sight.

The head of this legion of growers was their diminutive general, Dr. David Amoss. Those watching this grand march on that day were struck with one notable impression. The farmers moved not in a shuffling, unsystematic promenade down the boulevards. Erect and neatly dressed, they marched in step and with a sharp precision under the cause of their leader. Footmen, horsemen and even buggies were meshed together in a highly drilled and orderly review.

David Amoss, in keeping with his boyhood dreams, finally had his troops.

Encouraged no doubt by the Princeton rally, the Dark Tobacco Planters' Protection Association now put together the third annual membership meeting in Guthrie on September 22, 1906.

If there had been any doubts by anyone of the rising tide of this agrarian revolt, they were laid to rest on that day.

The little border town was simply overwhelmed.

Twenty-five thousand people, including entire families, poured into the narrow streets and onto the dusty fairgrounds in the sweltering heat.

Once again, this gathering cut across all social classes. The hard struggle and work of the Association had managed only in 1906 to raise the price level about half a cent a pound from the previous year, and the Trust was still spreading intense frustration by paying decent prices to the hillbillies. Yet, the grand gala in Guthrie on its third annual rally was still marked with enthusiasm, high hopes and excitement.

The existing prices seemed only to serve to make their mission more urgent and intense.

They gorged on barbeque and soda pop. The leathery and lean men of the soil languished under the huge oaks chewing Star Navy plug tobacco and smoking Duke's Best, both products of the American Tobacco Company. The more affluent planters puffed on cigars made by that same despised enterprise.

This puzzling and remarkable irony apparently went unnoticed.

They came from far and wide — Mayfield, Murray and Fulton, from the far west in Kentucky and from Paris and Martin in west Tennessee. Trains arrived and disgorged their loads from Nashville and other distant points.

At this meeting, more so than at the previous two, were large numbers of persons who were not tobacco growers. There were many non-farming supporters who rallied to the farmers' cause either through genuine sympathy for their plight or the economic compulsion of the boycott. And, of course, there were many hill-billy spies who came to feast on the barbeque and liquor while sponging important information concerning this organization's future plans.

Two things that the socially starved country folk of that day enjoyed were parades and speeches. At Guthrie that golden day they had a whole lot of both.

What a parade it was, taking one hour and ten minutes to pass through the dusty streets of this bulging little town.

Beginning at the downtown railroad station and led by the Chief Marshall, Colonel John B. Allen of Tennessee, it majestically weaved its way through the shouting throng of people who lined the thoroughfares.

Next to the mounted parade marshall was a dainty and impeccably attired Mrs. Felix Ewing, an accomplished rider now mounted on a muscular and glossy stallion of impressive stock. Also heading up that parade were the leaders of the organizations, proudly nodding to the applauding crowd as their horses carried them by in an easy strut. They were all there — the Fort brothers, Doc Amoss and others — all except the "Moses" himself.

Felix Ewing was sick that day. But he was close enough to the occasion, viewing this magnificent procession from the window of his hotel room overlooking the street.

Exquisitely dressed and shapely formed, a graceful group of Southern belles were next moved down the street on horseback, their bobbing plumes dancing in the dazzling sun.

After the ladies came carriages and buggies and surreys of all sorts and descriptions, their silken tassels glimmering. From these vehicles waved noted politicians and influential citizens of the day who were there to support the Association.

Then came the most impressive part of all — farmers on foot — thousands of them, moving down the street. They were divided into ten different groups, each one representing a community in the Black Patch. Each section was heralded by its own band. The loud discord of competing brass horns only added more noise to the clamorous event.

There were a thousand marching blacks placed at the end of the parade. They represented the great number of their race who made up the tenant farmer and sharecropper class. This group of people had been especially hard hit by the plummeting tobacco prices and had more Association members per capita than the whites.

In between the black and white farmers were floats of all kinds with the Association flag, a rich dark tobacco leaf placed against a white background.

The strands of "Dixie" and "My Old Kentucky Home" and other popular songs played by ringing banjoes and brass bands filled the humid air with music.

After the parade, which ended at the fairgrounds, thousands of people gathered to eat at long, wooden tables laden with food. Slowly, after much eating and conversation, they settled down for the afternoon speeches.

If a parade can be outmatched by speechmaking, this one surely was.

An impressive array of dignitaries were lined up on the newly constructed speaker's platform. Tennessee Governor Bob Taylor kicked off the rhetoric. He was a picture of the Southern gentleman: white suit, black tie and drooping silver mustache. He drolled on with homespun humor that tickled the sides of even the most calloused listeners. Then followed the Fort brothers, Mrs. Felix Ewing and other big names of the Mid-South. One such celebrity was Congressman A.O. Stanley of Henderson, Kentucky. He was by far the most eloquent speaker of all.

Stanley had been working arduously for the past two years in the halls of Congress attempting to have the tobacco tax lifted off the backs of the American farmer. It was reported on Capitol Hill that A.O. Stanley knew more about the growing, harvesting, cutting, packing and marketing of tobacco than any other man alive. So far his efforts had been defeated.

But, perhaps, just as importantly to the hearts of the Association members, he had been very much on the hustings, not politicking for himself but espousing the virtues of the Association and, at the same time, blasting the Duke Trust. He had done all of this, not to mention his many services as a lawyer which he had donated to the organization.

Standing tall and straight on the platform, Congressman Stanley cut an impressive figure. He was born in Shelbyville, Kentucky, on May 21, 1867, the son of Richard William Stanley, a minister and Confederate army veteran. His mother, Amanda, was the niece of Kentucky's 16th Governor, William Owsley. That accounted for his middle name which in later life was simply reduced to an initial. He attended Gordon's Academy near Nicholasville and Centre College in Danville, as well as Lexington's Agricultural and Mechanical College. He taught school for four years before being admitted to the state bar in 1894. He practiced law in Flemingsburg until four years later when he moved to Henderson. While in that picturesque west Kentucky town, he entered politics.

Physically impressive and well learned, he became a spellbinding orator. He was genial and enjoyed drinking with friends while engaging in discussions of politics and current events. Occasions such as the one at Guthrie brought out the best in Stanley. Sometimes it even brought out the worst — that being his well-founded reputation for occasional drunkedness. Stanley could even turn this vice to his advantage, however, with his quick wit under fire. This is evidenced by an incident which occurred when he ran for Governor against his friend, Edwin T. Morrow.

Morrow and Stanley had been traveling across the state tearing into each other as they stood on the speaker's platform. At one such speaking engagement on a hot summer afternoon in Somerset, Kentucky, the Hendersonian had once again drank too much. During the course of Morrow's speech, Stanley suddenly arose and staggered to the back of the platform where he vomited.

Returning to the front of the speaker's stand, Stanley beseeched with great aplomb that the audience excuse him for his action and said, "Every time I hear Edwin Morrow speak, it makes me sick to my stomach."

This type of self-confidence and charm, dashed with humor, made him a great favorite with these dirt farmers now resting in the Guthrie September shade to hear him speak.

Mopping the sweat from his large round and balding head with periodic strokes of his handkerchief, Stanley rocked back and forth on his feet, waving his arms in graceful gestures, weaving the entranced crowd into his complete control. He graphically reported the dire straits of the Kentucky and Tennessee tobacco farmer and forcefully emphasized the need for them to stick together. And, in a vehement and incisive manner which only political stump speakers of yesteryear were able to do, he tore into the despised Trust. Finally, he ended on a crescendo of eloquence which was followed by a thunderous roar of approval.

The smallest person there on that platform was Dr. David Amoss. But arising out of this multitude to greet him as he stood to speak was a welcome quite unlike the others. It was neither louder nor more prolonged, but different ... void of hoots and yells, but simply a deafening chorus of applause. To this speaker, unconsciously and without definition, they were saying something different.

With others, the crowd had exhibited appreciation, respect and even love. But for the 49 year old Cobb physician, it was more of a sense of acknowledgment.

While both the failing health of Felix Ewing and the seemingly unimproved plight of the farmers had not dampened their enthusiasm for the Association, there was no doubt that the Night Rider movement was seen as the best and most effective means of fighting the Trust. In fact, it was accepted by most members of the Association as a much needed part of tobacco organization. And, they were looking more and more to the General of the Silent Brigade as their leader.

As Amoss talked and as they listened, the gathering became completely serious. As if a dark cloud had moved to case a somber shadow over the group, the mood deepened.

Throughout the day and amidst the gaiety of the festivities, the Night Rider activity was the subject of most conversations. The Board of Directors of the Association at their morning meeting had taken up the matter very gingerly. It was believed by more than one member that things were going to get even rougher.

The militant gathering fully believed that the doctor from Cobb was in favor of taking his troops and doing whatever else needed to be done. And, as he finished his speech to the approving crowd, men shot quick but meaningful glances at one another as they shifted their Navy plugs from one jaw to the other.

Finally, the last words were spoken and the grand events of that day came to an end. While drunken revelers, prostitutes and young farm boys more interested in sowing wild oats than tobacco would carouse loudly about the town throughout the night, for most it was a time to head for home. In the gathering September dusk there were farewells and best wishes, sleeping toddlers and rattling wagons.

They quietly departed to all parts of west Kentucky and Tennessee. In spite of the spirited day of parades, picnics and eloquent speeches, they now receded into pensive moods. The stars came out and winked down upon this motley procession of home faring toilers of the earth. Many silently brooded as the wife and children fell asleep in the back of the wagon. Reflective thoughts ran across the minds of many a farmer that night as they rocked along toward home, the reins to their faithful beasts of burden loose in their hands.

Far away from this dreary, despondent scene and in the merry lights of New York, Buck Duke's heart was now fully recovered from his devastating marriage to Lillian McCreedy. He was once again dancing to the fancy of romance.

This new attraction was Mrs. Nanaline Holt Inman, the stunningly beautiful widow of a rich cotton merchant from Atlanta. From her home in the heart of Dixie, she had made frequent visits into the high society of New York City. There she met Buck Duke. Soon they were seeing each other regularly as she moved into a suite at the Hotel Webster in Manhattan.

The dazzling love affair helped to take Duke's mind off a little banny rooster of a man then occupying the residence of 1600 Pennsylvania Avenue. Teddy Roosevelt was listening with an ever increasing interst to those associates who were urging him to use the trust busting stick of his office and prosecute the Duke conglomerate as an illegal monopoly. The spunky Rough Rider had little sympathy for the tobacco trust which, led by Buck Duke, had tried ardently to defeat his nomination for President in 1904.

It would have no doubt bolstered the moral of the Kentucky and Tennessee dirt farmers tremendously on that September night as they journeyed homeward from Guthrie, Kentucky, to know that A.O. Stanley was not the only friend they had in Washington.

The President of the United States was preparing to take aim at the Trust of James Buchanan Duke.

And a damn Republican at that.

Chapter Five

As much as David Amoss despised the independent farmer who refused to join the Association, he was not blinded by this passion. For he knew that the hillbilly was, to some degree, the victim of circumstance. They were simply ordinary men who were either weaker or stronger than the rest, depending upon one's point of view, and mere pawns on the greater chessboard which was controlled by the Trust. These stubborn and sometimes arrogant individuals were the most convenient targets for the disgruntled farmers. And even though he condoned, encouraged and planned the violence that was inflicted upon them, he also recognized that they were striking only at the arms of the giant Duke conglomerate. It was necessary to inflict some jolt upon the heart.

Little David Amoss did not become the leader of this group of men only because of his audacity, adept organizational ability and toughness. More than anything else, he possessed brains.

And brains it would require, together with those other ingredients, to carry out the other phase of the Night Rider movement. That was the direct attacks upon the tobacco warehouses which banked the crops now purchased by the Trust.

It was much easier to burn that tobacco before it was sold to the Trust and while still hanging in the barns of the hillbillies. But, once again, the brilliant little doctor recognized a basic truth that guided his judgement. While it galled even him to see the despised and treasonous neighbors flaunt their greenback around, he realized that after the winter sales was the most devastating time to seek out that tobacco and destroy it. Then the American Tobacco Company had already paid out money and to lose the tobacco would be a double loss. Not only would they lose the crop targeted for the far flung markets of the world, but they would also lose the money that had been given for it.

The night riding farmers wanted most of all to get the attention of their hillbilly neighbors. Dr. Amoss wanted most of all to get the attention of the Wall Street moguls and the international trade barons.

So, late on those crisp fall evenings of 1906 after his family was down for the night, he and Guy Dunning talked in his living room. There, accompanied by the pale glow of the kerosene lamp while propping their feet in front of the red dying embers of a cozy fire, they plotted their strategy. Clarksville and Springfield, Tennessee, and Guthrie, Kentucky, may have been the main towns for the Association; but, without question, the unnamed and unofficial capital of the Night Rider movement was Princeton, Kentucky, the county seat of Caldwell County.

Princeton, Kentucky, in 1906 was a town of approximately 1,000 people. It had been settled around a large, resourceful spring by the first wave of western-moving whites in the late 1700's. Long before the white man ever invaded its perimeter, the rolling hills and woods were thickly populated with deer, buffalo and small varmints. An ancient and depressed pathway leading to the springs had been worn down for hundreds, perhaps thousands, of years of use by herds of game repeatedly finding their thirsty way there for water. Even today there is a street in Princeton named Varmint Trace.

From Eddy Grove, Princes Place and Princes Town named after Captain William Prince of Revolutionary War fame, it became a prosperous little country town, supported and maintained by the business of farmers who tilled the fine farmland surrounding it. After a fierce political feud with neighboring Eddyville which, at that time, was still a part of Caldwell County, Princeton became at last the county seat in 1817. By the turn of the century, it was bisected by the Illinois Central Railroad running on its way between Louisville and Paducah. At the time of Doc Amoss and Guy Dunning, it sponsored a gray brick courthouse in the middle of the town square, a stoutly built and sharply kept police station behind it, and numerous stores along with a fine fairground just south of town.

But, most importantly, to the eyes of David Amoss were two large tobacco concerns, namely, the J.G. Orr Factory on North Jefferson and the Steger & Dollar Warehouse on South Seminary just across from the depot. Both of these businesses were buying tobacco for the American Tobacco Company, the American Snuff Company and the Italian Regie, all part of the Duke Trust.

In late autumn of 1906, the insurance companies covering fire and casualty on both of these buildings received an anonymous

letter written in pencil, but grammatically exact and properly
punctuated.

It bore an ominous message,

"We are determined," the unknown writer wrote, "to put John
Orr of Princeton out of the tobacco business. The scoundrel has
bought and put up tobacco for the Tobacco Trust long enough." It
went on to place Steger & Dollar in the same ill-willed category,
but, according to the warning, they did not want to damage or
injure persons or businesses not directly involved in buying the
Trust tobacco.

"This is to notify you to cancel insurance immediately," the
warning concluded.

The Night Riders, at least at that early date, were still purists.

On the night of November 30, 1906, these Princeton tobacco
warehouses were freshly full of hillbilly grown Trust tobacco.

It was a Friday as the darkness shouldered the daylight aside
and houses began to glow through the heavy dusk from lamps and
newly stoked fires.

The weather was cold and windless and the sky was full of stars.
A perfect winter night, absent a moon.

By 10 o'clock, the streets had become deserted except for an
occasional horseman clipclopping home from a late engagement.

Houses began to grow dark as people snuggled in for the night.
There was an occasional bark of a dog or a metallic clang of a coal
scuttle.

Down at the police station, the wick was turned down and the
iron stove murmured softly as the easy banter of the two night
policemen began to drag, punctuated by yawns.

By midnight the town was dead and bathed in beautiful winter
silence.

It all happened so quickly that some of the deep sleepers would
remember it only as a dream.

Without notice, the ghostly shadows of masked men on foot
began to run silently along the streets. They were in six man
squads, each darting in a different direction. Gunny sacks were
tied to their feet to stifle the sound as they ran upon the wooden
plank sidewalks.

At the police station, the two drowsy cops were jolted to the
terrified shock of suddenly looking down the barrels of numerous
rifles and pistols as one of the hooded groups quickly invaded their
domain. The policemen were disarmed and left in the custody of
only a fragment of the group as the rest quickly retracted to the

streets and other businesses.

Simultaneously with the disabling of the officers, squads entered both the telegraph and telephone offices, placing their astonished and bewildered operator under the gun. An agile young rider quickly wiggled and pulled himself on top of the telephone and telegraph pole and cut the lines. All incoming and outgoing calls of the little sleeping town of Princeton were abruptly put to an end that night.

Another squad, carrying out its assigned duty, moved on the fire station and the city's water supply was cut, leaving the town without any means of fire protection.

Just as these small disguised advance parties were finishing up their silent tasks, a larger group of hooded and masked riders on horseback — over 200 of them — began to move into the main section of town from the south road. They, too were armed with rifles, shotguns and pistols, and their horses feet were covered. The mounts snorted steam into the cold frosty air. This sound, along with that of creaking saddles, pierced the silence of the slumbering town. Like a rising wind in the night, unseen but increasingly real, this gathering force moved upon the town.

Lights suddenly began to bring houses alive. The first gunshots rang out and bullets shattered the illuminated windows. The lights inside were quickly extinguished.

Doors were opened as sleep-drugged men in long nightgowns peered out through squinting eyes. "Stay in your houses!" the riders warned in rough tones, firing shots above doors which were quickly closed. Some citizens who escaped their homes were swiftly apprehended and retained.

A few citizens tried their telephones only to be answered by the Cumberland Telephone Office switchboard in a gruff tone, "The Night Riders are here."

Women screamed and men cursed. Dogs began to bark and children cried.

The main body of armed riders moved swiftly down North Jefferson toward the J.G. Orr Tobacco Factory. The lone night watchman meekly gave up to capture. In only a matter of minutes, the doors were broken down with axes, and kerosene was poured over the premises. After sticks of dynamite were carefully placed under piles of tobacco, the men hastily retreated outside to safety.

A torch was thrown into the large wooden structure which housed the dark tobacco for the Trust. It immediately became a raging inferno.

Now the streets of Princeton were almost as light as day, and the bright flames reached high into the sky. Soon the dynamite exploded, blasting parts of the burning building into nearby empty railroad cars which also caught fire.

For just a brief moment, the riders stood in awe of their own work. Swaying blazes of the fire reflected brightly off their covered faces where gaping and excited eyes peered out through small slits. They were watching over 200,000 pounds of tobacco go up in one big smoke.

Then they moved on to the Steger & Dollar Warehouse a few blocks away and repeated the process.

While the torches did their business, small units on horseback and on foot patrolled the streets to keep the local population in check.

A witness to all this, Gladys L. Carner, a small girl at the time, related her observations many years later:

> "We were living on South Jefferson Street in plain view of the Steger tobacco warehouse two blocks across on Seminary Street when the Night Riders burned that and the Orr tobacco warehouse in the north part of town. It was in the light of that fire that I saw one group of those masked men marching out South Jefferson Street to where their horses were hitched, ready for their getaway after their job was finished. I was only six years old but I can remember the sound of their heavy boots on that night of November 30, 1906. I was standing at our front door with my mother. We were terrified as other neighbors were also. My father had walked uptown to near the courthouse, before we understood what it was all about. Several other men who did the same thing got locked up in different places by the Night Riders but no one had seemed to notice my father. As the masked men passed our house, they were shooting guns in the air and yelled at us and others to 'get back inside.' "

With the sky ablaze with light, the leader of this band of invaders, Dr. David Amoss, rode to the courthouse square. There he raised something to his mouth and blew out three long blasts, the indescribable sounds of which seemed to be a mixture of that coming from a whistle and a horn. It was the signal to regroup and depart. First the footmen rapidly headed out of town in different directions to their waiting horses. Their departure was covered by a rear guard of armed horsemen. With their horseless comrades safely out of town, the main body of riders came closely together and in an unhurried and almost leisurely manner began their orderly exodus. As the heavens of the night were aglow with their handiwork, this band of satisfied outlaws began to sing in unison, "The fires shine bright on my old Kentucky home," to that classic tune of Stephen Foster's.

As the unusual chorus faded away in the night the town was left to the crackling and thundering sounds of two gigantic fires and an occasional roar of dynamite exploding.

People began to venture out, quietly at first, and then, satisfied that the dangerous invaders had left, they began to talk in loud and excited tones.

The fire brigade went into immediate action to contain the magnificent blazes which had already destroyed the warehouses. In spite of their efforts, a few houses in the Negro section of Princeton caught fire and burned, fortunately without any injury to life or limb.

Meanwhile, the Silent Brigade moved back into the backwoods from whence it had come. Its leader, David Amoss, could relax at last and lower the reins of his horse.

It had been a brilliant maneuver, honed to exact military precision and execution. Approximately 250 unlearned, some even illiterate, men had been led into the sleeping town. Communications had been cut, the civilian populace held under control, and the warehouses — sated with 400,000 pounds of Trust tobacco — had been burned to the ground, all without a single injury. Astoundingly, it had all been accomplished within one hour's time.

No doubt the heart of General David Amoss pounded with a euphoric sense of pride in this, his first, military outing.

And he must have known within his own mind that neither Nathan Forrest nor Stonewall Jackson could have done it better.

Amoss could also happily compute that the total loss of the destroyed tobacco would run between 75,000 and 100,000 dollars. He may even have broken a smile beneath his hot and scratchy mask when he considered the most heartwarming fact of all . . . the insurance companies for the tobacco factories had cancelled their coverage only a few days before.

The Princeton raid mesmerized the Black Patch.

When the last stick of dynamite rumbled forth from the bowels of the Steger & Dollar Factory, it signaled the opening volley of what was to continue over the next two years as the Black Patch War.

Up until the time of the attack upon the Caldwell County seat, the general public had perceived the Night Riders as simply a disorganized band of outlaws, flailing away at defenseless and isolated farmers in the middle of the night. But the capture of a whole town and the tremendous destruction of Trust property with such unerring competence made the Silent Brigade indeed deserving of that name.

And, most importantly to the purpose of Dr. David Amoss, the high starched collars of Wall Street had at last raised their eyebrows and glanced away from their market quotations, if only momentarily, to this impertinent and annoying clamor in the hinterland of Kentucky.

The angry and militant farmers were not by any means relegated soley to west Kentucky and Tennessee. In February, 1906, Virginia joined the Kentucky and Tennessee organization. The tongue twisting label was shortened to the Planters' Protection Association of Kentucky, Tennessee and Virginia. There were even some sporadic acts of violence in Virginia as well as in other tobacco producing states: Ohio, Indiana, West Virginia and North Carolina. But it did not come close to matching those highly organized acts of the Silent Brigade from the Black Patch.

Even in the burley growing regions of central Kentucky, there were occasional outbreaks of lawlessness, primarily dealing with the destruction of tobacco barns and warehouses. But nowhere else in the Bluegrass State — or in this country for that matter — was there another David Amoss. Thus the intricate Night Rider organization of west Kentucky and Tennessee was one of a kind.

Reports of the trouble in the Black Patch region were no doubt filtered through the corporate heirarchy and offices of the Trust to the man himself, James Buchanan Duke. After all, the dark tobacco trade was important to his international empire insomuch as a substantial amount of the leaf was exported to Italy, England and the rest of Europe for the use in snuff and plug chewing tobacco.

But the noise that Duke was hearing from down on the farm was muted somewhat by confidants and aides. In his busy and hectic life, reports were digested to bare essentials. At this stage in the game, he was reading the bottom line only, "The farmers are raising hell."

Naturally, he knew a lot of planters and farmers, most from his native land of North Carolina, and he believed that they were simply envious of his own success or frothing at the mouth because of the agitation from the news media. He placed the blame for the unrest squarely on the shoulders of the North Carolina press, vilifying it basically as a bunch of demagogues and socialists.

If Duke's divergent business interests and demands did not draw him away from any prolonged attention to the farmer nemesis, his personal life would.

About this time another embarrassment struck the Duke clan, now well noted for spicy encounters that would put the modern day television soaps to envy.

Buck's brother, Brody, was a high roller and lover of wine, women and song. This was not to mention his weakness for gambling. But, unlike the rest of the family, he was now unassociated with the Duke business venture and was constantly going broke. Yet, as if by genetics, he had his own grand business schemes going, which usually turned into catastrophic failures.

After two marriages, once widowed and once divorced, Brody married for the third time a woman from a less reputable district of New York. When the rest of the Duke family heard of this outrageous development, lawyers and detectives were called in. They suspected that the little damsel was more interested in getting in the family cupboards than in their brother's bed. After a whirlwind of cloak and dagger tactics and legal paperwork, Brody was committed to a private mental sanitorium. Three promissory notes of $5,000 each were discovered made payable by him to his wife of checkered reputation. Finally, Brody saw the light, or the bilking as the case was, and submitted to his family's demand. Contending that he could not even remember the marriage ceremony, and also alleging unfaithfulness on behalf of his wife, he obtained a divorce and the winds of controversy striking at gale force against the house of Duke subsided into a lull.

The winter months of early 1907 brought with them a peaceful interlude in the activities of the Night Riders. The Trust tobacco warehouses in the market towns of west Kentucky and Tennessee were now empty. The large wooden hulls, awaiting the next year's crop, now collected only cold air. The barns of the hillbillies, no longer laden with tiered plants of gold, ceased to be targets of the match and torch.

The followers of General Amoss were in a holding pattern. For the small towns in the Black Patch, it was a time for a collective, but guarded, sigh of relief.

Membership of the Association shot up during those months. Growing public support and the luster of the highly successful Princeton raid contributed not only to the growing image of the militants, but to its parent organization, the Association, as well.

But, if the ranks of the Association were growing during this time, there was also an increasing number of people moving away from the Night Rider intimidation.

They were leaving the country.

It was clear that the Black Patch was in the strong clutch of a violent uprising. Some people wanted no part of living there. Others — hillbillies or their families and friends — chose to switch rather than fight.

Most moved to the states of Indiana, Illinois, Missouri and Arkansas. Metropolis, Illinois — right across the river from the western end of Kentucky — became a popular refugee town for the harried exiles.

Residents of Montgomery and Robertson County, Tennessee, simply moved into other parts of the state where tobacco was not grown. There was even one large delegation from Kentucky which left by train for free or cheap land in Texas.

Most departed only to return years later.

A few found life more bearable within the familiar hotbed of unrest than on strange soil.

Jay Wesley Barefield of Trigg County, Kentucky, was such a person.

He was visited one night by 35 Night Riders who shot up his house and ordered him outside. There he was lectured sternly and warned to keep his mouth shut or else.

He forthwith moved to Arkansas. Just as quickly, however, he returned and immediately joined up with the Associaton.

Soon the spring sap of 1907 began to rise.

Plant beds were sown and covered. Night visits resumed.

The lash and torch were retrieved from their winter resting places.

It was a fresh new year and time for the hillbillies to see the error of their ways and pledge their next crop of tobacco to the

ABOVE: James B. Duke, (Photo
courtesy of Duke Endowment,
Charlotte, North Carolina)

RIGHT: Dark fired tobacco
ready for cutting. (Photo courtesy of George Everette)

ABOVE: Smoke escaping from barn during the "firing" of dark tobacco. (Photo courtesy of **The Rural Kentuckian**)

OPPOSITE, TOP: Washington Duke standing beside his first primitive tobacco factory. (Photo courtesy of Duke University)

OPPOSITE, BOTTOM: Site where the Stainback Schoolhouse stood in Robertson County, Tennessee.

ABOVE: Home of Charles Fort in Robertson County, Tennessee, president of the Dark Fired Tobacco District Planters' Protection Association.

OPPOSITE, TOP: Glenraven, the plantation mansion of Felix Ewing i Robertson County, Tennessee.

OPPOSITE, BOTTOM: The home of Dr. David A. Amoss in Cobb Kentucky.

ABOVE: Left to right on the front row, Benjamin Duke, Washington Duke, and James B. Duke pose for a picture at a North Carolina barbecue in 1904. (Photo courtesy of Duke University)

OPPOSITE, TOP: Unidentified persons standing in front of the office of Charles Meachem's "Kentuckian" in Hopkinsville, Kentucky, about the same time period of the Night Rider raid upon that town. (Photo courtesy of William Turner)

The Hopkinsville-Cadiz Road at the general vicinity of the shootout that occurred between the Night Riders and the pursuing posse on the night of the Hopkinsville raid. Note the bloody handkerchief left in the middle of the roadway. (Photo courtesy of William Turner)

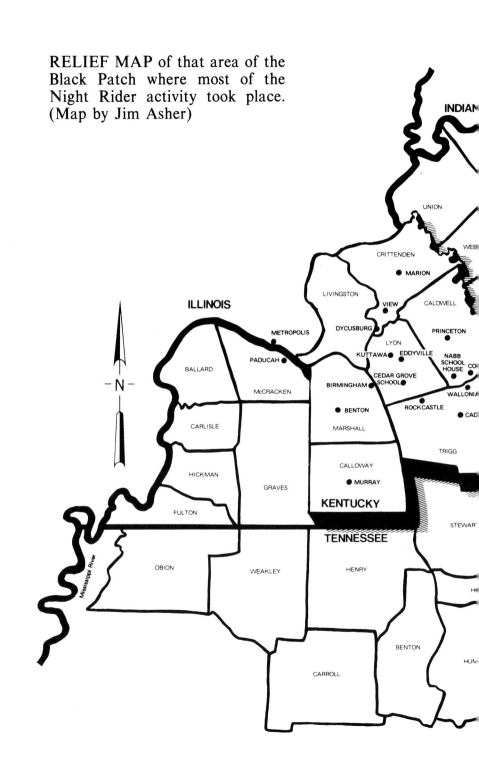

RELIEF MAP of that area of the Black Patch where most of the Night Rider activity took place. (Map by Jim Asher)

David A. Amoss. (Photo courtesy of Eloise Jacobs)

Crusty old W.L. Crumbaugh, County Judge of Lyon County, posed on the ready for a Night Rider attack. (Photo courtesy of Julian Beatty)

Mary Lou Hollowell. (Photo courtesy of Mrs. Robert Pasko, Princeton, Kentucky)

David A. Amoss. (Photo courtesy of Eloise Jacobs)

OPPOSITE, TOP: The home of Mary Lou and Robert Hollowell at the time of the attack upon them by the Night Riders as it appears today. The house and grounds reportedly are almost identical today as they were on that fateful night in May, 1907.

OPPOSITE, BOTTOM: The Cedar Grove Schoolhouse in Lyon County, Kentucky, as it appears today.

ABOVE: The home of Henry Bennett in Dycusburg, Kentucky, where he lived at the time of the attack by the Night Riders, as it appears today.

Christian County Court House,
Hopkinsville, Ky.
"The Second Largest Tobacco Market
in the World."

An early 20th century Christian County, Kentucky, circular boasting of its impressive courthouse as well as its main farm crop. (Photo courtesy of William Turner)

Association rather than to the Trust buyers.

Those that didn't would not have a crop.

While a large number of Night Riders would be required for a midnight whipping and lashing, the destruction of plantbeds was most times carried on better with only two or three men.

Following directions of their lodge, they would sneak onto the farm of the unfortunate subject under the cover of darkness and with hoe, grass seeds, salt or all of the mentioned, do their work. The smaller the number, the less likelihood of detection.

These men's specialty was the decimation of newly seeded tobacco beds. Soon they were disparingly labeled "hoe toters" by the bitter hillbillies. It was a label that was eventually given to all Night Riders by their enemies.

The loss of the young tobacco plants due to the Night Rider delinquency caused two unexpected developments in this farming region.

First, in late spring, when the victims came up empty handed and with the prospect of no cash crop for the year, they turned to foul means themselves. If a neighbor did not freely assist by giving him enough to make his crop, he would come up with a replacement by hook or crook.

Thievery of plants became a problem. Hillbillies ironically would sneak onto the lands of Association members, not with the intention of destroying their seedlings, but to desperately seize upon enough tobacco to get out their own crop.

The frantic and plantless farmers were no respecters of person. They even stole from other independent farmers, who may have somehow escaped the "hoe-toters." There may have been honor among some thieves, but not if they were hillbillies grasping for their livelihoods.

The other ramification from the loss of thousands of tobacco plants from the 1907 crop would be purely economical. It was a rather bizzare crop acreage allotment plan. As it would turn out, the volume of dark tobacco raised and sold at market that year would be substantially less than usual because of this illegal irradication of the early plants. Since oversupply had been one of the real, if less noted, reasons for the declining prices, the reduction in the crop size would help the degraded prices.

The imagination of the Night Rider lodges was boundless.

Hillbillies could be whipped, plant beds could be destroyed, and barns could be burned. But there were also ways of going after the Trust tobacco while it was in transit to the factories.

To prove the point, in mid-February, 1907, the Night Riders played their own rendition of the revolutionary Boston Tea Party.

The target of this maneuver was a prominent Lyon County buyer for the Rinaldo Tobacco Company — a Trust subsidiary. He was also a highly successful tobacco grower. H.C. Wallace had refused from the very outset to join the Association nor would he give up his allegiance to the Trust. As early as October, 1906, he had received his first warning letter from the Night Riders. After some investigative work of his own, he concluded to his own satisfaction that the letter had come from a respected Trigg County magistrate, N.E. Nabb. His attempts to have Nabb indicted by a Trigg County Grand Jury got about as far as a fish out of water. The only thing it served to do was to stir up more agitation toward him in that community of "hoe-toters."

Only Wallace himself was surprised when, on a cold February night in 1907, "unknown persons" entered his barn and detroyed 2600 pounds of tobacco which he had bought up and was preparing to ship to the Rinaldo Factory. He managed to salvage part of it and hauled three hogsheads to the Cumberland River town of Rockcastle on the Lyon-Trigg County line. There, on the evening of February 28, it waited shipment by packet boat up river to Clarksville, Tennessee.

In the still of night, twenty-five Night Riders gathered at the river, garbed, not in Indian attire as their New England predecessors had been, but disguised under mask and torch. With a relish of schoolboys, they splashed Wallace's heavy tobacco hogsheads off the pier into the deep muddy waters of the Cumberland River. So much did they enjoy this devilish work that they cleared the whole stock awaiting shipment. As the last hogshead went down the drink, they learned to their great embarrassment and regret that some of the leaf they had submarined actually belonged to someone other than Wallace. In fact, their faces no doubt turned crimson under their masks when they learned that the other victim was even a member of their own Association.

So, in this land of plantbed raids, nighttime whippings and other assorted evils, 1907 met its merry days of May.

Upon this untidy stage, already crowded with master spirits, walked a woman who could prove to be a match for them all.

Mary Lou Hollowell was a 40 year old brunette in Caldwell County, Kentucky.

She was good looking. This offended many of the women.

She was also opinionated and outspoken. This offended many of the men.

But, most importantly, she was also dutifully opposed to the Association and its militant arms.

This offended all of the Night Riders.

This staturesque beauty, along with her husband Robert, and twelve year old son Price, lived in the southern corner of Caldwell County within a brisk walking distance of both the Trigg and Lyon County lines. As the crow flies, her little frame house was only about five miles from the home of Doc Amoss in Cobb. It is highly probable that this kindly country doctor was the Hollowell family physician.

In the summer she and Robert successfully worked their small farm which included the growing of tobacco. In the winter she and Price would move into the town of Princeton where she ran a boarding house.

Mary Lou's controversial personality did not impair her business in Princeton. It was a popular gathering place, especially at meal time when some of the most respected and prominent people of this community, including judges, lawyers and other courthouse officials, would partake sumptuous food from her table. It was not unusual for David Amoss and Guy Dunning to visit Mary Lou's boarding house.

The coquettish hostess, immaculately dressed and flurrying among her guests, would — as people loved to say — serve dimples with her dumplings.

While the reviews of Mary Lou's reputation might be mixed, all agreed she was a character. Her living in town without Robert and her total disregard for the social mores of that time by unabashedly being seen alone with other men, raised both eyebrows and gossip. It is not known whether Mary Lou was in fact truly intimate with male company other than her husband. But it is certain that she was a liberated woman. In being so, she ruffled many feathers in 1907 Princeton.

And, there was no doubt as to who was the boss of the Hollowell family.

Robert Hollowell was a mild-mannered, quiet individual. By all accounts, he was a very good man, hard-working, sober and discreet. He was ruled by his dynamic, charismatic wife and appeared totally happy with this arrangement.

Mary Lou lived and breathed daily in a social maelstrom.

Robert's brother, John, who lived nearby, was one of the leading
Night Riders in the county and a very close associate of Doc
Amoss. His wife and Mary Lou were not on the best of terms; her
sister-in-law carrying a deep jealously for this abrasive beauty,
suspecting that she was friendlier with her husband than family
ties required.

Mary Lou's brother, on the other hand, also resided close by and
was much like her — a bitter opponent to the Association and all
that it stood for.

In the midst of it all, Robert's frail and failing old mother lived
just across the field and within easy view of Mary Lou's home.

There, suffering away as only mothers understand, she observed
the deepening strife between her own blood.

And to cap it all, Nabb Schoolhouse, the meeting place for one
of the most active Night Rider lodges in Kentucky, was only a ten
minute leisurely walk from the Robert Hollowell farm.

Needless to say, this little neck of the woods crackled and
popped with tension. While the town of Princeton was buzzing in
the aftermath of the December raid, Mary Lou was in a perfect
position to gather information about the grand event.

For the most uninterested person, it would have been impossible
not to overhear conversations between prominent citizens and
courthouse officials at the boarding house table. For a bright and
curious matron such as Mary Lou, it was a simple matter to put
the whole thing together.

She eagerly picked up on unguarded statements made by Association members and even Night Riders who should have been
much more careful and discreet in their discussion of business.
And, of course, many a man's willpower weakened and their
tongues loosened under the seductive and beguiling prodding of
Mary Lou. She was also perceptive enough to pick up on things
within the Hollowell family itself, even if relations were strained.
Her brother-in-law, John, had no doubt been one of the prime
movers in the surprise attack upon the county seat.

In April of 1907, just before she would close her boarding house
for the summer and return with Price to the country where Robert
remained in the care of a Negro cook and housewoman, Mary Lou
took a bold and dangerous step. She requested to appear before
the Caldwell County Grand Jury concerning information she had
about the Night Rider raid upon Princeton.

The all male panel listened in stoned silence. Many, if not all,
were Night Riders.

To their horror, she actually called names of some of the people involved with the Silent Brigade. More especially, she gave information about the raid upon Princeton.

To no one's surprise, including no doubt Mary Lou's, the Grand Jury did not return any indictments.

In retrospect, one has to wonder about Mary Lou's intentions. She was a very observant and knowledgeable citizen, familiar with the people of that community and most certainly knew that the Grand Jury was stacked with "hoe-toters" who would never take any affirmative action against their own kind.

That being the case, one must ponder why she even bothered.

It quickly becomes apparent that Mary Lou was looking for a fight. She seemed obsessed at throwing the gauntlet and challenging them right across their own threshold.

Personal bitterness and spite many times is more intense and vicious within the family circle. It was no secret that she and her sister-in-law were irreparably at odds, hardly on speaking terms. Two of Robert Hollowell's brothers were strong Association members and at least one of them a Night Rider.

It seems then that Mary Lou's personal attack upon the militant farmers' group may well have been incited by her own personal resentments against the Hollowell clan. The Night Rider movement may simply have provided a place to draw the battlelines.

In any event, if it was trouble she was seeking, it was trouble she got.

On the night of April 18, a "hoe-toter" squad was dispatched to the Bob and Mary Lou Hollowell farm.

They were, through the experiences of the past year, "professionals." The plant beds of Mary Lou and Robert were almost within a stone's throw of their house. They were destroyed quickly and silently without a bark from their yard full of dogs.

Robert soberly surveyed the damage the next morning with stoic acceptance. Mary Lou blew a gasket.

Storming around the house spewing venom and generally venting her spleen was not enough. Up and down the countryside, in Princeton and in Cobb, at church, and anywhere one or more would listen, she not only preached against the deed, but pointed her dainty finger at three neighbors and called their names — one being her brother-in-law John Hollowell.

She must have realized, especially on the heels of her unsuccessful grand jury trek, that her loud and persistent accusations would be of no avail. But it evidently helped her release the searing anger and frustration bearing down on her soul.

However, on the night of April 30, she apparently did more than just complain. For, on that evening, the seed beds of three farmers in Mary Lou's neighborhood were mysteriously scraped clean. The unfortunate victims just so happened to be the same persons that the outraged Mary Lou had been accusing of like deeds on her own farm.

Now the shoe was on the other foot. This Night Rider lodge was, with the rising sun the following morning, up in arms. The sheriff was notified.

He came immediately.

A creeping selfish hillbilly plant bed being destroyed was one thing. But the audacious and unlawful acts of perfidy against good upstanding Association members was something else. This demanded prompt and thorough investigation.

As the lawman and a couple of deputies stomped around the dew-drenched weeds surrounding one of the violated patches, interesting and intriguing pieces of evidence developed. ·

First, there were tracks. They were followed easily through the damp grass and soggy ground to the doorsteps of Ned Pettit, a black tenant farmer who worked from time to time for Robert Hollowell. But most important of all was the discovery at the scene of the crime of a small crumpled daybook. After examining the pages thoroughly, it was concluded to belong to none other than Steve Choate, the hired hand of Robert and Mary Lou.

Choate was quickly visited, apprehended, and questioned. It didn't take long for him to break. What was obvious to the investigators from the very outset now became fact.

According to Choate's confession, Mary Lou had paid him and Pettit $10.00 apiece to scrape the plant beds.

By noon of the first day of May, the case was wrapped up. Choate and Pettit were charged and lodged in jail. Now all attention turned to Mary Lou.

No additional warrants were taken that day. No questioning was done and no arrests perfected. The law went home and the matter was turned over, temporarily at least, to the Silent Brigade.

Summons were issued.

Throughout the afternoon, notices were sent out.

As the darkness enshrouded the neighborhood of Mary Lou Hollowell, armed horsemen began to arrive at the little schoolhouse. Thirty-five of them in all tied their horses to the hitching post and nearby saplings. They didn't even enter the building but met in the darkness under a sky blinking with diamonds.

There was not much said. After the gathering was complete, masks and hoods were pulled on, adjusted into place, rifles and shotguns checked. Then, at the hour that most good country folk were slumbering in their beds, they began their silent march on foot across the fields.

Mary Lou, Robert and Price were all asleep when their visitors arrived.

Dogs began to bark. "Up close!" yelled the Night Rider in charge, and the group surrounded the dwelling.

There was still no sign of any movement within the house. Then they opened up with gunfire. Bullets and shotgun blasts fell upon the wooden fixture as the deafening noise broke open the cool spring air.

Windows shattered, and cascaded to the ground. Mary Lou was immediately awakened by the first blast. She was clad in a clinging, well-fitted flannel gown which accentuated the enviable lines of her shapely form. Her long, black hair fell down around her shoulders.

She quickly rolled to the floor and frantically crawled to the bed of little Price. Pulling him along and ignoring his screams, she dragged him to a large wooden trunk and placed him between it and the wall for protection. By this time, Robert was also on the wooden planking beside her.

The shooting continued and flying glass and splintered wood filled the room. A spray of buckshot caught Mary Lou in the neck. She screamed out in anguish to no one in particular, "I've been shot!"

"That's what we meant to do!" came a rough and masculine retort from outside.

"We're coming out!" she screamed again, this time her anger beginning to swell up inside to match her fears.

The shooting stopped.

Out into the small yard Mary Lou staggered, bleeding badly around her neck and face. Robert, also scantily dressed, followed feebly behind, blinking and searching the masked faces. Young Price, sobbing continuously, peered out the door and slowly moved out of the house as full attention was paid to his imperiled parents.

The assailants quickly surrounded the pair. Some held up lanterns which encircled the victims in a dim glow. The flickering flames also cast leaping shadows off of the menacing masks, out of which beady eyes peered and rough, cursing voices arose.

At first the couple, especially Mary Lou, were chastised verbally for their acts against the Association and Night Rider members. Then three men grabbed hold of Robert and buggy whips appeared. While his arms were pulled wide of his body and he was held against a tree, the lashing began. He yelled out in pain.

Mary Lou screamed and rushed to his aide but was quickly beaten with fists and thrown to the ground. There she was struck repeatedly. While she was lying there withering and bleeding in the dirt, a husky young Night Rider stepped forward and placed a swift kick of a heavy boot to the buttocks of this prostrate, but still dashingly attractive, brunette.

With that came the piercing and high pitched exclamation of a female voice from one of the disguised faces, "This is sweet revenge for me!"

Lulu Hollowell, the despised sister-in-law, had not been able to turn down the visit. No doubt for the only time during the entire Black Patch War, the Silent Brigade had the benefit of a masquerading feminist.

Her husband, John, was also there assisting his confederates in drawing the blood of his own brother. Their anguished mother sat in her upstairs corner bedroom just across the way and anxiously looked out the window at the family violence.

The beating and lashings of Robert and Mary Lou continued through the poignant and terrified screams of little Price who stood helplessly by while his parents were brutalized. It no doubt seemed like hours. In fact, it was all over in just a few minutes. Robert sunk to the base of the tree, his nightgown shredded and matted to his bleeding back. Mary Lou lay unconscious on the ground.

Then, with nothing further to do, the visitors quietly filed out of the small yard through the open space and onto the dirt road which led to the empty fields. One last departing threat was given to the helpless victims. Loudly proclaimed and couched in profanities, the message was clear, "Get out of the county and never come back or you will be killed."

Quickly, the attackers were gone, disappearing into the night. The sounds of nature flushed with katydids and crickets returned, mixed with the groans of Robert Hollowell, the sobs of a little boy, and the curses of a revived Mary Lou.

The first rays of sun breaking across the Caldwell County countryside the following morning found the Robert Hollowell farm deserted.

The heartbroken and hysterical old mother was the first there to offer aid after the Night Riders had left. It was with a heavy and woeful spirit that she tried to attend to the wounds of Robert and Mary Lou and to calm her dazed and bewildered grandson. The task was made more agonizing no doubt by the knowledge that such pain and suffering of her own had been at the hands of her own also.

Through the remaining dark hours of the night, the maimed and halting couple packed their personal belongings into a few old trunks and departed from the little home place as dawn was streaking the eastern sky.

Mary Lou's wound, though superficial as it turned out, had caused a lot of bleeding and was quite painful. She was alarmed, now that her life was apparently out of danger, about the cosmetic effects of the injury. No greater grasp upon the soul wrenches like the vanity of a beautiful woman. So, before going into town, she stopped for medical attention, unbelievably, at the home of David A. Amoss, M.D., Cobb, Kentucky.

Robert took little Price with him to his brother Archer's house where they remained for about two weeks while winding up his farming operation and selling his land and livestock.

It was imperative, however, that the despised Mary Lou depart from the county immediately and not stand upon her leave taking. So she headed for Princeton. There she requested the local livery stable to pick up her trunks which were still sitting at home awaiting delivery to the railroad station. Even this seemingly routine task was not easy during this volatile time.

Wiley Jones, former sheriff and the owner of the stable, directed his hired hands to take the large drummer buggy and go to the Hollowell farm to pick up the luggage. The cowed and quivering employees flatly refused to go when they discovered the location of the pickup.

Jones, never known as a timid sort, became agitated. He recruited a friend and went himself. As they arrived at Mary Lou's house, they found 17 men sitting across the road on a pile of lumber. The place was obviously under surveillance.

Not to be intimidated, the two men casually spoke to the onlookers and proceeded to carry out their duties by loading the trunks and returning to town. Jones would subsequently be called to task by the Night Riders for "aiding and abetting Mary Lou" and came within an eyelash of a whipping himself.

By mid-morning, Mary Lou was on a train headed for Paducah. She was soon to be joined there by her husband and son from whence they traveled to Oklahoma and resettled for awhile.

Within a few days after their departure, Mary Lou was indicted along with Steve Choate and Ned Pettit by a Caldwell County Grand Jury for scraping the plant beds of their neighbors.

The Night Riders of Caldwell County dusted their hands and congratulated themselves on a job well done. It was a masterful stroke, a great example for any other wayward souls that might be thinking about following Mary Lou's example of defiance. The female miscreant had been beaten, banished and a criminal charge placed dangling over her head for good measure.

The problem of Mary Lou was behind them. So, at least, they thought.

In the summer of 1907, Buck Duke was 51 years of age and took on his second marriage in three years. He and the lovely Georgia peach, Nanaline Holt Inman, were wed on July 23, in Brooklyn, New York. Earlier in the year, anticipating such an event, he bought property at Fifth Avenue and 78th Street in New York City for the construction of a palatial Georgian mansion which would be valued at $1,600,000.00.

The same year that ragged and sweat stained farmers in the Black Patch were losing their shirts on tobacco, Duke's personal fortune was only $200,000,000.00.

In addition to the Fifth Avenue property, Duke also owned a grand estate in New Jersey where he and his new bride would spend much of their time. The grounds at Somerville, known simply as Duke's Farm, was an extravagance of unbelievable dimensions. Consisting of 2,200 acres, it supported a dairy of 250 blooded Guernseys. There were also fine horses and a half mile trotting track. He imported gardeners, architects, horticulturists, stone masons, sculptors, and stained glass artisans from abroad to construct what was described by some as a "veritable fairyland". The estate had paved streets, stone bridges, artificial lakes, lagoons, water fountains, and luscious gardens. The house was composed of fifty rooms and a greenhouse covered by 110,000 square feet of glass. There Buck Duke pursued what may have been his only known hobby — growing orange trees, melons, peaches, nectarines, grapes and his award winning orchids.

The spacious and beautifully kept front lawn was graced by two large granite lions carved and shipped from China. Next to the lions was an impressive life size statue of the martyred William McKinley whom Duke admired deeply, having contributed great sums to the campaign of the ill-fated President.

His lavish living was not confined to these grounds nor to New York. He and Nanaline also purchased "Rough Point," the old, picturesque Vanderbilt mansion at Newport which perched above the rocky Atlantic coastline and its crashing breakers.

By all appearances, Buck Duke was living a life on top of the world.

Physically, he was still impressive.

Standing over six feet tall, he looked like the typical Scot with his large head and red hair. His eyes were bright and clear. In dress, Duke attired himself simply, somewhat carelessly, until under the influence of his later wife, he became more fashionable and better groomed. His manner exuded self-confidence and, while normally rather reserved, on occasion he became effervescent and, with a little booze, would sometimes lapse into loud and boorish conduct.

In politics, like all tycoons of the day, this son of a Confederate soldier was a Republican. He worked hard against any candidate that was associated with the populist cause of the day, having little confidence in the common people. He, like all leading industrialists and commercial giants during the first years of the 20th century, looked upon the upsurging labor movement as composed of Communists and anarchists.

And, like other leaders in big business, he detested President Teddy Roosevelt.

From the time that he went into the White House the little Rough Rider had ideas of taking on all the big monopolies of the day. They were, in his opinion, in direct violation of the Sherman Anti-Trust Law passed by Congress in 1890. As early as 1906, the knowing public eagerly and wistfully braced for the fight. One North Carolina headline bannered, "Teddy About to Jump Onto Buck; the Trust Will Hear Thunder!"

As his heart danced with romance and anticipation of his upcoming marriage to Mrs. Inman, Buck Duke's sunny blue sky was darkened by large drifting black clouds.

On the muggy, summer morning of July 10, 1907, a man by the name of James C. McReynolds walked into the Federal Courthouse in New York City. He was a lawyer for the United States of

America. On the clerk's counter he laid down the death warrant
for the Duke Trust. It was a lawsuit charging James B. Duke and
twenty-eight associates of violating the Sherman Anti-Trust Act
of 1890.

David Amoss wasn't the only little man of that day who knew
how to fight.

The hillbillies were not organized.

Independent souls do not good associates make.

Most opposition by farmers to the acts of the Association and
the Night Riders was composed of a one on one confrontation.
The individuals who defied the militants made up a very thin
minority and, with the exception of a spirited few, either took their
lumps and left the country, or endured stoically. The ranks of the
hillbillies were not sufficiently in force or with adequate leadership
to stage any kind of an effective resistance.

The closest the hillbillies came to any type of organized operation was in Robertson County, Tennessee. There it was led by Ben
H. Sory of the small community of Adams.

He was a formidable individual having previously served as
sheriff of that community and known throughout the area as a
bold and fearless man.

Sory was a buyer for the Duke combination of the American
Tobacco Company, the Reggie and Imperial companies. In addition to his tobacco factory, he also ran a business in Adams. From
its very inception, he vigorously fought the Association and used
both his position as buyer and that of considerable prestige in the
community to coax some farmers into falling in line behind him.

The local Night Rider lodges of these north Tennessee counties
feared and respected Ben Sory. For this reason, they too used
extra precaution and peaceable means in their attempt to bring
him over to their side. They knew very well that he could not be
intimidated.

Sory quickly became tabbed "King of the Hillbillies" and many
thought a comparable balance to both Ewing and Amoss. He was
even able to elicit some respected men of that area as his lieuten-
ants and had spies within the Association itself.

The "King" organized a band of armed men to protect his own
tobacco factory in Adams. Finally, however, it was not the lash
and torch that got him but the boycott. It forced him to close his
store, board up his tobacco warehouse, and move to Clarksville

twenty miles away.

He left behind his friend, Thomas Menees, a member of the Sory resistance movement who lived in Cedar Hill. In addition to a small store in that village, Menees owned a threshing machine which he took from farm to farm harvesting wheat. In July of 1907, forty Night Riders surprised the armed hillbilly guards sleeping around the machine, disarmed them, and dynamited the thresher into scrap iron.

When Sory heard of the dastardly misfortune which had befallen his friend, he became incensed and immediately boarded a train to come to his aid. As fate would have it, the large, raw-boned ex-lawman encountered one of the Association's leaders, Colonel Joel Fort, on the same car. Ben Sory, not a man to tangle with in the best of times, was highly agitated and on edge by the latest Night Rider mischief.

The sight of Joel Fort was too much. Words were exchanged and Sory proceeded to beat the living daylights out of the right hand man of Felix Ewing. Only the intervention of the conductor, flagman and other passengers finally restrained Sory from killing Fort barehanded right there between the aisles of this jostling train coach. The outsized and defeated combatant survived with broken glasses, two less teeth and injuries to his head and throat.

The assault upon the popular Fort brought anger and consternation to the camps of the Silent Brigade. Amoss, now the universally recognized leader of the underground army, was sent the word.

Ben Sory went to the top of his list. But he would prove to be one of the few whom the Night Riders never bested.

Hillbilly attacks in Robertson County, like the violent upheaval throughout the region, cut across family blood.

Tough Ben Sory's cousin, Dr. Frank Sory, also of Adams, Tennessee, was a strong and adamant member of the Association. While walking down the street late at night on August 6, 1907, two men unexpectedly leaped out of the darkness and stabbed him.

Seriously wounded, he nevertheless managed to pull away, draw his pistol and unsuccessfully fire several shots at the escaping attackers. The physician survived but the news went out to lodges far and wide. Night Riders flocked in from all over but the would-be murderers were never apprehended. Frank Sory had received written threats on his life from the hillbillies just a few days before, just as had the president of the Association, Charles H. Fort.

Fort's eloquent response printed in the local newspapers to those challenges against his life was typical of the tenacious and deadly struggle which had enveloped Robertson County and the entire Black Patch.

"I will not resign," he retorted. "I will stay with the organization until removed by the people who elected me. It has fed more hungry children, paid off more mortgages, and put clothes on more poor children than any other organization that ever existed. I will keep on working for the Association and if need be will die in the ditches with the rest of the boys from the furrows."

Chapter Six

If James B. Duke ever heard of Hopkinsville, Kentucky, it is not known.

But he no doubt knew of it, if only to a shallow degree. It is almost certain that, under the dim light of a late night lamp, he poured over the map of his scattered warehouses throughout the South. Like a miser fondling his gold, he must have surveyed the deep wells of his wealth.

Hopkinsville, Kentucky, in 1907, was — as it is today — one of the most prosperous and energetic towns of west Kentucky. It was a city of 8,000 people situated in the heart of prime agricultural land and, more especially, dark tobacco country. Only a few miles from the Tennessee line, it was a market town for people of several counties from both states. This county seat of Christian County was blessed with the economic nourishment of two railroads — the Louisville and Nashville and the Illinois Central. The transient lanes, along with its proximity to Clarksville and Nashville, made it a vital crossroads for the Black Patch and a natural center for the tobacco trade.

Within its confines were located two of the largest Trust warehouses in the entire region. They were the Latham Warehouse at Ninth and Campbell streets and the Tandy and Fairleigh Factory, a few blocks to the south.

The city itself provided considerable support for the interests of the Trust, including that of the city officials. This, no doubt, was due to the fact that these warehouses coupled with the numerous employees and buyers contributed much to the local economy. At any rate, during this summer of the farmers' discontent, Hopkinsville, Kentucky, was not exactly a Night Rider haven even though a large Association warehouse was located next door to the Tandy and Fairleigh building.

To David Amoss and Guy Dunning, Hopkinsville was almost hometown. From Cobb and Wallonia it was only a 30-minute train ride or a leisurely morning trip in a buggy. During the summer months of 1907, both Amoss and Dunning had this bustling little city ever on their minds.

No sooner had the glowing embers cooled from the debris of the Princeton warehouses than General Amoss and his lieutenant placed a brand new set of plans upon their audacious drawing boards.

They refused to be intimidated by the apparent opposition of the local citizenry in Hopkinsville. In fact, the scathing editorials and written attacks against the Night Riders by Charles Meacham who was both editor of the **HOPKINSVILLE KENTUCKIAN** and mayor of the city only whetted the appetite of the Silent Brigade. Neither was the Cobb physician nor his sidekick awed by the fact that a local company of the state's militia was stationed there under the leadership of the courageous Major E.B. Bassett.

Amoss and Company didn't scare easily.

Rumors of a Hopkinsville raid by the Night Riders had been circulating ever since the Princeton attack. But Amoss knew that a move on that city would be a much greater undertaking than that which they had so successfully accomplished the past December.

On the night of January 4, 1907, almost within a month of the Princeton raid, he dispatched some spies — mere observers — into the middle of Hopkinsville. Then he caused a hoax telephone call to be made to Mayor Meacham warning that the Night Riders were on their way. The mayor, already tense and paranoid by the flying rumors, reacted quickly and with force. City and county officials were immediately assembled and plans made for the defense of the city. Extra police were called in and the sheriff organized an armed posse of citizen volunteers. They were stationed around the warehouses and on the roads leading into the city. The militia, Company D, was activated and moved into play.

Then they waited.

Nothing happened.

But valuable intelligence was gathered by the spies who subsequently made their reports to the commander.

With this knowledge, Amoss and Dunning looked over the city map of Hopkinsville. Late into many nights, the two friends talked and planned. They took stock of the various lodges within the Christian County area, their manpower and resources, including the quality of men in leadership roles.

Amoss became obsessed with the prospect of an organized assault upon the city of Hopkinsville, the success of which would make the Princeton venture look like an afternoon stroll.

David Amoss knew Hopkinsville like the inside of his medical satchel. He had first visited the city as a child and later lived and went to school there. Streets, buildings and landmarks were as familiar to him as the environment of his own little town of Cobb.

Not only were Amoss and Dunning familiar with the city, but now they were able to anticipate the likely response to a known attack. The General soberly recognized that the highly organized city and county law enforcement, as well as the state militia, would pose a formidable defense. It might even prove disastrous. He, like all good military leaders, had great concern over leading his men into a bloodbath.

Secrecy was the key.

The town had to be hit as Princeton had been, totally unexpectedly and while sound asleep.

To this end, Amoss decided upon two courses.

First, Guy Dunning and he would be the only two people in the world to know the exact date of the raid until the very day of its occurrence.

Secondly, an effort was undertaken to bolster and increase the Night Rider membership in Hopkinsville itself. This would give their efforts extra strength by way of a fifth column and, most importantly, would enhance considerably the chances of knowing if the secrecy of their movement was violated at the last minute and the town alerted.

In April, 1907, an intense campaign was undertaken to increase the Association membership within Christian County and especially Hopkinsville. This drive was highly successful and by October several hundred new members had written their names upon the rolls of the Association. Here one thing became crystal clear. While the Association openly and officially denied any involvement with the Night Riders, it always played defensive tackle for their efforts. There can be no doubt that a strong and frequently used line of communication was in place between David Amoss and Felix Ewing.

While the date for the actual strike would be locked within the prodigious heads of Amoss and Dunning only, the details of the raid were dispensed throughout the lodges which would participate. Basically, according to the General's plans, five Kentucky counties would provide the troops. Caldwell, Calloway, Christian, Lyon and Trigg were all alerted. Plans were passed by word of mouth to the respective colonels and, through the summer months of 1907, the individual lodges were drilled over and over as to their expected roles.

Amoss traveled about meeting with the leaders of the different lodges. Little Cedar Grove School in southern Lyon County was a convenient and popular meeting place for the planners of this bold venture.

Behind pulled shades and the flickering light of coal oil lamps, they contrived and schemed. Amidst chalk dust, the miniature school desks of children, and a soot sodden Old Glory standing limply in the corner, grown men talked of burning buildings and terrorizing people.

At last, late one evening in early November of 1907, David Amoss and Guy Dunning pulled back from the kitchen table and heaved a collective sigh. The date was set for November 19.

On that day, the word went out. It was, after all these months, hardly unexpected. At about 9 p.m., approximately fifty riders from Calloway County passed through Cadiz to join a hundred more from Lyon, Trigg and Caldwell Counties. Around midnight, Night Ridgers from the five county area some two hundred strong gathered near the small town of Gracey, eleven miles west of Hopkinsville.

It was a rather unsettling night. The riders were tense and the horses jittery. A stiff wind was blowing into a gale and the temperature was unusally high for that time of year.

With all forces present and accounted for, the telephone lines leading from that spot into Hopkinsville were cut. But just as the riders fell into place and prepared to commence the final stage of their journey, a lone galloping horseman came upon the group, whipping his way from the direction of Hopkinsville.

The rider pulled to a rough halt in front of Dr. Amoss and began speaking in an excited, gasping manner.

Word of the Night Riders' approach had reached the city.

Extra policemen and the state militia, along with a hundred or more citizens, were on the ready.

Amoss remained silent as the words sank in. He peered at the rider as all other eyes focused upon the little doctor.

It was the hour of decision.

The messenger bothered him as much as the message. He didn't know the man and no one could immediately vouch for him. It could be a trick — a turn coat who would, through deceit, turn a well-prepared army back from a finely planned attack upon a sleeping town. It must have seemed like minutes to the soldiers of the Silent Brigade. Amoss pulled off his mask and leaned into the man's face, searching, unblinking. Then, with the briskness of crackling ice, he made the decision.

The raid was off.

The leader turned his men away, and they slowly and silently passed back through the night toward the direction from which they had come. The hunched and darkened riders retreated with mixed feelings of relief and disappointment.

The little General had made the right decision. The report from the frantic horseman had been correct. A city, somehow alerted and armed, was waiting for the masked force to fall upon them.

In that moment of decision, something other than the credibility of the message had entered Amoss' mind. Following closely those warning words in his ears was the howling wind. A flaming warehouse in that gale would have most likely turned upon the entire town, destroying the property and possibly the lives of innocent people. That dark and frightening prospect came down upon the leader of the Silent Brigade at a most crucial moment.

If the leader of the Night Riders was discouraged by the turn of events he did not show it. Lesser men may have considered the task too formidable. After all, the town had been on virtually a perpetual alert since the Princeton raid. It would appear to be impossible to surprise a city of such size and preparedness.

But Amoss and Dunning were unmovable. They set the new date between themselves for the night of December 6, just two weeks away.

Before dark on the appointed day, riders began to move along the lonely trails and backroads of the five western Kentucky counties. From the remote hills and hollows of Calloway County and the river bottoms of Lyon, they came one by one to assemble at various lodges and then move out as a group into the gathering dusk toward Hopkinsville.

Lodges at the northern points met at Wallonia. Those from Calloway and the western parts of Trigg joined up at Cadiz. After about an hour of reviewing their tactics and listening to the prayer of a minister, they moved once again to the same meeting place near Gracey. Here the entire force, approximately two hundred and fifty troops, came together. At the direction of Amoss, a few buggies were brought along in case of casualties. The General himself rode in one.

Spirits among the troops were high. The night was quiet and windless but still unusually warm for that time of year. The roads were good and the mood was jovial, almost festive.

During the afternoon hours, spies had been sent into Hopkinsville both to notify the local members of their coming and to report back to the advancing army any apparent alert of their approach.

At the I.C. Railroad, just two miles west of town, their number was increased to three hundred when local riders fell in with the rest. Also, one of the spies returned from town and met them with good news. The road was open and all was clear in town. A shot of optimism surged through the armed band of militants.

Then, the well-prepared and laboriously studied plans were put into effect.

All but twenty-five horsemen dismounted and fed their horses in preparation for the long and possibly hurried trip home. The others rode on into the sleeping burg. They acted as an advance patrol for the protection of the main raiding party which was to follow.

Some of the men were left with the horses while the others knotted in closely to receive final words from Amoss. After pulling on their masks and checking their weapons, about two hundred and fifty began their march on foot into town. Meanwhile, on the streets of downtown Hopkinsville, the fifth column was making its appearance. Throughout the previous day, numerous Night Riders from out in the county had filtered into town and casually, without notice, had remained lounging around livery stables, hotel lobbies and with friends. Upon receiving word of the arrival of their confederates, they immediately masked and armed themselves and moved out onto the thoroughfares of the quiet and slumbering town.

James O. Nall picks up on the action in his book, **The Tobacco Night Riders of Kentucky and Tennessee:**

> Shortly after 1:00 A.M., the Night Riders marched in by the I.C. depot with the order and precision of an army. They turned right, into Ninth street, one small squad stopping at the depot, another going out Water street to guard the Seventh street bridge over Little River. The other squads proceeded one block east on Ninth to Main street, from where Squad No. 2 went north to Sixth street and captured the police station and the officers on duty. Squad No.3 went south on Main street to Eleventh street and took charge of the Home telephone office. Squads Nos. 1, 4, 5, 6, and 7 continued east on Ninth where one squad took charge of the armory at Ninth and Virginia

streets, while another took charge of the Cumberland
telephone office between Virginia and Liberty streets,
another stopped at the Liberty intersection, and still another took charge of the fire department between Liberty
and Clay streets. Squad No. 1 continued east on Ninth to
the L & N depot and Latham tobacco factory, as the
Night Riders already in the city masked themselves and
moved in on the streets listed to aid in the activities ...
All these movements took place within a few minutes.
Each squad operated with precision, all plans of capture
having been made in advance. Some one yelled: 'The
people of Hopkinsville have made their brags that we
would never come here, but By God! we're here.'

So, as in Princeton and with equal ease, the Night Riders took
control of the town. The police station, fire house, and even the
armory for the state militia were all arrested and placed out of
commission. All communications with the outside world were
severed when a squad broke through the locked doors of the
Cumberland Telephone Office and, at gunpoint, made the attending women leave the switchboard and accompany them back to the
streets.

Any citizens making a light in their house or curiously peering
out of their doors were met with a full side of bullets and buckshot
above their heads. The sounds of gunfire and the pungent smell of
burned powder permeated the air.

With Amoss and his troops having early subdued the populace,
a group of Night Riders headed toward the Latham Warehouse. It
was quickly and expertly put to the torch and the leaping flames
lighted the sky. At the same time, the aroma of flaming tobacco
filled the air.

Then, with the building beyond saving, they marched up Campbell Street to the Tandy and Fairleigh Tobacco Factory and
commenced to set it afire.

Inside this building was Ed Shanklin, the night watchman.
Aroused from his sleepy stupor by the clamor in town and the
bright glow of the inflamed Latham Warehouse, he opened the
door to see what was going on. His eyes fell upon the Night Rider
group moving down the street straight to his location. Quickly he
grabbed his rifle; but, before he could offer any effective resistance, the old wooden structure was rattled by a barrage of gunfire. Obviously outmanned, and now thinking only of his own life,
he quickly headed down into the dark basement. The dull thump-

ing of his runaway heart soon clashed with the sound of the front door of the large warehouse being smashed to the floor.

Shortly came the unmistakable sounds of men running and shouting just above his head. He lay still until he heard the pattering footsteps recede and disappear as the invaders retreated to the streets. Then came an ominous quiet with only the faint echoes of the outside world reaching into his haven. But soon a low snapping crackle became audible, slowly growing louder. Looking out the small basement window located just over his head, he saw a terrifying glow.

The warehouse above him was engulfed in flames.

Frantically, he searched out the small entrance through which he had descended into this predicament. He was promptly turned back by the searing inferno on the main floor. Temperatures in the basement were rising, and his nose and eyes smarted at the incinerated tobacco. Quickly, he smashed a window with his rifle. With great effort he was able to pull himself up to its jagged opening. Wiggling and twisting through the small casement, Shanklin wormed himself into the blessed night air and safety. Only his agility and strength kept him from being baked alive within the bowels of this tobacco furnace.

The Night Riders gleefully watched the Trust tobacco go up in smoke. Their contented expressions suddenly disappeared, however, for the intensity of the flames which were consuming the Tandy and Fairleigh Factory was so great that the Association's own storage warehouse of R.M. Woodridge located next door had caught fire. It too was rapidly going the way to destruction. Word of this unexpected development was quickly forwarded to Amoss at his command post near the courthouse. He immediately ordered the release of the fire wagons. Accompanied by armed Night Riders, the wagons came but were unsuccessful in their attempt to save the Woodridge building.

With their main goals accomplished, and while some of the Night Riders helped combat the burning of their own warehouse, others turned to general mischief. They kept up a continuous stream of gunfire around the city, shooting into several buildings and keeping the populace at bay.

One man living near the I.C. Railroad depot was wounded when he failed to douse his light as commanded. Another one, an L & N switchman named J.C. Felts, was wounded in the back when he attempted to move some boxcars away from the Latham Warehouse in direct disobedience to a Night Rider order.

With the Trust property sufficiently done in, one group of Night Riders turned to a little personal chore of their own. Prior to coming to town, the excited group of raiders had talked among themselves of a special project which, if accomplished, would place a crowning touch upon the event. They vowed, if given enough time, to seek out and whip Mayor Charles Meacham, the adamant and aggressive adversary of the Night Rider movement. At the very least they intended to destroy the instrument through which he assaulted their cause — the newspaper building of the **HOPKINSVILLE KENTUCKIAN.**

It is reported that Meacham, hearing the commotion from his home, frantically hurried downtown only to suddenly wish that he hadn't. Running smack dab into this rolling avalanche of lash, torch and destruction, he sought out an escape as soon as he discovered the foolery of his outing. One small group of riders, recognizing the onionhead mayor and hardly believing their good fortune, gave chase. Meacham darted down a blind alleyway next to the Baptist church only to be followed fast by his armed and vengeful pursuers.

To his horror, and to the Night Riders' delight, the darkened lane came to a dead end up against a brick building. Fearfully, and at the same time resigned to his fate, he turned slowly to face his would be assailants. Out of the corner of his eye, he saw the metal door of a coal chute fixed close to the ground in the building to his right. In an instant, and before the Night Riders could react, he had pulled the hatch and propelled his long, lanky form through the opening, sliding down into the dark but secure basement of the Hopkinsville Baptist Church. The efforts of the pursuers were unexpectedly thwarted just when the prize catch seemed to be in their hands. But the attackers — devout church men themselves — gave up the chase rather than invade the house of God with ill will in their hearts. However, Night Riders chuckled from that day forth, and everyone ridiculed Charles Meacham as "the only sprinkled Methodist saint saved in a water-dunking Baptist church".

The mayor's newspaper building was not as fortunate as its owner. It was shot into and entered by the Night Riders. Once inside, they proceeded to wreck havoc, breaking up the furniture, throwing type all over the shop, smashing the linotype, and squirting ink on the walls. As a grand finale, they shoved rolls of paper out the back door and tore into the press with axes.

Lindsay Mitchell, a buyer for the Trust Imperial Company, was visited by the Night Riders that night also. He refused to come out even when his home was shot into. His wife appeared, pleading with the disguised raiders to leave and telling them of the sickness of their child. This failed to move them in the least. Finally, Mitchell appeared and was struck repeatedly with the butts of the outlaws' guns until his face was a mask of gashes and cuts. Then he was promenaded around the streets of Hopkinsville and compelled to view the burning building of the Trust warehouses before being allowed to return home.

The fire power which consumed the city on that night was phenomenal, especially in light of the fact that none of the residents were killed. Thirty-two bullet holes were counted in the room from which the pastor of the Methodist Church had curiously looked out. Eight bullet holes were found in the home of Judge W.P. Winfrey. Over one hundred and seventy-five filled the office of the city judge. Many other buildings were riddled with bullet holes, windows shattered and wooden doors splintered. Miraculously, it was all done without loss of life.

One defiant resident returned the fire, however. From the upstairs room overlooking a main city street, he fired into the Night Riders as they went about their business. This opposition was hardly noted at the time, so one-sided was the affray.

No one knew for sure how it happened.

The little commander, David Amoss, was scurrying about directing the battle in and around different circles of activity. Near the L & N depot and next door to the raging Latham Warehouse, Amoss was shot in the head. Whether it was from the lone resident sniper or from his own troops by accident was never known for sure. Still conscious, but bleeding badly, he continued to lead the attack, holding a blood soaked bandana to his wound. Finally, with all the damage to the county seat completed, he sounded the signal to regroup and prepare to leave the battered city. The troops were gathered and all quickly accounted for. For the first time for many of the Night Riders, their eyes fell upon the wounded leader. The men were quickly alarmed by what they saw. Amoss' head and shoulders were drenched in blood. Suddenly feeling weak, their leader placed Guy Dunning in charge of bringing the Night Riders out of town, warning him to maintain a strong rear guard to take care of any group which might form and give chase. With that admonition, Amoss was placed in a commandeered livery stable rig and rushed out of the city to seek medical treatment for his wound.

After Amoss was whisked out of danger, the remaining attackers quickly fell in behind Dunning and in an orderly fashion left the burning warehouses, bullet laden buildings and startled citizens.

One rider started it and the rest quickly picked up the standard refrain, "The fires burn bright on my old Kentucky home." Soon they were gone, and the dazed city was left to the excited citizens who began to recover from their shock as they moved out onto the streets.

Almost as soon as the last fading sound of the Night Riders' farewell song passed from the night, Major E.B. Bassett, the county sheriff, and an irate and embittered Charles Meacham were about the town rounding up a posse. After some effort, five members of the militia, four citizen volunteers, and a deputy sheriff came together under the leadership of Major Bassett. It was the best retaliatory force the city could muster. Six were on horseback and the remainder in a wagon.

Armed and chomping at the bits, the motley group thundered out of town to give chase to the masked marauders.

What followed next is right out of a wild west picture show.

Outside of town, the entire Night Rider group was back on horses moving eastwardly along the Cadiz Road. They were in high spirits. The rear guard Amoss had mandated was either nonexistent or passing the ceremonial jug. In any event, it ignored its duty and simply fell in behind the rest.

It was but a couple of miles out of town when the pursuing officials caught sight of the tail end of the rear attachment. Spurring their horses on, they rapidly closed the gap. When the Night Riders finally saw the posse hot on their heels, they too put whip and spur to their mounts and the chase was on. Through the darkness of this winter night galloped the frantic horsemen along the tree-lined country road. At times, the posse would pull close enough to exchange shots with the fleeing band — flashes from their muzzles blinking through the black night.

Beating down the dirt highways, the two groups sustained a grueling drive all the way past Gracey and into Trigg County.

At one point, Major Bassett overtook several riders who were in a carriage. Leaning off his mount, he managed to leap onto the vehicle, pistol in hand, and ordered them to surrender. Undaunted and apparently unimpressed by this herculean feat, the driver of the rig applied his whip with force and the carriage lurched

violently forward, throwing Bassett over the side as his near cap-
tives escaped down the road. Miracuously, the bouncing major
survived the horrendous fall unhurt.

About seven miles west of Cadiz, the law caught up for the last
time and fired into a buggy carrying George Gray and Clancey
McKool. Gray was killed by a shotgun charge through his body
and McKool was wounded. A squad of riders turned back to assist
their comrades and a pitched battle took place. Finally, the Hopkinsville force retreated, taking with them McKool's bullet riddled
hat and Gray's bloody handkerchief.

The Night Riders had sustained their first casualties. Gray's
body was simply returned to his home by his fellow riders. No
explanation was needed or expected. His family was merely told
that he had been ambushed while traveling to a "singing."
McKool received a gaping wound to the back of the head, but he
miracuously survived with the assistance of a Trigg County physician, J.H. Lackey.

While the rest of the riders were making their desperate and
exhausted way home, David Amoss, now weak from his loss of
blood, was taken to the home of Dr. W.C. Haydon in Wallonia.
Haydon, a young physician, arose from his bed and quickly examined his older friend under the dim light of a kerosene lamp. After
cleaning blood and cutting away some hair, he was relieved to find
that the bullet wounds — three in all — were superficial. While
the General had lost a great deal of blood, a few sutures and a skull
cap bandage provided him with ample treatment. Amoss then
returned the four miles to his home in Cobb by himself, just as the
gray streaks of dawn began to appear in the east.

The violent west Kentucky night finally came to a close, and the
darkness was pushed away by the morning light of December 7.
Two tobacco warehouses in Hopkinsville, belonging to the Trust
tobacco buyers, lay in ruin as the dying embers smoked for days.
The state fire marshal arrived in town and began an investigation
which lasted for weeks.

After the raid, Company D of the state militia was placed on
continual guard duty and local volunteers joined in night watches,
believing erroneously that the Night Riders were planning another
raid to retaliate for their wounded and killed.

Property damage to the Trust companies was staggering. The
loss of the warehouse buildings themselves was placed at over
$30,000.00, not to mention the tobacco which was destroyed. One
large city newspaper placed the total damage inflicted by the

Night Riders on that noisy December night at $200,000.00
If Doc Amoss wished to shake the eye teeth of the national interest, he was successful. Reverberations of the raid ran up and down the country and into the board rooms of Wall Street. The New York papers spoke about the lawlessness of the wild Kentucky men and the unleashed violence in the backwoods. The Sunday morning edition of the **NEW YORK TIMES** on December 8th, bantered the headlines: "Four Hundred Night Riders Shoot and Burn." The distinguished paper began this leading story by saying:

> Anarchy broke loose again in Kentucky's dark tobacco district at 2 o'clock this morning when a body of four hundred Night Riders wearing masks and heavily armed descended upon Hopkinsville, a little city of ten thousand inhabitants, shot up the town, laid waste property valued at $200,000, beat a tobacco buyer into insensibility, and shot a brakeman.

The Big Apple's own **HARPER'S WEEKLY** would subsequently run an exaggerated and grossly distorted account of the "Battle of Hopkinsville."

Down in James B. Duke's own home state, the antics of the Silent Brigade received front page coverage. Residents of Charlotte, North Carolina, casually opening up their Sunday morning papers, were greeted by the dark headlines: "Band of Five Hundred Night Riders Masked and Heavily Armed Shoot Up and Fire Kentucky Town."

Back in the Black Patch, the Night Riders' casualities did not substantially tarnish the glorious success of their masterful military feat. The reputation of the brave little general was only enhanced and enlarged upon by the shedding of his own blood. Spoke the CADIZ RECORD of the Night Rider leader:

> He was tall and erect, except shoulders stooped, was a man of middle age. His short, iron gray whiskers were visible below the mask he wore. He gave his orders in quick, emphatic tones. His step was firm, elastic and spring. His manner was watchful, but cool and free from excitement. He wore a brownish overcoat and a black slouch hat, both old in appearance. His legs were long, wide apart, and slightly bowed at the knees. He walked with a peculiar swing. He carried an army pistol with a barrel about eight inches long.

One New York firm had a personal envoy in the beseiged city on the night of its misfortune. A drummer from a Manhattan business concern had refused repeatedly to travel to west Kentucky to market the wares of his employer, citing the Night Rider menace in the area as too hazardous to risk. Finally, his disgruntled and impatient boss informed him that he would either work the territory or be fired.

So the timid soul caught a train for Hopkinsville and arrived — as fate would have it — on the night of the grand invasion by the masked outlaws. Arriving around midnight, he grabbed a quick bite to eat and then went to his hotel room. He was subsequently awakened with a start by a Night Rider bullet shattering the window of his room. Cowering under his bed throughout the terrible ordeal, he remained in his room, scared out of his wits through the sleepless night. The next morning he wasted no time making his groggy way down to the telegraph office to send a short but important message to his employer. "Arrived Hopkinsville midnight — Stop. Checked into hotel at one — Stop. Night Riders filled room with bullets at two — Stop. I quit — Stop."

Chapter Seven

Sooner or later, at least in Kentucky, all things turn to politics. Only three days after the Hopkinsville raid, Augustus E. Willson was sworn in as Governor of Kentucky, being one of very few Republicans in this century to hold that office. He succeeded young J.C.W. Beckham, a Democrat, who, at the age of only thirty-one, had succeeded William Goebel. Goebel had been assassinated on the capitol steps on January 30, 1900. Beckham had successfully run for re-election four years later.

Beckham, originally a country boy from Nelson County, really didn't know what to make of the Night Riders.

At heart, he symphathized with their cause. Fellow Democrat, A.O. Stanley, no doubt kept him abreast of the good men who were at the heart of the upheaval. On the record and officially speaking, Beckham condemned their acts of violence. But that was about it. He ignored repeated requests by some citizens to send troops into the troubled region. He was not a strong governor and was more interested in building a new capitol than becoming embroiled in the controversial tobacco war raging at the other end of the state. Besides, at about the time that the Night Riders' efforts were becoming most intense, Beckham was counting down to the end of his term. By law, he could not seek re-election and so did very little. And that was exactly what the Night Riders wanted.

The Republican candidate that year was a horse of a different color. Willson was a city boy out of Louisville. He had joined a distinguished and affluent law firm of that city after graduating from prestigious Harvard University. His ancestors were starchy New Englanders. If Augie even knew what a plant bed was, it would have shocked half of the Commonwealth.

As a city slicker and Republican of that day, Willson followed the philosophy of such past leaders of the GOP as the martyred

President William McKinley and Senator Mark Hannah of Ohio. They were all strongly aligned with the interests of big business. And, as an urbanite, Willson was more concerned with the image that the state portrayed to the rest of the world than in grappling in the dirt with the economic problems of the countryfolk.

The Democrats fielded a nondescript and lightweight candidate against Willson by the name of S.W. Hagger. Law and order, and more particularly the Night Rider menace, was a burning issue in the campaign. Of course, Hagger was saddled with the Democratic record of being a soft touch on the lawless uprising.

Willson, on the other hand, came at the Black Patch militants with his gloves off and received strong support from Democratic discontents in the western part of the state who were growing tired of the violence. County Judge, A.J.G. Wells of Calloway County, stumped across Kentucky making speeches in favor of the candidate from the opposing part. "We have had a belly full of men riding hooded by night, dispensing justice after their own diseased and distorted notice of justice. We have seen enough of the torch and black snake. Let us elect a fearless man who will root out these masked cowards and send them to the penitentiary where they deserve to be," Wells proclaimed.

And the influential **COURIER JOURNAL,** more especially the distinguished editor Henry Waterson, himself a strong Democrat, jumped ship in favor of the Willson candidacy. Speaking editorially to the subject of the day, he said, "Let us stamp out this blight that is disgracing our fair state. Let us cease hanging our heads in shame that Kentucky has become known as the worse governed state in the Union."

It was no secret that Willson was a candidate of the Trust. As a lawyer, he had been an attorney for the American Tobacco Company. James B. Duke, who had himself at one time declared William McKinley and Mark Hannah the greatest men of his time, no doubt approved of the thousands of dollars poured into the Republican campaign for the governorship of Kentucky.

Ironically, the thing which bolstered Willson's campaign more than anything else was the success of the Association.

The Night Riders were winning the war.

In fact, many people across the state who may have originally sympathized with their effort, now thought the battle had been won and they should abandon the lash and torch. There was good reason for this belief.

Tobacco prices were up. The 1907 dark crop was a short one, due in large part to the Night Riders' activities of plant bed scraping and dramatic raids which destroyed thousands of pounds of tobacco. The price of leaf climbed to over eight cents a pound. This had been the target figure of the Association when it first began back in 1904.

There were ten major Association warehouses throughout the Black Patch in the towns of Clarksville, Springfield, Paducah, Mayfield, Murray, Hopkinsville, Russellville, Cadiz, Guthrie and Princeton. All were doing a land office business. At the end of 1907, the Association handled ninety percent of the tobacco grown in the area. Members of the Association were now receiving the best prices for their labors, and it was no longer profitable to be a hillbilly. In fact, it was downright hazardous, considering that much of the tobacco was lost by the Night Rider attacks once it was placed in the barn. The Trust companies, much to their chagrin, were now being forced to purchase the Association tobacco as soon as it hit the market.

Prosperity was returning to the impoverished farmlands. Once again tired, labored and worn men could feel the jingle of money in their pockets. A new spring came to their walk as they moved about town, paying off old debts, including mortgage notes.

The merchants, at the same time, were realizing an economic shot in the arm.

The Trust companies, however, downplayed the success of their arch nemesis by contending that the rise in prices was due simply to "natural conditions." Interestingly enough, they had also attributed the fall in the farmers' fortune a few years back to the same thing. The tycoons of Wall Street would never concede that the underproduction of tobacco between 1904-1908 which drove prices upward was the result of the Night Rider efforts.

But the Association and its members, including those of the Silent Brigade, expected no more from the despised Duke and his cronies and could care less what the public relations firm of big business was putting out.

What really galled them, however, was that the dude from the city — a Republican no less — Augustus E. Willson, was using the upswing of the economy in the Black Patch to his own political advantage. "The work of the lawless men is finished," Willson announced. "Why not unsaddle the Night Rider? Let them disband and return to decent living. Tobacco is back to its long time price. If there is a Trust, it's licked. Elect me. A vote for me is a vote for the lawabiding and decency and peace."

If there is a Trust.

That phrase portrayed the true colors of the Republican candidate who, in spite of the strangling monoplies interwoven into the business fabric of this country, in spite of the starvation tobacco prices that existed prior to the Association, in spite of the Anti-Trust suit then pending against the Duke combination; in spite of all this, he still refused to disparage, even in the slightest, his big business friends.

On November 5, 1907, to the great disappointment of the farmers of west Kentucky, Augustus E. Willson was elected as the thirty-sixth governor of the Commonwealth of Kentucky, defeating the Democratic candidate by eighteen thousand votes. It had been one of the most hotly contested elections in the history of a state not known for powder-puff politics. Three days before Willson's inauguration on December 10, his Democratic predecessor, Governor Beckham, gave in to the tidal wave of public panic with almost an apathetic shrug and activated Company D of the state militia at Hopkinsville. With that farewell gesture, the young former chief-of-state moved from the Governor's mansion, leaving the Night Riders at the mercy of Willson.

And Willson was itching to get at them.

The new governor quickly appointed Major Phillip P. Johnston, a former Confederate soldier, as his Adjutant General. Johnston made a quick trip to Hopkinsville and, upon his return to Frankfort, reported that the city was in a state of frozen fear with the anticipation of a Night Rider return visit. The governor immediately ordered Company H of the state militia from Louisville to proceed to Hopkinsville and relieve the local troops from duty and to set up a camp to protect that city.

The Black Patch War was now official.

For the second time within fifty years, one group of organized Kentuckians was at war against another. Military encampments, hopefully seen for the last time by the weary eyes of the old, were once again placed upon the troubled land.

To some extent, Governor Willson was responding not only to growing public sentiment mainly from other parts of the embarrassed state, but also from within the very thick of the turmoil.

Various county judges and other officials, noticeably Judge Wells of Calloway County and Mayor Charles Meacham of Hopkinsville, were beseeching the chief executive to roll out the army.

Officials in other parts of the state where there was sporadic violence among the tobacco growers were also pressuring the Governor.

If A.O. Stanley had been the one inaugurated as governor of Kentucky in those closing days of 1907, the war may well have been over. He was revered by the farmers and no doubt could have coaxed them into laying down their arms. But Stanley was still fighting for them on another front in Washington D.C. in attempting to provide some tax relief.

Willson was neither liked nor respected by the Night Riders or the Association. This was not simply because he was a Republican — although that certainly did not endear him to the citizens of this Democratic Gibraltar of the West. And it was not just because he was a slick city dude with a Harvard education. But the farmers saw him as insensitive and ignorant of their severe economic problem.

They had good reason for this belief.

In late December, Felix Ewing invited the Governor to personally travel to west Kentucky, review the tobacco problems in the Black Patch first hand, and discuss it with the Association and its members.

He refused the invitation.

To be completely fair, Ewing also refused a similar invite to Frankfort by the Governor in late December. In any respect, Willson's refusal to visit the farm leaders of west Kentucky raised the hackles on the neck of Ewing. In an open letter to the Governor published in local newspapers, the Association leader questioned the Republican Governor's sincerity. In conclusion, he went right to the heart of the question which was burning upon most every farmer's mind:

> The Chief Justice of the Supreme Court of the State of Kentucky has said there are enough laws on the statue books of Kentucky to put down the nefarious methods of the Trust. You have sent many soldiers to Hopkinsville. Will you use the full influence of the highest office in the state to do this; will you assemble at Frankfort the equivalent of one hundred soldiers and good lawyers to protect to a full extent the interest of the tobacco planters at the state's expense?

Willson offered many rewards for the apprehension and conviction of Night Riders and proclaimed that he would pardon anyone who killed one of the culprits in the mask.

Then, in a speech in Louisville, he showed his complete ignorance of what was actually going on in the Black Patch. "The
trouble is," he raged, "and I call your attention to this now
because it is an important thing to consider, if this is wholly due to
the wrongful acts of the tobacco Trust, why haven't some of your
tobacco producers done something to the Trust, either in court or
to its property or to its men? My neighbors, from the beginning of
this trouble to now, there has not been a finger laid upon a Trust
man or a Trust piece of property, or a Trust pound of tobacco."

These obviously false statements must have startled not only the
militant farmers but the Trust executives as well. Battered tobacco
buyer, Lindsay Mitchell, still recovering from his December beating, must have also done a double take.

Soldiers would eventually be sent to Marion, Eddyville,
Kuttawa and Murray in west Kentucky and to other locations in
the central part of the state.

The Bluegrass uprising by burley farmers was of the same mood
as their western brothers but was spontaneous and disjointed,
lacking any sustained or organized movement. It was quickly
extinguished and the troops recalled.

Military units in the Black Patch, however, settled in as an
occupying force. The soldiers not only guarded the cities but also
carried out other duties such as patrolling the roads at night,
guarding hillbillies and Night Rider traitors. They also attempted
to raid lodge rooms and arrest members of the Silent Brigade with
very limited success.

The militia was moved to Paducah on a couple of occasions to
aid the local police when it was reported on two separate dates that
the Amoss army was moving in. Such scares were without any
substance whatsoever. An idiot David Amoss was not. Although
the largest city in western Kentucky may have confined large
quantities of the Trust tobacco, it was never even considered for a
raid. Almost three times as large as Hopkinsville and with hardly
any local support for Night Riders, it would have simply been
impossible to capture.

Like garrison soldiers down through the ages, the Kentucky
state militia would soon become almost as much a problem for the
local people as the evil they were supposedly combating. It was
composed of young boys, mostly from farflung reaches of the
state. Bored by the general inactivity, they turned to drink, local
girls, and fighting, either among themselves or against hometown

boys. In most towns, they wore their welcome down to the seams long before they were recalled.

"Hell, we had rather have the Night Riders!" exclaimed one irate citizen voicing the general sentiment.

Editor and owner of the **MURRAY LEDGER,** O.J. Jennings ran an editorial which pretty much summed up the feeling of the Murray citizens concerning the occupation of their town by the state militia:

> "Does Calloway County need an armed force to correct present conditions? Does she need, as the **PADUCAH SUN** describes, the soldiers here 'strapping six foot mountain boys armed with Krag-Jergensen rifles and big army Colts to shoot into our citizens?' Does she need them to serve warrants on men charged with crimes? Does she need them to summon the witnesses to appear before her juries and judges? Does she need them to aid her grand jury in the discharge of its sworn duty? Does her county seat need them to prevent an attack from citizens of the county? Does her sheriff need them to apprehend lawbreakers when he may command and take with him the power of the county to aid him in the execution of the duties of his office? I contend that she does not need them for a single purpose set forth or for any purpose whatsoever."

At about the same time as Willson was gaining control of the state, the Law and Order League sprung up. This was a group of citizens throughout the state whose posture toward the shenanigans in the tobacco fields was compatible with their newly elected governor. Local chapters were formed in each of the counties of the tobacco districts of both Kentucky and Tennessee. It was composed of people who opposed the Night Riders and was devoted to giving full support to all officials who would bring the desperadoes to their knees. The League was lent considerable prestige by its selection as their president, General Simon B. Buckner, a Confederate Civil War hero and former governor.

By and large, however, this group of moralists spoke well, had nice meetings, enlisted good people into its membership, and that was all. Judge Wells, who became one of the chief leaders of the group, went about proclaiming that "Night Riding will become as dangerous as hell fire."

But lip service was about it for the League. It didn't put a person in jail nor raise an arm to defend a single leaf of tobacco. Soon it went the way of all well intended but vaguely purposed groups. It simply disappeared.

In Tennessee, very little action was taken by the powers in Nashville against the Night Riders. The problem was limited mainly to Montgomery and Robertson Counties and was not on as large a scale as that of its northern neighbor. So Governor John Issac Cox simply followed a similar course to that of his Kentucky contemporary, Governor Beckham, and ignored the uprising. His successor, Malcolm R. Patterson, followed practically the same course. The latter did offer some reward money for information leading to the capture and conviction of the outlaw farmers. Patterson also threatened on occasion to call out the state militia. But, all in all, that was about it for the Volunteer State as far as executive action was concerned.

The winter winds swept up the broad concrete canyons of New York City. It was December 23, 1907.

Shoppers scurried along the sidewalks with their Christmas wares. The thumping of a Salvation Army drum blended with the metallic carol played through the half-frozen lips of the street corner trumpeter.

This teeming megapolis had become not only the commercial center of the world but the main gateway to America, full of diverse and varying hues of people, dialects and cultures.

Hordes of shabbily-dressed, hollow-eyed immigrants of all origins shuffled through the processing centers of Ellis Island and into their ethnic settlement within this city of nations. Italians, Irish, Poles, Orientals, and others packed into their nooks and crannies to begin their new way of life that was miserably poor, but free.

The city was also the home of the very rich, elegant and industrious. Wall Street clattered with business as men, expensively dressed in tailored suits and bowler hats, hurried through the turnstiles of affluence. Fifth Avenue and Broadway displayed the most lavish mansions and expensive shops. Theaters paraded out the finest entertainment on the face of the earth.

On this winter morning, the New York City population had been up to its usual busy self. Reverend Charles F. Ajed, the minister of the prestigious and healthily attended Fifth Avenue

Baptist Church, had just the day before severely castigated his rich congregation for not contributing more to pay off a past church deficit. Mr. and Mrs. John D. Rockefeller and their son were in their pews, and, when the service was over, seven thousand dollars had been raised.

World famous Italian singer, Enrico Caruso had just the afternoon before performed to a full house at the Metropolitan Opera House. Internationally known conductor, Mahler Gostav, had just, on that same date, arrived from Vienna in preparation for his performances on the works of Beethoven, Mozart and Wagner.

Even then, on this winter day in 1907, the Big Apple was already the place of the bizarre, the unexpected and the unusual. A falling piece of glass from a skylight in the Natural Arts Club had narrowly missed decapitating a number of women attending a reception for some play goers. Although it fell directly onto the heads of some of the female guests, they were saved from injury by the extremely large hats they were wearing for the occasion.

All of this activity was simply one day's sampling of this action-packed metropolis.

The electrifying and stimulating commotion of this city had from the very first captivated Buck Duke.

And so it was business as usual on this, his fifty-first birthday, as he sat in his massive office at 111 Fifth Avenue, totally oblivious to the busy, yuletide scene outside.

Many problems, both large and small, besieged the tobacco king as he leaned back in his chair and wistfully peered across the elegant room to the opposite wall. There, hanging in contrast to the rest of the plush headquarters, was the picture of the first log house factory of the Duke enterprise many years before in North Carolina. Standing beside it was his revered old father, Washington Duke, dead now for almost three years.

Buck chewed and puffed on one of the many cigars he would consume that day. His attention presently turned to the matters at hand, and they included a vast assortment of subjects.

Much more of his time than people realized was taken up with comparatively small personal matters of special interest to him. His own fleet of expensive and temperamental automobiles received much of his conscientious attention. These included two Hotchkiss and a Renault, premium models of the day. On this birthday, Buck Duke had directed that his devoted and competent secretary, R.B. Arrington, have his electric Brougham placed in cold storage for the remainder of the winter.

There was also the bothersome lawsuit out of New Jersey which he had to give attention to and which had arisen out of the transporting of one of his vehicles from the city to the Somerville estate. An irate equestrian had filed suit for several hundred dollars for damages he alleged were caused by a runaway horse spooked by a Duke automobile.

Although the lawsuit was for a mere pittance as far as Buck Duke's money went, he contested it as a matter of principle, not believing that he was liable. Then too, the wealthy tobacconist could not afford to concede out of mere convenience every claim filed against his interest as it would undoubtedly encourage endless suits from sponges attempting to scrape a few coins out of his deep pocket.

So, while the Christmas spirit flowed freely in the wide avenue below him, Duke was attempting to have his lawyer obtain a continuance of the trial of this small matter until February or March. The extra time was needed in order to locate witnesses in his behalf who were currently out of pocket.

Then there was also a much heavier matter which occupied Buck's mind on this anniversary of his birth. He was preparing his defense for a much more serious legal albatross which was hanging around his neck. This was the government trust-busting action against him and his mammoth tobacco empire.

It was the most crucial and consuming problem in his life.

Buck's mind darted with a sharp crispness from one pertinent point to another as he listened to the counseling and advice of his lawyers. As was his habit when he was deep in thought on matters of great import, he nervously and unconsciously fidgeted with sheets of paper, ripping them into small fragments which drifted onto a haphazard heap on the floor underneath his seat.

Neatly filed away within his office was a letter he had received days earlier, now relegated to office history.

It was an invitation from the new governor of Kentucky, Augustus E. Willson, urging him to personally attend a tobacco conference in Frankfort, Kentucky, to discuss plans for settling the tobacco troubles of that state which had led to increasing unrest. He had not attended the meeting, now two days past, but had sent one of his attorneys instead.

As Duke had suspected, the parley had broken down into a total fiasco with growers and buyers, as well as state officials, shouting at each other. He regretted that he had even bothered to send a respresentative.

For James B. Duke, the problems in the backwood tobacco
lands of Kentucky and Tennessee were simple. The law was being
broken. Innocent growers were being attacked and maimed by
hooded outlaws. Trust property was being destroyed and thousands of dollars were going down the drain without adequate
protection from law enforcement. He was not by nature one to
understand the subtleties of human nature. He would bargain,
cajole, intimidate, charm and wrangle across the tables of commerce better than any man. But, with people who made excuses
for their own economic failures by blaming others, he had little
patience. The rural hoodlums and ruffians should be caught and
punished. Why they had not received their just due before now was
beyond him. But, maybe things would change in Kentucky, he had
opined, with the new Republican governor. After all, from what he
heard, the Kentucky chief executive was of the right political bent.

For now, he had little time for such matters. His mind was
directed to the main uncheerful problem at hand: that was Teddy
Roosevelt and his tenacious Trust busters. Not even the Christmas
hoopla nor his birthday could distract his attention from this
worry.

As thousands of Night Riders sat around their winter fires on
New Year's Day, 1908, they must have pondered what the upcom-
ing months would bring in this savage struggle with the huge Duke
Trust and the stubborn hillbillies.

More than one must have also wondered where it would all end.

A majority of Kentuckians clearly agreed with Augustus Willson that there was no reason for the violence to continue any
further since the movement had obviously obtained its goal.

With solid money for tobacco pouring into the pockets of tobacco farmers in that winter of 1907-1908, one question became
obvious. Why didn't Felix Ewing and David Amoss declare a
victory over the Trust, savor the economic win, and retire the
mask, lash and torch in a flurry of celebration?

The answer to that question still remains a mystery. But one
battle does not a victory make. There were numerous considerations, no doubt, bearing down upon the minds of the Association
and Night Rider leaders which compelled them to keep up the
pressure.

First, their successes had not come easily. A very complex and
intricate organization had been put into place. Inactivity would

allow it to deteriorate, if not completely fall apart. Their masterful efforts must not be thrown away, they most surely agreed, until the war, and not just the battle, had been won.

Also, the farmers of west Kentucky and Tennessee were not thoroughly familiar with the economic winds of the day. The **WALL STREET JOURNAL** could probably not be found within a single household in the Black Patch. They were familiar only vaguely with the Trust machinations, but not in depth. Most knew that the Federal government had stepped into the affray but were about as knowledgeable of the Sherman Anti-Trust Act of 1890 as they were of classical music. So, to them, the high prices of tobacco were brought about by fighting for them, and fighting would be the only way they would be maintained.

Amoss and Ewing saw the situation in much the same way except for more sophisticated reasons. The Trust was not to be bickered with. Its power and resiliency had been all too over-whelming in the past to believe that it was beaten. They were like kids on top of the neighborhood bully, afraid to either let go or let up, apprehensive that a recovered villain might render more de-struction than ever. So, to flail away was the only safe course, at least until the Feds had completed their work and Mr. Duke and Company were brought to their knees. Lingering doubts, in spite of clearing skies, hung like a dark cloud over these leading mili-tants.

And, so, the war continued.

Chapter Eight

The traditional New Year Day's portions of black-eyed peas and hog jowl had hardly settled in their stomachs when the Night Riders took to the roads again. A month had not elapsed from the night of the Hopkinsville raid when a small group, approximately fifty-five in all, raided Russellville, Kentucky, between midnight and 1:30 a.m. on Friday, January 3, 1908.

Except for the numbers involved, it was almost an exact duplication of technique and execution as that used in the two previous raids. Two local merchants were wounded when they failed to obey the abrupt orders of the masked invaders. Other than that, there were no casualties and no armed resistance was given the Night Riders while they were in town, and they easily departed without pursuit. Their efforts had inflicted over thirty thousand dollars worth of damage to two warehouses which were burned to the ground. The orderly movements of the troops, including the takeover of the vital services of the city, were flawless and even more fluid than their attacks upon Princeton and Hopkinsville. It was the most dramatic crime committed within the city limits of this elegant Logan County seat since the masked Jesse James robbed the Nimrod Long Bank some forty years before.

Newspapers were not only depicting a common thread in the manner of the growing number of raids, but also in the leader of the attackers.

Reported the **CADIZ RECORD** after the Russellville raid, "It is considered the man who is dominating the Night Riders is a man of rare ability with excellent military training. This is based on the wonderful discipline in the raids of Hopkinsville and Russellville. The riders marched in a way that could only be the result of training. The man in command had a perfect military bearing. He is believed to be the mysterious genius who is the moving spirit of the Night Riders."

It may have been mysterious to some but was becoming more obvious to most.

The cold days of winter settled in. For most farmers, it was a time to mend and repair worn-out tools and rigging. Livestock had to be tended constantly and protected from the frigid weather. But there were some, especially the single gents, who still found time to while away their nights recreating in the bright lights of town.

Eddyville, Kentucky, was a popular river town. Its three rowdy saloons were as wet as the muddy Cumberland River that silently slipped by.

It was already an ancient little city, being one of the frontier towns of the state. Settlers had lived there before 1800 and, for years, it was the westernmost outpost in the Commonwealth. Great and famous men and women had visited there: these included Andrew Jackson, Aaron Burr, Jenny Lind and, most likely, General Lafayette.

It was also the town of the worst of men as well. For high upon the hill hovering over the city and overlooking the broad river valley was the medieval castle of the Kentucky State Penitentiary. Built in the 1880's, it was still a primitive and brutal place to be. Twelve-year-olds were occasionally incarcerated there and fractious inmates were hung by their arms from metal rings fastened to dungeon walls.

In contrast to the somber facade of the giant stone-faced structure and the grim existence within, the life of the rest of the town was rather light and gay. Carnivals and circuses made Eddyville a regular stop, and summer showboats whistled into the landing frequently, their calliopes blasting away popular tunes to the gathering crowd.

On cold, dark winter nights, the town taverns became the warm beacons of merriment. Clinking glasses and the low roar of masculine voices mingled with the mellow chords of a nicolodean and the occasional ringing of a banjo. Menfolk from miles around gathered during this brooding, lonesome season to mix good whiskey with manly fellowship.

A frequent customer to the Eddyville night life was Henry Bennett from Dycusburg, Kentucky, a small Crittenden County river hamlet about ten miles downstream.

At forty-eight years of age, Bennett was a highly successful business man, speculating on tobacco and purchasing it for the Trust warehouses in Paducah. He also owned a distillery, a tobacco factory, a farm and a general merchandising store in Dycusburg. His huge, multi-gabled house graced the top of a hill on the main road leading down into the town.

His brew was sold to captains, passengers and crews of passing Cumberland River packets as well as other good customers within the area. These diversified businesses allowed Bennett to pay the hillbillies gold dollars for their leaf, an extra enticement in those hard pressed days.

His progeny matched his material wealth, having six children by his first wife who had died and another offspring by his second spouse. By any standard of the day, Henry Bennett was affluent and well-to-do.

Physically, he stood only five feet six inches tall, a proud, brash and abrasive sort who strutted about with the brag and bravado of a bantam rooster. Bennett refused to join the Planters' Protection Association. The Night Riders warned him several times to stop buying up tobacco for the Trust. This was as good as the little scrapper wanted. Bouncing about the area, both on business and socially, the entrepreneur flaunted his independence and made light of the Silent Brigade. Worse yet, he taunted the likes of Guy Dunning and David Amoss. With the Willson troops now patrolling the backroads of the country, Bennett no doubt felt rather secure in his bluster.

It was a dark, crisp evening around the first of Feburary when Henry Bennett was enjoying one of his frequent visits to an Eddyville saloon. As usual, it was a full house. Typically, after having had a few drinks, he became more voluble and began to aim his barbs at any Night Rider sympathizers who might have been in attendance.

Finally, with the whiskey taking hold, Bennett reasserted his stand against the blasted militants and blatantly charged any of them there to do anything about it. A heavy silence rolled over the gathering. He received no challenge — at least not then.

Word of this latest confrontation went out far and wide, all the way in fact to the doorsteps of the little country physician in Cobb. A few nights later, a group of Christian County horsemen began their silent trek down through Cadiz to Eddyville. Their number increased considerably as the dark night wore on, picking up fellow members along the country roads of Trigg and Lyon Counties. By the time they had passed through the deserted streets of Eddyville and Kuttawa, their number, by some reports, was as high as three hundred men.

The eight miles of lonely road which led from Kuttawa to

Dycusburg was sparsely populated. A young teenager by the name of Doyle Polk had been visiting his girlfriend in the Crittenden County town and was returning home to Lyon County on foot when he was suddenly frightened out of his wits by stumbling directly into this long, mysterious column of muted riders. After a closer look, he was able to make out the uncovered faces of a few men from his home neighborhood near Kuttawa. His acquaintances quickly returned the recognition. Then the Night Riders did what had become a rather common practice under those circumstances. They forced the lad to climb upon a horse behind one of the riders and continued on their way. This kept the youth from sounding an alarm concerning that night's activity and also assured that he would keep quiet in the future since, unwittingly as it might have been, he would be an accomplice in their crime.

Not far from the Henry Bennett home, they crossed an old iron bridge with wooden flooring. A man living nearby just north of the Bennett house was awakened by dogs barking. He peered out his door to see the riders, now hooded and masked, pass his house. The string of horsemen, two abreast, was so long that he could still hear the hoof beat of the last of the group clattering upon the wooden floor of the bridge a good half mile away.

The procession shortly pulled to a stop and the riders dismounted. A few scouts broke out and scampered up the road to where the large house on the hill was now darkly silhouetted against the night sky. After satisfying themselves that their target was at home and that no warning of their coming had been given, they quickly returned to their waiting confederates.

With one small group, including the newly recruited Doyle Polk, tending the horses, the rest of the ill-willed band moved up into the yard of Henry Bennett and, with rifles, pistols and shotguns at the ready, surrounded the house.

Then their leader yelled, "Henry Bennett! Come out!"

There was no response from the dark dwelling.

They continued to shout, but Bennett refused to come out.

Finally, one exasperated rider cried out, "We'll burn him out! Bring the torch!"

With that, Henry Bennett emerged from the house carrying a pistol in his hand. He was ordered to drop his weapon but only the tearful beseeching of his wife — seeing that he was no match for this herd of gunmen — caused him to obey the order. The pack of rabid militants pounced upon him with a violent rush. He was quickly ushered to a nearby tree, penned frontward against the bark, hands bound around the trunk.

What followed then was one of the most brutal, cowardly and unnecessary maimings of the Night Rider movement. The poor man was thrashed about, whips ripping away his shirt and under-clothing. Some of the riders broke off the limbs from a nearby thorn tree and proceeded to lacerate his body until his back was red with blood. One long thorn tore his cheek and broke off in his flesh. His howling screams fell upon unsympathetic ears. Someone shot a pistol and a bullet tore through Bennett's ear, barely miss-ing the fatal mark. He was kicked repeatedly as he slid to the base of the tree unconscious as one rider spiked him with a spur, the rowel breaking off in his thigh. Finally, they left off their battering and withdrew, leaving Bennett a bloody lump lying on the ground.

Next, they moved on down into Dycusburg and called out W.G. Groves, the foreman of Bennett's tobacco warehouse. The main ardor of their vengeance had been spent on the despised Henry Bennett, but they still contained enough venom in their whips to give Groves a good lashing.

Quickly, the torch was put to Bennett's warehouse and distillery. An unusual blue blaze leaped and bounded with such intensity that the light of the fire could be seen all the way to Eddyville.

Elderly Bill Dycus, also a buyer for the Trust tobacco who lived near the warehouse, was awakened by the noise. Clad only in his long nightgown, he moved out onto his front balcony to bravely view the happenings. Night Riders were stationed throughout his yard, firing their weapons into the air. Dycus, however, being a jovial and friendly sort, was well liked by the local Association members in spite of his attachment to the Trust interest, a rare bird indeed in those days. One masked carouser, seeing him on the balcony, simply yelled, "How do ya like that fire, Uncle Bill?"

Dycus squinted his eyes and peering out over the raging inferno finally replied, "Let'er burn, boys!"

Then, giving the whole ordeal a quick wave of his hand, he disgustedly turned around and went back inside to bed.

With all the damage done, the raiding party reassembled, hur-ried back to their waiting horses and remounted. Slowly they plodded back down through the muddy roads on their return trip home, leaving Dycusburg to bask in the firelight.

A crowd of people had gathered on the streets of Eddyville in those early morning hours, attracted by the strange glow in the northern sky. As the long column of riders weaved past the peni-tentiary and down through the main part of town, the curious onlookers asked what they had been doing.

"Ask Henry Bennett," came the testy and somber response from underneath a mask.

David Amoss and Guy Dunning had not been along on the Dycusburg trip. Though they no doubt approved of it and probably helped plan the venture, it is reported that the two men did not encourage the excessive brutality.

Bennett almost died from the beating and had to be hospitalized in Paducah. He received occasional death threats until September when he finally gave up and left the state. He meandered around for a time, finally ending up in Jeffersonville, Indiana.

It remains a great mystery as to how quickly it took Bennett to recover from the Night Rider beating. Or, for that matter, that he ever recovered at all. There is some reliable evidence that, within only a few weeks, he was back on his feet in full form, dappered up and frolicking at his favorite Eddyville saloon. Other accounts say that he never fully recuperated from the horrible mauling and that he ultimately died from the injuries over two years later. Of one thing, however, there is no doubt. Etched into his tombstone today in the Dycusburg Cemetery is the bitter inscription of a mourning wife, "Killed by the Night Riders."

Within a week of the Dycusburg escapade, the Night Riders traveled to View, Kentucky, another small Crittenden County hamlet between Dycusburg and Marion. Their intention was to pay a visit upon A.H. Cardin who operated a large tobacco factory on his farm and was considered a turncoat by the Night Riders since he had previously served as county chairman for the Planters' Protection Association. He had severed that relationship and continued in business as an independent grower and buyer, purchasing at times for the Trust and thereby aggravating the Association members. It was a long trek for these riders who came from Trigg, Caldwell and Lyon Counties. On the way, they passed through Fredonia and a squad took charge of the telephone office and blocked all direct communication to the outside. With Fredonia under their control, the main body then moved on toward View — six miles to the north — and were joined by Crittenden County riders on the way.

They were sorely disappointed, however, when they reached the large Cardin house and, discovered after firing several volleys, that no one was at home. Nevertheless, the riders burned his residence as well as his factory which contained thirty-five thousand pounds of tobacco. After their business was done, they rejoined the rear guard detachment at Fredonia and continued their long way home. It was after daylight when the last of these nocturnal horsemen finally placed their lathered mounts back into their stables.

They had made a ride of over sixty miles through the worse roads of winter with approximately two hundred riders taking part. It had been a grueling ordeal, one of the most lengthy of all the Night Rider activities, and had been carried out successfully only because most of the veterans from previous outings had participated.

Twice within that February week, the Night Riders had moved through Eddyville on their way to Dycusburg and View.

Now, with those outings behind them, they turned their attention to the home of the Kentucky State Penitentiary.

Eddyville was the county seat of a divided Lyon County. The Night Riders were well within the majority, but the opposition to them was made up of a few influential and aggressive men.

Division of loyalties and deep emotional rifts on matters of public concern was nothing new to this county. During the Civil War, the community had been overwhelmingly on the side of the Confederate cause. Their own General Hylan B. Lyon had been a most brilliant and devastating hit and run tactician for the rebel cause. He and his troops had used dashing and surprising raids to burn numerous courthouses behind the Union lines in west Kentucky.

But, there was also a small pocket of Union symphathizers in Eddyville. They were treated with disdain and invective of the severest kind. After the war, these Union sympathizers, no longer able to live within the bitter resentment of that town, traveled two miles down the river and, under the leadership of former Ohio governor and Union soldier Colonel Charles Anderson, set up a brand new town named Kuttawa. Thus, over the following years, the two towns grew out of this Civil War discord into two rivaling neighbors. The bad blood between them carried on down through the years, long after the reason for it had been forgotten.

Living in Kuttawa in the winter of 1908 was Walter Krone, the county attorney. He was a competent, bright young lawyer and used all the powers of his office to combat the antics of the Night Riders. This courageous prosecutor tried desperately but unsuccessfully to bring charges against the outlaws for acts of criminal mischief in the county. Needless to say, he was bitterly despised by this secret fraternity.

Also on the same side with the county attorney was W.L. Crumbaugh, the elderly and highly respected county judge who lived in Eddyville. Eddyville City Police Judge C.W. Rucker and former city lawmen, Preston Fralick and L.M. Wood, were also members of this small and dangerously thin minority that, openly and without reservation, opposed the forces of Dr. Amoss.

Firmly entrenched as a recognized leader of the far more populous side of this great divide was the sheriff, Sam Cash. He was a devoted member of both the Association and its militant arm.

S.M. (Morgan) Martin was the thirty-three year old town marshal of Eddyville. He was a rather worldy and reflective little man, having fought in the Phillipines during the Spanish-American War. There he had been exposed to the ghastly results of violence, bringing home pictures of the native dead stacked up along the road like cordwood. In addition to his police duties, he was also a barber and dabbled in the timber business. As a man, his sympathies ran with the Night Riders. As the town marshal, Martin typically took his duties seriously.

Customarily, Marshal Martin patrolled the town at night insomuch as the sheriff was available to take care of matters during the daylight hours.

On the afternoon of February 16, 1908, Martin casually sauntered downtown and happened to meet Sheriff Sam Cash on the street. He exchanged pleasantries with the hefty lawman and just as they were parting ways, Cash suggested with a wink, "Morgan, if I were you I would go in a little early tonight." Rumors had been flying for days about an organized raid on Eddyville by the Night Riders. They had been incited no doubt to some degree by the militants' recent tours through the old settlement on their way to Dycusburg and View. Martin took Cash's hint as a clear indication that there was going to be a hot time in the old town that evening.

Darkness fell and Martin strolled the streets of his city. The hours passed toward midnight and nothing unusual happened. The rowdy saloons wound down to a few inebriated stragglers and finally they too staggered off down the quiet deserted streets.

The bewitching hour of midnight struck and Martin finally decided that the whole thing had been a joke and that Cash had been "pulling his leg." He headed up the hill toward home looking forward, not unpleasantly, to a good ribbing the next day.

As the retiring town marshal sat on the side of his bed to remove the boots from his feet, something out of the corner of his eye caught his attention.

Fixing his attention to the front window of his bedroom, he saw them moving down the street. In front of his house came the Night Riders.

Riding two abreast, masked and with gunny sacks over the feet of their horses, they appeared to be floating down the darkened thoroughfare past Martin's dwelling.

Unknown to him at that time, the town was already full of Night Riders, over three hundred in all. Coincidental with his departure from Main Street, a group had tied their horses outside of town on the Cadiz Road and moved in unnoticed on foot. Another sizeable cluster from "between the rivers" had commandeered the ferry and had made an amphibious landing.

By the time the part-time barber/part-time lawman had hurriedly put his clothes back on and started out the front door, he heard the low rumble of dynamite blowing the tobacco warehouse to smithereens.

One cannot think that the lone officer of the law was in any great hurry to descend into the unknown perils of downtown. But duty called and downtown Martin went. To his surprise, he found the streets relatively deserted with only a few curious citizens venturing out to see what was going on.

Then Martin heard the distinctive sounds of buggy whips snapping and popping and weapons being fired down on the river bank behind the row of wooden stores. The full force of the invaders was at the business they did best — flogging and whipping outmanned and terrified victims.

At that time Martin made a very judicious and logical decision. He turned on his heels and went home.

As he explained many years later, "What could I as one lone man do? All that gang against me and even the sheriff one of them?"

S.M. Martin went on to live a rather remarkable life, becoming mayor of Eddyville and active in various business schemes and civic matters. He ran for public office numerous times, including a race for sheriff at the age of ninety-six. While in his nineties, he constructed his own non-denominational "tabernacle" for general worship and gospel singing. As a centenarian, he traveled to the Holy Land, he received a personal letter from the President of the United States and, while laying plans for another political campaign, was killed in 1977 at the age of one hundred and one when the car which he was driving accidentally smashed into a tree. On that long ago winter evening of February 1908, S.M. Martin's sense of public duty had clashed with his common sense and the later won out. Such sound discretion, no doubt, contributed greatly to his subsequent long life.

What the town marshal of Eddyville did not see that night was quite a show. The Night Riders took over the telephone office and placed guards around the houses of those they had come to punish. One of the leading merchants was forced out of his home and compelled to open his hardware store in order to provide a sufficient number of buggy whips for their immediate use. At approximately one o'clock in the morning, and in full charge of the town, the "whipping party" began.

First was the hated police judge, C.W. Rucker. The largest squad of riders proceeded to his house and, after shooting out the doors and windows, finally managed to force the magistrate to meekly stumble out of his home with his hands high above his head. He was quickly ushered to the river bank behind the drug store to await the congregation of other subjects sentenced to the inevitable thrashings.

The tribe then visited other homes, twelve altogether, including Preston Fralick, the former city marshal. After being forced out of his warm confines, he came hastily and partially dressed, blinking and disheveled, out into the cold.

"Here was a fellow that said he would sit on the river bank and shoot down the Night Riders as they came across," yelled one of the riders. "Alright," chimed in another, "we'll take him down to the river and see what he can do." Joining the dozen white men on the river bank were eight Negroes, including a man by the name of George Gordon. All were then warned to stop talking against the Night Riders and the blacks were told to leave town.

Gordon, a Negro schoolteacher, had been victimized by mistake. Just the day before he had moved into the house of the man the Night Riders were actually after. In the dark confusion of this turbulent night, it was simply a matter of mistaken identity.

None of those whipped had direct dealings with tobacco. They were simply people, including the blacks, who had been overly outspoken and active against the Night Riders. Some were considered by the community as "undesirable citizens."

After the gathering at the river — for baptizing with fire and not water — the invaders went to the home of elderly Judge Crumbaugh. The old man came stumbling out of his house, his nightgown whipping about his knees in the cold winter night and his white whiskers blowing in the breeze. One of the men admonished him that they had already whipped a number of men that night and only his gray hair was saving him from the same fate.

The crusty old judge was neither impressed nor intimidated.

He raised his slender bare arm and shook his bony fist at them. Pointing to the massive structure covering the hill behind them he warned, "You scoundrels! I'll work till my last breath to put everyone of you behind those gray stone walls!"

The riders, amused by the old man's spunk and in deference to his age, simply chuckled underneath their masks and let him be.

By that time, it was getting up into the early morning hours.

The man they wanted most lived two miles away in Kuttawa. That was Walter Krone, the county prosecutor. They had a quick discussion on whether to move out to the county's twin city or save it for another time.

Because of the hour, they decided against it.

It was almost four o'clock in the morning when the Night Riders began to make their way back out of Eddyville toward home. As it was, they barely made it in before the first streaks of morning light came falling.

S.M. (Morgan) Martin had been asleep for hours.

The military genius of David Amoss and Guy Dunning was clearly shown by the daring raids of February 1908. They cleverly planned the Eddyville attack to occur after those at Dycusburg and View. A look at an early century roadmap of western Kentucky would show the wisdom of this strategy. Geographically, it was almost impossible — unless the horsemen went far out of their way — to travel to Dycusburg and View from their common meeting place at the juncture of Lyon, Caldwell and Trigg Counties without passing through Eddyville and Kuttawa. Amoss wanted to make sure that those places remained "open" cities until the Crittenden County treks were completed.

The leader of the Night Riders was right on the mark. A few days after the incursions of February 17, the soldiers of the Commonwealth moved in to occupy the cities of Eddyville and Kuttawa.

The road to Dycusburg and View was slammed shut, only however, after the horse was already out of the barn.

Chapter Nine

It would be impossible to chronicle all of the activities of the Night Riders in west Kentucky and Tennessee in those frantic and frenzied months of 1907 and 1908. Much of the violence and suffering was never reported and probably not even known except by those directly involved. How many whippings, plant bed scrapings, burned barns and dynamited farm machines there were during that era is impossible to say.

But a compendium of those acts of lawlessness that we know about gives a graphic picture of this turbulent period in the Black Patch.

* * *

Walter Krone, the county attorney for Lyon County, had been lucky during the early morning hours of February 17, 1908. That was the night that the Night Riders had run out of time in their Eddyville raid and had passed up traveling two miles to Kuttawa to impose punishment upon the young prosecutor. But his good fortune did not hold.

In May of 1908, Krone was beaten by Night Riders and on August 3, 1908, an assassination attempt fell short when shots were fired through the window of his home, barely missing his head. In October of that same year, he was again attacked in his law office by an individual carrying a huge stone. Krone would eventually leave the state along with Eddyville Judge, C.W. Rucker, but not before carrying out a few plans of his own.

* * *

Night Riders visited Brandon Hurt who lived near Kirksey in Calloway County. All telephone lines to his house were out. Hurt, who was included on the Association's black list had been warned not to deliver his tobacco to the Trust. The only tobacco barn on his farm was destroyed by fire, including all of the valuable leaf within it.

* * *

In January, 1908, one mile from Adairville, Kentucky, the barns of Jessie Burr and Cress Strickland were burned around midnight one evening. Neither of these men were members of the Association and a nearby barn belonging to Association member, Pink West, was not disturbed.

* * *

In Hopkinsville, Kentucky, Press Rogers, an aged farmer, was brutally beaten by masked men who condemned him for selling tobacco to the Trust.

* * *

In Paducah, Kentucky, County Judge R.T. Lightfoot received a letter signed by the Night Riders warning him that his "tongue was too long" and that they would get him "if he didn't look out." Insurance companies in that city announced that they would cancel all policies on tobacco warehouses due to the actions of the Night Riders.

* * *

In Adams, Tennessee, the farm of Hugh C. Lawrence and Wash T. Vicker was visited with a total of thirty eight thousand pounds of tobacco burned. Lawrence and his son were wounded and two Negro tenants were unmercifully beaten.

* * *

In Christian County, Lucian Means, a prominent farmer, was whipped for selling tobacco outside the Association. B.A. Gregory's home in Hopkinsville was visited by masked men who set fire to his residence and repeatedly fired through his window, narrowly missing his wife and baby.

* * *

In Calloway County, the home of Richard Spann was burned by the Night Riders and the family barely escaped cremation.

* * *

McCracken County farmer and road supervisor, J.T. Lutrell received a letter signed by four hundred Night Riders warning him not to attempt to work the roads or he would be punished.

* * *

Near Port Royale, Tennessee, farmer Dee Foust was visited by Night Riders and a thresher taken from his barn and burned.

* * *

Two Negroes were shot and killed and a third wounded in Clarksville, Tennessee, by a private night watchman of Ben Sory when they attempted to set fire to his tobacco warehouse there. While blacks were not known to be active members of the Night

Riders, many people in this community believed that, in this instance, they were nevertheless working as saboteurs for that group. Other reports, however, raised basic questions about their motives since one of them had been dismissed from employment at the warehouse just a few days before.

* * *

After Night Rider nemesis Ben Sory moved his business to Clarksville, Tennessee, rumors abounded that the forces of David Amoss were planning an attack on that city.

On the night of March 9, 1908, a telephone message was sent from the small village of Sango, Tennessee, to Sory. It warned that the Night Riders were on their way. The local law enforcement agencies were alerted and braced themselves for the onslaught. Impatiently, Sory himself led a small resistance team and headed east toward Sango to meet the outlaws.

What followed was an unexpected turn of events which ended in a bloody mess.

Sory and his five sidekicks, armed to the teeth, set up an ambush near the Sango community expecting the full group of Night Riders to pass by on their way into Clarksville. Hidden behind trees and lying in the weeds beside the road, the defenders nervously waited in the darkness.

Meanwhile, and unknown to Sory and his group, at Port Royale, seven miles north of where they waited, a group of Night Riders, approximately thirty in number, were playing havoc with that little community. They captured the telephone office, cut the wires, and whipped a hillbilly spy. Without the slightest intention of attacking Clarksville, this Tennessee lodge then broke up in smaller groups and headed for home. As fate would have it, however, a clutch of seven of these Riders, on their leisurely trip home had to pass the way laying Sory and Company.

As they rode into the ambush, the waiting gunmen rose up and commenced firing. They killed one Night Rider, Vaughn Bennett, and wounded his brother Earl before the others escaped into the night. Two of the horses also lay dead on the road.

Two of Sory's accomplices were subsequently tried for the murder of Bennett and were sentenced to ten years in the penitentiary. That verdict, however, was reversed on appeal and a subsequent trial in Nashville resulted in the men's acquittal. Despite anxious anticipation and the liveliest of rumors, a Night Rider raid on Clarksville never materialized.

* * *

An attack upon Golden Pond, Kentucky, in Trigg County on April 23, 1907, by thirty-five riders resulted in the town being shot up and the Trust warehouse of W.R. Wilson, along with ten thousand pounds of tobacco, being burned. The assault upon this small community located between the Cumberland and Tennessee Rivers was facilitated by the capture of a ferry boat and numerous skiffs at Canton, Kentucky.

* * *

Stephen P. Moseley of Roaring Springs, Kentucky, was the unfortunate recipient of much Night Rider attention. After refusing numerous invitations which were, in actuality, veiled threats to join the Association, the Night Riders first paid him a visit in March of 1907 and sowed his plant beds with grass seed. They returned one month later and dug up his other beds: in one they packed up a mound of dirt to ominously resemble a grave. Still later, they again returned and cut his telephone lines and scattered shotgun shells around his house as a warning. Hoping to end his troubles, Moseley finally joined the Association. But this hard nosed lodge of Night Riders was not convinced of his sincerity. On July 23, 1907, approximately one hundred of them forged an attack upon his house and riddled it with gunfire, splintering the floors and breaking the windows. Moseley himself was wounded and his wife was injured from flying debris. His children barely escaped serious injury. It was enough for Moseley to sell his farm and move out of the county.

* * *

On the night of January 28, 1908, the Silent Brigade went looking for John Heath in Dawson Springs, Kentucky. He was a buyer who had committed the unpardonable sin of purchasing tobacco as an independent and then selling it to the Trust.

Heath spent the night in the Arcadia Hotel thinking no doubt, that the public accommodation would offer him a secure sanctuary from the Night Riders.

No so.

First, the militants shot up the place, yelling for him to come out. Then, to the horror of the management and the occupants of that fine facility, they stormed into the hotel looking for him. Sweeping through the building, they beat on doors with their rifle butts, calling for their man. Finally, Heath surrendered and the Night Riders escorted him across the Tradewater River and whipped him with hickory branches. Shortly thereafter, he sold his warehouse and departed for Oklahoma, leaving the state for good.

* * *

Calloway County, Kentucky, was one of the leading dark fired tobacco producing areas of the state and, predictably, there was a lot of Night Rider activity there. But this outlaw fraternity was thwarted to a substantial degree by County Judge A.J.G. Wells, an adamant and fearless opponent of their tactics.

Dorothy and Kirby Jennings, in their work, **"The Story of Calloway County,** 1822-1976," make a very perceptive observation about the battle lines in that county. The appraisement can be applied to the entire Night Rider territory: ". . . the membership of the Association was closely aligned to the sympathizers of the Confederacy. Non-Association growers were identified more with the Union. In additon, it should also be noted at this time that the Union was identified with the Republican Party and the Confederacy with the Democratic Party."

The hillbillies were also quite active and militant in Calloway County, retaliating to Night Riders at times by damaging Association warehouses and the property of its members.

For some reason, the exchange of threatening letters and notes seemed to have been more prevalent in Calloway County than in most other communities. Many hillbillies received the same message tacked to their gateposts or stuck in their plant beds. Often, threatening and portentous tokens were left with the notes. Typical was the note received by Henry Pace from near Kirksey, Kentucky, which was draped around a rifle cartridge containing three matches. It said, "If you deliver your tobacco outside the Association, we will tend to you in a rough way for we don't aim to have any scrubs as you to impose on the people any longer. Now we are watching you and if you sell this tobacco, we will get you and your barns for we are tired of being fooled with by you and your kind! Night Riders."

The Silent Brigade planned a raid upon Murray for the night of March 23, 1908. One of their main goals was to see that Judge Wells got a good thrashing. Their plans were discovered, however, and the town alerted. This caused the attack upon the Calloway County seat to be postponed only after the masked men had begun to gather on the appointed evening in the eastern part of the county.

The venture was primarily put together by the lodges from Calloway and Trigg Counties and was set again for April 2. Suspecting another attempt by the Night Riders to invade Murray, but not knowing the designated date, Judge Wells implored Governor Willson for state troops.

Through sheer coincidence, a detachment of the state militia marched from Hopkinsville to Murray, arriving at that city around four o'clock on the very evening of April 2. At the same time, the Night Rider lodges in Trigg and Calloway were gathering to visit the popular town with altogether different purposes. Two opposing armed camps, like the Biblical armies of Saul and David, moved virtually within shouting distance of each other. But Governor Willson's boys got there first and, once again, this time for good, the Night Rider raid upon Murray was called off.

Later that summer, a small guerilla group did manage to sneak into town and, underneath the nose of the bored and listless occupational militia, inflicted about twenty thousand dollars worth of property damage.

* * *

On June 7, 1908, in Lyon County, Kentucky, Herbert Hall, brother of a Night Rider informer, left his home in Lamasco to go to a neighbor's farm to work. His head was practically blown off by a shotgun blast at close range by a Night Rider appointed to the job. His body was hidden in a nearby swamp and tied down with rocks. That evening, however, it broke loose and emerged. He was buried in a shallow grave and, over a period of time, additional layers of dirt were washed over his remains. It was never known by anyone except the perpetrators of the deed where Hall was buried. He was one of many who just simply disappeared to an unmarked grave.

* * *

L.B. Morris, a well known citizen of Calloway County, was visited and taken from his home and severely whipped. That same week, A.H. Perry was visited by Night Riders, taken from his home and beaten as was Roland Norsworth two nights later. All three men were non-members of the Association.

* * *

On the night of July 14, 1908, about twenty-five Night Riders kidnapped Tom Stevens, an alleged Night Rider traitor of the Lyon-Caldwell County area. They took him to an abandoned well, bound him with wire and chain, then threatened to drown him in the bottom of the shaft. Protesting his innocence, he miraculously talked them out of taking his life. Boasting the next day that they had been "taken in" by Stevens and that he was in fact guilty as charged, the riders attempted to kill him the next night by firing into his house. He once again narrowly escaped death and left the state for Indiana.

* * *

Julian Robinson, a witness who had been subpoenaed to a Night Rider trial in a civil action, was killed from ambush near Otter Pond, Kentucky, on July 9, 1910.

* * *

One hundred and seventy-five to two hundred Night Riders visited the home of Al Perry near Mallory Schoolhouse in Calloway County. When Perry came out of his house, the captain of the participating lodge spoke with him briefly. Then a vote was taken among the Night Riders present on whether to whip him or let him go. The decision was to inflict the punishment, and Perry was immediately put to the lash.

* * *

The Trust warehouse of Palmer and Brown in Hazel, Kentucky, was destroyed by fire on Saturday night, May 31, 1908, along with five thousand dollars worth of tobacco.

* * *

John F. Dalton of Knight, Kentucky, on the Tennessee River in Calloway County, mistook his wife to be a Night Rider and killed her on the night of September 8, 1908.

* * *

August 31, 1908, a fire hit the city of Murray, destroying stores all along one side of the court square. Night Riders were believed to be responsible for the arson, based to some degree upon the fact that the owner of one of the stores was openly defiant of the Night Rider activities and had published his opinion the previous week. Following the fire, a panic-stricken city council passed an ordinance which legalized the shooting down of known Night Riders from the window of anyone's home.

* * *

The Night Riders invaded two railroad cars at Otter Pond in Caldwell County on March 3, 1907, and destroyed the tobacco out of sixteen hogheads by tramping it into the ground. The tobacco had been sold and was on its way to the American Snuff Company, a Trust conglomerate.

* * *

Near the small community of Oak Grove in Christian County, the thrasher of John Fields was dynamited. The helper who was feeding the machine at the time was blown some distance, receiving a broken leg and other injuries. On the following August 21,

Fields himself barely missed an explosion when working on another farm. Picking up a bundle of wheat to put into the thrasher, he discovered four sticks of dynamite hidden within the sheave.

* * *

In May of 1907, the Night Riders scraped plant beds in the Blue Springs community in Christian County on the farms of F.B. McCown and John M. Rice. The outlaws left notes which said, "If you want to raise tobacco, you must change your way of selling. This is a warning. If we have to come back, something else will be done."

* * *

Night Riders took an independent tobacco buyer by the name of Mr. Wicks from the home of William West in Christian County and whipped him with a stick. He was told, "Go back to Hopkinsville and stay there. If you ever come to this neighborhood again, you'll look up a limb." West had received numerous other warnings prior to this assault.

* * *

On August 14, 1907, in the town of Fredonia, Tennessee, the business of W.E. Wall, a prominent farmer and businessman, was burned. Wall had previously been a member of the Association but had withdrawn. His leaving the organization apparently embittered the Night Riders deeply. Subsequent to their parting ways, Wall sustained not only the burning of his business but the destruction of five plant beds, his residence, two barns, and a steam engine. He finally sold all of his property and left the community.

* * *

Shortly after the state militia moved into Hopkinsville, subsequent to the successful Night Rider raid, a young Negro woman was shot and killed by a soldier guarding the I.C. Depot. The sentinel was shooting at two men slipping along in the dark when they refused to obey his order to stop. The ricocheting bullet went through a Negro cabin and fatally struck the victim.

* * *

Leonard Holloway of the Night Riders' commander's own home town of Cobb was accused of being a hillbilly spy, supposedly infiltrating the ranks of the Silent Brigade. On May 17, 1908, he was taken from his home by a band of Night Riders and never seen again. It was assumed that he was murdered and placed in an abandoned barn that was, a few days later, burned into ashes.

* * *

Actual clashes between the Night Riders and the soldiers stationed throughout the Black Patch were surprisingly, even unbelievably, rare. There were shots exchanged in Eddyville when about a hundred Night Riders creeped into the edge of town to harass the uniformed defenders sometime after the February raid of 1908. Also, in July of that same year, there was a running gun battle between the militia and the militants at the home of Henry Bennett. A detachment of seven state troops had been stationed there to guard his property. No one was injured in the skirmish.

* * *

There was a close call at Princeton on September 19, 1908, during their annual tobacco festival. Plans had been made by the Night Riders to make a surprise attack upon the soldiers in the afternoon and to shed blood if necessary. However, cooler heads prevailed and, at the last minute, there was only some pushing and shoving.

* * *

Four warehouses belonging to the American Snuff Company were burned by the Night Riders in Mayfield, Kentucky, on April 11, 1909, with a loss of over three hundred thousand pounds of tobacco valued at twenty five thousand dollars.

* * *

Attacks upon the small Cumberland River town of Rockcastle in Trigg County continued throughout the Night Rider era. In addition to the "hogshead party" that occurred on February 28, 1907, the Night Riders made other frequent and devastating visits to that village. On August 23 of that same year, thirty Night Riders paid a visit to Johnson Hendrick who ran a hotel there. After firing several volleys into his place of business, they called for him to come out and then warned him to quit making threats against them. Apparently they were not satisfied with his subsequent conduct insomuch as, in November, they returned and burned down his hotel, three other residences, a blacksmith shop, two stables, a warehouse, the post office, and two other businesses, one of which belonged to Hendrick. On New Year's night, 1908, the Night Riders came back and finished off the town, Hendrick's general store, and another warehouse. Rockcastle, which had been a teeming and prosperous river town, never recovered from these devastating attacks.

* * *

Generally speaking, the Night Riders' standard of retribution and punishment was even-handed. Family members participated in whipping parties on many occasions against their own kin. One of the more interesting and amazing examples of this impartial approach concerns an infraction committed by none other than the second in command of the entire Night Rider army — Guy Dunning. In April of 1907, Dunning loaded his wagon with grain and hauled it across the bumpy roads to Cadiz for grinding at the mill of W.C. White. Dunning had obviously not given much thought to whom he was giving his business because White was a non-Association member and was on the Night Riders black list for having formerly handled tobacco for the Trust. Nonchalantly going through the business of having his grain ground and loaded into the back of his wagon, Dunning then headed for home. Just as he was crossing the muddy Fort Creek near his home, fifteen Night Riders descended upon him. They were members of Dunning's own lodge. They sternly chastized him for doing business in violation of the Night Rider boycott. Then they "ordered" their commander not to do business with White again and proceeded — to Dunning's astonishment — to dump all of his flour and meal into the water. This group at least was no respecter of persons.

* * *

Probably the deadliest acts of violence did not occur under the flaming torches of masked horsemen or in their whipping parties. The rift between the Association members, including Night Riders, and the hillbillies carried over into the social circles of the day. Fights would break out at church parties, school functions, political gatherings, picnics and other gala events where the representatives of the two opposing groups would come and mingle. These so called "amiable" assemblies were sometimes smothered by the tension of bad feelings between individuals there. The consumption of moonshine, the encouragement of comrades, and the apparent security in numbers would often lead to an explosion of tempers and fights between unmasked and freshly scrubbed Night Riders and their independently brazen counterparts. A single word or gesture in this seething atmosphere might set off an altercation with fatal results. This occurred quite often, one example being an incident in Princeton, Kentucky, between Orbie Nabb and Henry Wilson.

Nabb was a Night Rider whose legitimate job was pricing tobacco for the Association warehouses. Wilson, on the other hand, was an adamant — even militant — hillbilly from the northern part of the county. He had helped plan a hillbilly raid upon the town of Princeton to burn the Association warehouses —

a "turn about fair play" for the Night Riders successful Princeton invasion. The hillbillies got justifiably "cold feet" concerning their venture, however, when the Night Riders got wind of the scheme and rode to town in force, heavily armed.

Arising out of that episode were hard feelings between Nabb and Wilson. Bitter words were exchanged between the two, including death threats. Feelings were still bitter a few weeks later when Nabb and Wilson were both in attendance at the Henrietta Hotel in Princeton to view the beautiful chorus girls in the dance show, "The Isle of Spice." It was such a popular showing that the repeated applause continued the production past midnight. Finally, the curtains closed for the last time and the show came to a thunderous end as the satisfied and predominantly male spectators began shuffling to the exits. Nabb was fortunate enough — or unfortunate as it turned out — to have a late date with one of the young starlets of the show. He was proceeding back up the steps into the theater to meet his lady friend when he met Wilson coming down. The two men were suddenly wedged face to face by the jostling crowd. Neither would budge to let the other pass. Before Nabb could get his own weapon out, his armed adversary had blasted away, causing him to turn and fall mortally wounded down the steps onto the sidewalk before the horrified stares of the show crowd.

Wilson, as quick on his feet as he was on the draw, made a sudden dash to his horse, took to his mount, and galloped off up the street and out of sight.

Governor Willson subsequently pardoned Wilson for the murder of Nabb.

* * *

Another such tragedy at what was supposed to be a festive occasion of merriment was the death of Anexia Cooper. He was shot and killed by a group of "off duty" Night Riders when an altercation broke out at a Lamasco picnic. The victim's brother would be heard from later.

* * *

Chapter Ten

Dr. MacDonald in Robert Penn Warren's fictional book, **"Night Riders,"** said it best: "... the good Lord never got any thousand or so men together for any purpose without a liberal assortment of sons of bitches thrown in ...."

Somewhere along the line, the noble purposes of the Stainback schoolhouse got waylaid and the main mission lost its innocence.

During those hectic months of 1908, the battles of the tobacco Night Riders became enmeshed with other violent activities totally divorced from any redeeming values whatsoever. As in most every movement where people move under the cloak of darkness and in disguise, the idealism of the initial fight became tarnished. The white banner of the Night Riders was dragged through the mud, sometimes by its own members, but most times by hoodlums who could care less about tobacco prices — or anything else for that matter.

First was the racial issue. Down through the years since that era of discord, the Night Riders have been labeled with the unshakeable reputation of being a racist clan of terrorists bent on imposing violent injury upon Negroes.

This, of course, is simply a bum rap. But the misconception is quite understandable.

One must follow the Silent Brigade carefully, examining the morals and values of the day as well as the other unrelated racial atrocities of that period, and bring the hooded horsemen and their cause into proper focus.

Some basic facts must first be established.

The Dark Tobacco District Planters' Protection Association of Kentucky and Tennessee, from its very inception, welcomed and encouraged black membership.

The Negro sharecropper and tenant farmer suffered most from the plummeting tobacco prices. That is perhaps why, ironically, the blacks had a higher percentage of membership in the Association per capita than did white farmers, especially in Tennessee. There was also, of course, an ulterior motive for the Association to encourage its members to treat Negroes cordially. It was feared that, if things got too hard on the black farmers, they would migrate to the cities, leaving a labor shortage in the Black Patch.

With the parent organization being without racial interest, the membership of the Night Riders was equally free of any special ill will toward the black minority. David Amoss and Guy Dunning were too interested in chastizing the white hillbillies and inflicting damage upon the Trust buyers and their property to satisfy what racial prejudice they may have had. The issue was simply not relevant to their cause. The fact that Amoss adopted some organizational technique and ritual from the Ku Klux Klan was simply a matter of form and not substance. While there is no evidence that any Negroes were active members of the Silent Brigade, that fact alone connotes nothing for that age of practicing apartheid.

It is to be remembered that the not too distance past saw a strictly segregated way of life in Kentucky and Tennessee, even in times of war. For the Negro group to march in the rear of the grand Association parade in Guthrie was one thing, fine and accepted to the social mores of the day. But to saddle up and ride under disguise, imparting injury and punishment upon fellow whites was strictly for a "whites only club."

But what is doctrine of the church may not always be practiced by its members. Even though the Night Riders were not a racist organization under definitions of that day, neither were they a group without racists.

Peeping into the pictures of some of its "legitimate" activities are indications that a few of the Night Riders used the lash and torch to vent their own personal grudges against blacks. Suspiciously, for instance, there seemed to have been little philosophical rationale, if any, for the burning of Negro shanties at Hopkinsville and Princeton and the beatings of 'undesirable" blacks at Eddyville. It is safe to deduct that a few of the Night Riders would move out of line occasionally and, in the heat of battle, pick on a few blacks.

But, considering the magnitude of their incursions, such infractions were few. And the Night Riders of David Amoss — to the best of all available records and reports — never carried out an organized visit to a man's home at night to inflict a whipping simply on the basis of the color of his skin.

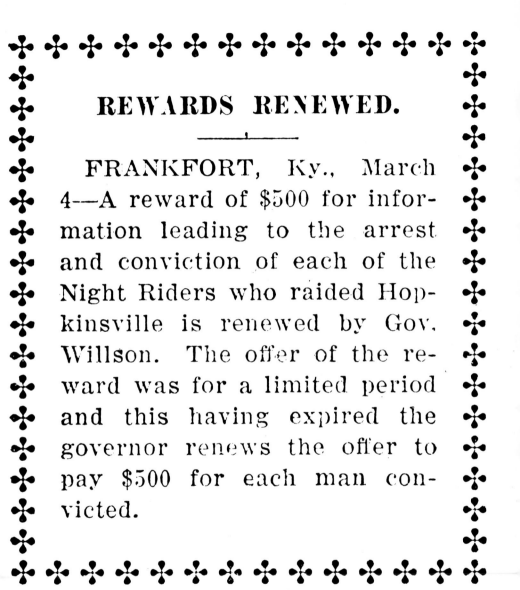

REWARDS RENEWED.

FRANKFORT, Ky., March 4—A reward of $500 for information leading to the arrest and conviction of each of the Night Riders who raided Hopkinsville is renewed by Gov. Willson. The offer of the reward was for a limited period and this having expired the governor renews the offer to pay $500 for each man convicted.

Publication of the reward notice run in the Hopkinsville paper during the time of the Amoss trial. (Photo courtesy of David Riley, **Kentucky New Era** Editorial Staff)

ABOVE: Members of the Kentucky State Guard, Company D, or th "Latham Light Guard" mounted for Night Rider patrol near Hopkinsvill (Photo courtesy of William Turner)

OPPOSITE, TOP: Members of the Kentucky State Guard, Company I the "Latham Light Guards" in camp for Night Rider surveillance. (Phot courtesy of William Turner)

OPPOSITE, BOTTOM: The home of Dr. W.C. Haydon, Wallonia, Ker tucky, where David Amoss was treated for his wound on the night of th Hopkinsville raid.

OPPOSITE, TOP: OPPOSITE, BOTTOM: ABOVE: All pictures of the devastation brought upon the tobacco warehouses as a result of the Night Rider raid on Hopkinsville, Kentucky. (Photos courtesy of William Turner)

IN THE NIGHT RIDER DISTRICT OF KENTUCKY TROOPERS GOING ON DUTY.

ABOVE: Members of the State Militia on patrol in western Kentucky. (Photo courtesy of William Turner)

OPPOSITE, TOP: Sanford Hall, one of the Night Rider traitors. (Photo courtesy of William Turner)

OPPOSITE, BOTTOM: Major E.B. Bassett of the Hopkinsville state militia on horse back during the Night Rider trouble. (Photo courtesy of William Turner)

TOP: Christian Co. Circuit Courtroom during the trial of David Amoss. The Night Rider leader is on the stand in lower center of picture. (Photo courtesy of William Turner)

BOTTOM: The bitter inscription on the tombstone of Henry Bennett in the Dycusburg Cemetery.

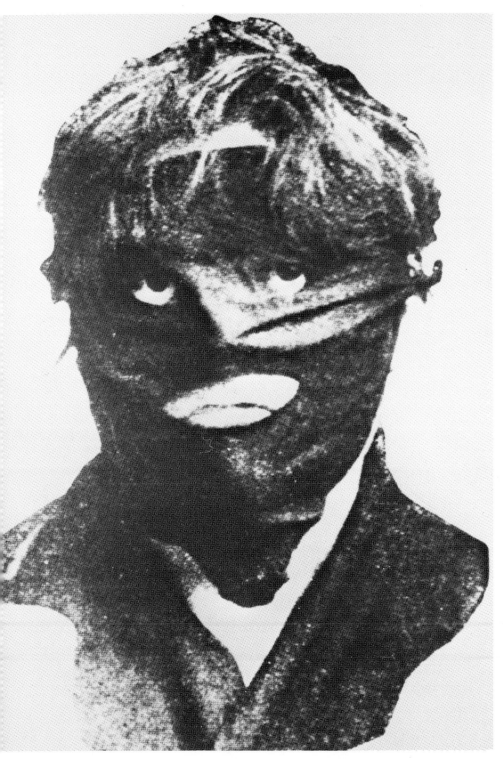

k worn by the tobacco Night Riders in the war 1904-08. (Photo courtesy
Winston Coleman Kentuckiana Collection, Transylvania University Li-
y)

ABOVE: Dr. and Mrs. David A. Amoss and daughter Harvey made during the Night Rider trial, March, 1911. (Photo courtesy of William Turner)

BOTTOM: Pictures of Milton Oliver and Sanford Hall as depicted on the front page of the Hopkinsville newspaper, **Kentucky New Era** during the David Amoss trial.

T OUTLAW CLAN

ld "Don't strike the man
Heard later some of
e careful and don't get
'e's no doctor in the
not present at any
meeting with Dr. Amos
d did not think he had
h him since then about

ılned by Judge Bush:
Lyon county, before go-
He became member of
ective Association after
ght Riders. Joined at
house in Caldwell
ter or spring of 1907,
ceton raid. First heard
ak of raid at Nabb's
Heard him at Cedar
structions about whip-
llonia was the place set
on night of Hopkins-
'ent there about dark.
there. Meeting was ın
time—not over hour.
was lighted by lamps.
ıe on in direction of
Did not see Dr. Amos

Two of the Confessed Night Riders

MILTON OLIVER.

SANFORD HALL.

ABOVE: Unusual picture of the jurors who deliberated on the fate of David Amoss. The jurors who determined the fate of David Amoss: (left to right, first row) R.S. Lindsay, Ed B. Moss, Horace M. Henderson, F.B. Wagoner, Dan E. Foster, E.F. Griffen; (left to right, second row) Sheriff Lowe Johnson, W.D. Hord, J.T. West, J.R. Fears, E.H. Majors, Joe Davis, John H. Williams, Deputy Sheriff Jewell W. Smith. (Photo courtesy of William Turner)

ABOVE: Members of the State Militia on patrol in west Kentucky during the Night Rider uprising. (Photo courtesy of The Kentucky Filson Club)

OPPOSITE, TOP: Commonwealth Attorney Denny P. Smith. (Photo courtesy of David Riley, **Kentucky New Era** Editorial Staff)

OPPOSITE, MIDDLE: Lindsay Mitchell, tobacco buyer for the Trust, who was severely beaten by the Night Riders during the Hopkinsville raid. Note bandages on the chin and head. (Photo courtesy of William Turner)

OPPOSITE, BOTTOM: Circuit Judge J.T. Hanberry, about the time of the trial of David Amoss. (Photo courtesy of David Riley, **Kentucky New Era** Editorial Staff)

The tombstone of Dr. David A. Amoss in Millwood Cemetery, Caldwell County, Kentucky.

crypt of James B. Duke within the Duke Chapel at Duke University.
to courtesy of Duke University)

The statue of James B. Duke in front of the chapel at Duke University (Photo courtesy of Duke University)

Ned Pettit, for instance, who was hired by Mary Lou Hollowell to scrape the plant beds of neighbors along with Steve Choate, was a black man. Yet he received the same treatment in court as did the white Choate. In fact, within the community, Choate was apparently cast about in a rougher manner by the Night Riders than was Pettit. But if one blinks at history and does not examine carefully the Night Rider movement, these masked tobacco riders will be unjustly cast in with other less savory groups of that time.

Lurking in the highways and biways of this rural setting, there were bad men secretly harboring evil intent. Hoodlums, ruffians and racists were quick to see an opportunity in the Night Rider movement to carry out their own sinister schemes under the camouflage of the tobacco war. And, this, they did repeatedly.

Either as individuals or in small groups, persons not even belonging to the Association, let alone the Silent Brigade, donned masks and carried torches to the homes of their personal enemies. There they carried out their own personal vindictiveness with a violent ardor.

Boundary line disputes, wife problems, political differences, and even family squabbles were sometimes settled physically and with injury in a similar mode and fashion as that of the tobacco militants. To the unknowing public, only hearing about the misdeeds, the pattern seemed the same and the Night Riders got the blame.

At about midnight on March 9, 1908, a band of about a hundred men stormed down upon the little Tennessee River town of Birmingham, Kentucky, in Marshall County. Their announced intentions were to "run all niggers out of Marshall County" and they proceeded to assault the pitifully small black section of town.

The ruthless invaders poured down a rain of gunfire upon a defenseless dwelling. Out of the house of Negro John Scruggs came return fire of a rifle shooting at the attackers. With that, the house was targeted and riddled with bullets. Old man Scruggs and his baby granddaughter were both killed. After the houses were set ablaze, the murderous culprits stormed out of town.

This senseless and cowardly slaughter had nothing to do whatsoever with either tobacco or the Night Riders. It was a racist attack by a local group of hoodlums known as the "Negro Chasers." Their acts of violence as well as repeated threats against this besieged minority soon drove all the blacks out of that county. The wounds of racial terror have healed slowly. At this writing, over seventy years later, there are still no blacks within the Marshall

County population of approximately twenty-five thousand people.

Only two weeks after the tragedy at Birmingham, a group of forty Negro Chasers whipped and fatally wounded black Tom Weaver of Golden Pond, Kentucky. This incident too was unrelated to tobacco but was part of a drive by a small group of bigots trying to run all the Negroes out of "between the rivers."

Probably the most reprehensible and dastardly crime committed upon the Negro population in western Kentucky occurred near Hickman, Kentucky. A Negro man by the name of Dave Walker had been accused of cursing a white woman, as well as pointing a gun at a white man. A group of local ruffians — caucasian type — set fire to Walker's house. Then they shot all six members of his family, one by one, as they made a frantic escape from the burning building. Walker, his wife, and two young children all died as a result of the attack.

These criminal atrocities and other similar racial assaults occurred during the same period of time as the Night Rider attacks against the Trust and hillbillies. They were completely divorced and totally unrelated to the efforts of David Amoss and company. But, because of similarities of the modes and methods used, right down to the mask and torch as well as threatening notes signed as "Night Riders," history has erringly lumped all these acts of lawlessness under the Night Rider banner.

Then there were the vigilantes. These were average citizens, highly reputable and in agreement with the Night Rider purposes and means, who sought to expand upon it. "Citizen Committees" made up of numerous masked horsemen paid nightly visits to people in the community who needed "correcting." A lazy father or unfaithful husband would be dragged out of bed at night, whipped and directed to mend his sinful ways.

One such lesson was imparted upon an indolent husband and father who failed to provide firewood to keep his family warm. The group of night visitors took him from his house and, to the tune of snapping whips, escorted the man to the woodlot forcing him to cut a cord of wood and stack it near the house. After the whipping, the recalcitrant was left with the final instructions to take care of his family or they would be back and give him more of the same. It was reported that the victim became unusually zestful at his household chores from that time on.

These types of visits were quite common. No doubt many Night Riders were involved, possibly even instigating the measures. But they were not "official" excursions of the Silent Brigade and certainly not sanctioned by its leadership.

How many Night Riders, hillbillies and other persons were actually killed during the Black Patch War, not to mention those injured and run out of the country, is open to speculation. It was reported in one newspaper's report of events that as many as sixteen Night Riders were killed within a few months in 1908. That most certainly was an exaggeration, but exact figures will never be known because there were few accurate accounts recorded at the time. Some, especially highly despised hillbillies listed upon the Night Riders unofficial hit list, simply disappeared without any evidence as to the perpetrators of their demise. And the families of Night Riders were careful to conceal information of their loved ones falling in an unlawful battle. This is evidenced by the rumor that a most secret and mysterious funeral took place in Trigg County, Kentucky, only a few days after the Hopkinsville raid. It was speculated that an unreported casualty within the ranks of Dr. Amoss had succumbed to a mortal wound received in that affray.

Of one thing there is no doubt. It was a bloody enough era for everyone. The tide of public opinion which had bolstered great support for the Night Rider movement at first was beginning to turn. People grew tired and even appalled at the violent and brutal misdeeds of the time, including misbehavior of the Night Riders which had been previously condoned.

The prestigous publication, **THE SATURDAY EVENING POST,** sounding off through writer H.L. Beach, dramatically summed up the aura of terror caused by the farmers insurrection of west Kentucky and Tennessee: "Because of it, men sit by night with rifles in their hands to guard their crops and barns. Because of it, cities have been called to arms and resist threatened attack and destruction of property. Because of it, every night in nineteen counties in Kentucky and Tennessee, men sleep with bolts drawn, windows barred and weapons within reach. It has created unrest, suspicion and terror. In a word, it has driven peace from the land."

In those early months of 1908, James B. Duke was not well. His weakened condition had required him to remain confined to his bedroom at 82nd and Fifth Avenue in New York City for days at a time.

The federal prosecution against him and his company was moving into its crucial stages. His deteriorated health made it necessary for him to give his testimony in the matter by deposition from his home. Duke's bed chamber was turned into a courtroom with James A. Shields, the U.S. Commissioner, taking the testimony.

Beginning February 25 and continuing for three complete days, Buck Duke was questioned and cross examined concerning his motives and actions in building the Duke international tobacco trust. The U.S. prosecutor from Tennessee, James C. McReynolds, who was destined to become a justice on the highest court in the land, was present and in a most genteel and courteous manner probed the commercial life of Buck Duke.

Duke denied any attempt to form a monopoly.

He defended all of his actions, proclaiming that he was a strong believer in the unrestricted give and take of the market place. Then responding to the allegations that his efforts had, in fact, reduced competition in the tobacco field and had lowered prices to the growers, he boldly stated, "Competition in buying leaf is better for all concerned. The farmer has got to have a good price for his tobacco or he won't grow it. We are just as much interested in the farmer as we are in the consumer."

This testimony, of course, would be rebutted later by a large quantity of evidence produced by the prosecution, including statistics covering the entire industry which showed that the American Tobacco Company had created a monopoly which controlled the trade, both domestic and foreign.

But the seasoned warhorse of a lifetime of competition was, by all accounts, a good witness for himself. His lawyers, at least, felt that he had held his own against the government prosecution in spite of his apparent poor health. Here one must wonder if Buck Duke didn't outmaneuver the government a bit. There is absolutely no evidence at all that the head of the American Tobacco Company was malingering during these times. But it seems only logical that, if Duke had the strength to withstand three days of grueling and tiresome questioning within his own home, he surely had the stamina to travel just a few blocks away to the Federal Courthouse for trial.

But James B. Duke got the government right where he wanted it, on his own turf. It is a fundamental and universally accepted business stratagem and concept of the high rollers to lure the opposition onto your own home floor when the chips are down. The tobacco tycoon followed this precept precisely in what was shaping up to be the biggest battle of his life. In that one encounter, at least, he succeeded and put the government attorneys on the defensive.

This idea of Duke's use of psychological intimidation is strengthened significantly by the fact that, within only a few days following the conclusion of his testimony, he had miraculously recovered sufficiently enough to pack up his gear and leave New York City for Charlotte, North Carolina, on business.

The business to which he was attending was not tobacco but power — hydroelectric power.

Ironically, it had been during another illness Duke had suffered some five years past when he stumbled onto the idea which was to become a major industry in the southeast.

In 1905, Duke had been confined to his New York home with a severe case of erysipelas of the foot. This acute and infectious skin inflammation was treated by his physician who was also a native North Carolinean. Dr. W. Gill Wylie became almost his sole companion during these healing times, and their conversations one day turned by chance to the doctor's own personal investment in a South Carolina power plant. This led to the expressed opinion shared by both men that the Carolinas were in great need of a chain of hydroelectric dams which would generate electricity for the entire region. Duke, as he could when the subject was business, turned eloquent when proclaiming how oceans of water were going to waste while Carolina mills bought coal from other states with which to generate their power. It was, in his opinion, time for the exploitation of their "white coal."

Duke was somewhat familiar with the mechanics of hydroelectric generating, having built a small plant on the Raritan River in order to light his fantastically embellished New Jersey estate.

W.S. Lee, an engineer and native of Lancaster, South Carolina, was immediately beckoned by Duke to his Fifth Avenue domain. There, accompanied by his doctor and with his foot still wrapped and propped on the ottoman, the tobacco economist plied the brilliant young technician with questions, quickly learning the cost and potential of his scheme. Finally, to his astonishment, this thirty-two year old engineer left the Duke home with one hundred thousand dollars and instructions to purchase the real estate for the construction of a hydroelectric dam on the Catawba River at Great Falls, near Charlotte, North Carolina.

The Southern Power Company was then formed by Duke and the North Carolina plant went into operation in March of 1907. Other dams were constructed, and slowly, over the years, a giant productive electrical grid began to take shape under the hand of

James B. Duke. His dream of linking the plants together to provide hydro power for industrial use throughout his home region
materialized.

And, of course it made him money.

It was reported later that Buck Duke had boosted the profit
from the electric business by some intricate corporate scheming.
He supposedly would build a dam for one million dollars and sell it
to his own corporation for eight times that amount. Then he would
approach the state utility regulatory commission and have rates
set on the greater amount. If this technique was used, it was totally
legal, shrewd and another example of Duke's genius. Of course,
had the consumer of the electric services been fully aware of the
matter, it might have been considered otherwise.

By early March, 1908, Buck Duke was out of the blustery winds
of New York City and fully recuperated as he rolled along in his
plush, private railroad car across the red clay soil of North Carolina toward Great Falls. He was joined in Charlotte by his able
engineer, Mr. Lee, and they proceeded to inspect the dam site and
its operation. This South Carolina dam on the Catawba River was
ideally situated on that part of the stream which maintained a
constant level and steady flow of power. Duke found the visit, as
always, stimulating and, at the same time, relaxing.

He had developed an obsession with the fluid power of breaking
water. Dams and fountains fascinated and mesmerized him, much
in the same manner as piddling in the greenhouse at Duke Farm.
So captivated was Duke by cascading water that he would later
have a fountain installed at his Charlotte mansion which periodically gushed its stream more than eighty feet into the air.

On March 9, 1908, Buck was back in Charlotte preparing for his
rendezvous with Mrs. Duke who was coming in from New York.
Both of them would then proceed to depart for an extended trip
across the continent to the west coast on business. Duke found his
private car unsuitable and made inquiry through his secretary,
Arrington, who had remained in Manhattan, if a more comodious
and comfortable one could not be provided. He was assured by his
trusted aid that one of the finest which the railroad had to offer
would be at his disposal by the time they reached New Orleans.

As he was ensconced in this rolling opulence, transversing the
American continent, he looked out his window at the serene
countryside passing by him. At about that same time, Ben Sory
and his five armed abettors engaged an unsuspecting group of
Night Riders in a bloody ambush in the rough and tumble backwoods of west Tennessee.

Chapter Eleven

The ides of March, 1908.

Plant beds had been burned, seeded and covered. The sheeted patches spotted the countryside throughout the tobacco region as winter, worn down by age, was about to be shoved out the door.

Farmers went about their early spring chores of clearing and mending fence rows, breaking their garden spots, and forking manure from the stables. Muscles ached from the relatively inactive winter months, but spirits embraced the outdoor work with the renewing hope which comes with every spring.

No one paid much attention to the lone rider who slowly made his way through the Caldwell County backroads and farmland.

He was a deputy marshal for the United States of America.

Erect in his saddle with a wide brimmed hat set down close to his eyes, this federal agent spoke hardly a word as he went about his work.

Moving up the winding muddy lanes, he caught laboring farmers in the midst of their work. Routinely, almost with an air of boredom, the marshal pulled a folded paper from within his coat and handed it to the puzzled farmer. Then he turned his mount and slowly rode off, leaving the recipient of his brief attention quizzically studying the document which he had delivered. This, or similar type occurrences, was repeated numerous times within a very short distance of the little Nabb Schoolhouse.

Through their own haltering deciphering, sometimes with the aid of a neighbor or friendly parson, each and every one finally wrestled from the strange language of the message one gloomy but inescapable fact.

Mary Lou was back.

After the assault upon her and Robert by the Night Riders, she quickly left the county under heavy guard for Paducah. Robert, along with little Price, followed a couple of weeks later.

All three were still stunned from the violent ordeal they had been through. Robert especially was suffering mentally and was close to a nervous breakdown. Nevertheless, he managed to obtain employment.

Mary Lou, easily the stronger of the two, quickly began to recover both physically and emotionally. Her combative and resilient spirit resurfaced. Within a few weeks, she was once again her old pugnacious self. Flushing with both her beauty and her pride, she decided to go to war.

After her indictment in Caldwell County for plant bed scraping, she went to the very able attorney in Paducah by the name of John G. Miller. This distinguished barrister was in the prime of his lawyering career. A native of Caldwell County himself, he had moved to Paducah many years before to practice law. He was a highly respected lawyer and his professional duties called him back to Princeton from time to time to handle legal battles.

Mary Lou's visit to Miller's office was not only to secure his services for her defense against the criminal indictment. She also wanted to sue her assailants for monetary damages for the dastardly depredation committed upon her and her family.

Miller's law firm insisted that he not take the lawsuit. Defending her was bad enough. But to go after the Night Riders on their own turf was suicidal in the most literal sense.

Miller was appalled at the injustices which had been perpetrated upon the Hollowells. As a lawyer, he was also challenged by the prospect of seeking monetary damages against the now famous nocturnal raiders. The attorney at law also had secret plans of dissolving his association with his present firm within a very few months. He declined to take the suit of Robert and Mary Lou for the time being but encouraged them to return and see him within a few months. Oddly enough, the Caldwell County authorities were not pursuing the criminal prosecution of Mary Lou — apparently happy, simply, to have her out of their hair.

Robert and Mary Lou, along with Price, moved to Oklahoma and lived there for a few months. But Robert's emotional condition worsened and Mary Lou yielded to his wishes to return to their native state. Almost as soon as they had moved back to Paducah, Mary Lou was once again back in Miller's office beseeching him to move on their case. By this time he had parted ways from his previous law firm and had formed a partnership with his son. This development completely freed him to take on the matter if he chose. But, before he tied himself to the cause of this fiery-eyed lovely, he wanted to be assured to his satisfaction that she was completely innocent of the charge of scraping her neighbors' plant beds. To his great surprise, Mary Lou dramatically fell down on her knees right in his office and raising her right hand exclaimed, "I swear to you that I had nothing to do with the scraping of that plant bed, have no knowledge of who did it, and am as innocent of that charge as an unborn child — so help me God!"

John Miller was impressed.

He agreed to represent her in the lawsuit on the condition that she and Robert, along with Price, once again move out of state. This family, seemingly without a country, wearily agreed and trudged off to Evansville, Indiana, where Robert once again obtained a job.

John Miller's mind was turning.

He was well aware that he could not file a civil lawsuit against the Hollowells' attackers in Caldwell County, even though Mary Lou insisted that she could identify each and every one. Obtaining a verdict against the Night Riders within a state court in the Black Patch would be like passing through the eye of the proverbial needle. As Miller knew all too well, most of the court officials were Night Riders. Secret signs and gestures would be passed between defendants and prospective jurors assuring the defendants that there would be twelve men tried and true for one side only. Such an attempt would be, in fact, a charade.

Besides, his own client could not dare cross the boundary line into her home county in fear of certainly being arrested and jailed on the indictment now pending against her.

Still, there was a way.

A path untried and unproven. Yet one well worth the try.

The last days of 1907 passed and the frenzied months of 1908 began to unfold. Members of the Silent Brigade went about their destructive ways without a thought of their erstwhile female nemises and certainly unknowing of her quietly whiling away the time in Evansville waiting for the opportune time to strike.

When John Miller walked into the Federal Courthouse in Paducah on the blustery day of March 2, 1908, he was representing residents of the state of Indiana. They were Robert, Mary Lou and Price Hollowell. The defendants named in the pleadings within his leather briefcase — thirty in all — were residents of Kentucky. The first one listed was John E. Hollowell, Robert's brother. The only woman defendant was Lulu Hollowell, a sister-in-law.

The lawsuit against these citizens of Caldwell and Lyon Counties was for fifty-thousand dollars in damages for each Robert and Mary Lou and twenty-five thousand for Price. The figures were well above the amount required by the United States Constitution for the federal court to take jurisdiction.

So the Night Riders were in federal court instead of state court for the first time based upon a suit between residents of one state against residents of another and the matter in controversy exceeding ten thousand dollars.

The importance of bringing the Hollowell litigation into the federal court for the Western District of Kentucky would soon become all too plain to the defendants. No longer would they be tried by people of their own immediate community who were sympathetic and perhaps even avid supporters of their cause. The jury wheel of the United States Court would include names of people from the entire western half of the state, including Louisville, the hometown of the best known Night Rider hater of them all — Governor Willson himself.

The often repeated refrain, "We fear no judge nor jury," was not falling from as many lips of the Silent Brigade these days after the federal marshal had completed his rounds of serving legal papers upon the Night Rider defendants.

Naturally, David Amoss was immediately advised of the developments. This — the federal court approach — was one stone the Night Rider lawyers had left unturned. General Amoss had been assured that his forces were not in danger of being thrown into the court of the United States since all their misdeeds were crimes against the states of Kentucky and Tennessee, not the Federal government.

Assembling his staff quickly, including Guy Dunning, the Night Rider leadership discussed the "Paducah case" as it became called.

Amoss, more than any of the rest at the time, completely comprehended the seriousness of the situation and the ingenuity of Miller's plan. To many of his confederates, the legal action was just the latest in Mary Lou's harassing tricks, bothersome but not necessarily alarming.

But the dimunitive commander was quite somber as they pondered the matter. His normal buoyance was reposed, almost subdued. He was looking at, not only the Hollowell action, but the threat of an avalanche of suits further down the road if this one proved successful. Amoss was not forgetting that the money— or the lack of it — had forged the movement from the beginning. His troops could not withstand any substantial financial reverses. He could lead them anywhere — but not back into penury.

Lodge meetings were called by Amoss throughout Caldwell, Lyon and Trigg Counties for the purpose of discussing Night Rider strategy.

It was an entirely new twist — the head scratching over defending a lawsuit. These earthy farmers had become quite proficient in mastering the precision of mass troop movements and lightening strikes upon unsuspecting citizens. Now their energies would have to be directed, to some degree at least, toward going to court.

First, lawyers were retained. Ward Headley of Princeton, W.H. Yost and Ruby Laffoon of Madisonville all became attorneys for the defendants. Laffoon would have better moments, especially his election as Governor of Kentucky over twenty years later.

Contributions were collected from the hard pressed farmers during their meetings to help pay the legal fees in the "Paducah case." Fifty cents per member was assessed. It doesn't seem like a tremendous amount in retrospect, but at the time it added up to over five pounds of dark fired tobacco for each man.

Headley quickly took charge as lead counsel for the defense team. He accused the Hollowells of filing action for revenge in response to Mary Lou being indicted for the scraping of plant beds of at least one of the parties being sued. Said the Hopkins County mouthpiece, "The plaintiff is the woman indicted for having two tenants scrape the plant beds of her neighbors and the tenants are now in the penitentiary having pled guilty. She was indicted and is now a fugitive from justice. This suit is brought for revenge and the defendants anticipate no trouble in showing their absolute innocence."

Preparing the case for the Hollowells was a torturous and frustrating chore for Miller. He made repeated trips to Princeton to interview prospective witnesses only to be met constantly with shifting accounts from obviously cowered and frightened people. The entire community was up in arms, rushing to the support of the "fine, innocent, upstanding citizens" who were being maligned and abused by the trumped up Hollowell allegations. Miller's life would not have been worth a plug nickel in Caldwell County during those days.

Robert and young Price Hollowell were considered merely harmless role players pulled along by the domineering dame. But Mary Lou was not without her supporters in her own home county either. Granted, they were few and far between and very hesitant to even speak upon the subject.

Miller correctly anticipated that the defense would try to discredit his star witness by attacking her character. This no doubt would be done by parading a stream of witnesses through the courtroom attesting to Mary Lou's bad reputation. Thus he concentrated his efforts in seeking out and recruiting those rare breeds indeed who not only spoke highly of his client, but possessed the courage to do so in open court and in defiance of the warped sentiments of the community.

From one day to the next, prospective testifiers would renege, change stories, disappear and adeptly dodge Miller's attempts to visit them. Numerous subpoenaes were issued, but he was never sure of who would show up for trial or what they would choose to say on that particular day. One such witness was F.G. Lester who was supposedly a character witness in favor of Mary Lou. Excitement and tension of the prospects, however, got to him. When finally sworn and put on the stand by Miller, Lester stated that Mary Lou's character was bad.

Threats were made against the life of the plaintiff and even Miller armed himself in anticipation of foul play.

On his visits to Princeton, small knots of men wandered by giving him the evil eye. Even old friends treated him like a side dish no one ordered.

In this pressurized and volatile atmosphere, the days slowly passed toward the trial date of April 21. Reports went out that a special train of five hundred Night Riders would be moving into Paducah on the appointed day as "spectators." Governor Willson quietly set about ordering in the state's troops to be on hand when the trial began. Two armed guards were assigned to be a constant escort for the Hollowells.

A few days before the trial got under way in Paducah, an unusual and significant ad appeared in the Princeton newspaper. It was an open endorsement of the character of all thirty defendants in the Hollowell suit, declaring them to be persons of the highest character and repute. It boldly proclaimed that they were in "every way honest and good people" and went on to express a belief in the complete innocence of the charges made against them in the lawsuit. Then followed a list of the sponsoring citizens. Hardly a person of any political, economical or social position was missing as it included the presidents of both of the local banks, the county judge, county attorney, county court clerk, circuit court clerk, commonwealth attorney, mayor of Princeton, city police chief, county school superintendent, and numerous other county officials, two Baptist ministers, doctors, lawyers and various others.

When the trial date arrived, Paducah was braced.

Although they did not all arrive on one train, the number of militant partisans for the defendants easily reached the predicted five hundred.

The state militia was also there in force.

Robert and Mary Lou had not dared to travel from their home in Evansville over the conventional route through Henderson, Marion and Smithland. Instead, for security reasons, they had to transgress western Indiana, the southern part of Illinois to Brookport across the river from Paducah. There they were provided with an armed escort for the rest of the trip.

As soon as Mary Lou and Robert walked into the courthouse with their lawyer, Mary Lou was immediately arrested by the sheriff of McCracken County on the Caldwell County bench warrant pursuant to her indictment. The Night Riders who crowded the hallways looked on with satisfaction believing they had struck the first and perhaps fatal "legal" blow of the contest. Now they were sure she would have to be escorted back to Princeton for trial and the present civil matter continued. At least, they surmised, she would be a plantiff in the present suit in shackles and handcuffs, thus casting her as a fugitive from justice before the eyes of the jury.

But the Night Riders had underestimated the legal prowess of the astute John Miller. In anticipating just such a maneuver, he had a man of substantial means on hand and the paperwork ready. Within minutes, a sufficient bond had been posted before the local magistrate and Mary Lou was free to pursue her duties of the day — suing Night Riders.

Technically, the suit which was pressed on the day of trial was that of Robert. As part of his strategy, Miller elected to try first the claims of the broken, emotionally wrecked father and husband. This decision was made no doubt for numerous reasons. First, in case the jury did not take a liking to Mary Lou's spunky ways, it could render a verdict for the plantiff nevertheless, resting in the satisfaction that it was for Robert who no doubt would garner more compassion.

Also, there was a peculiar Kentucky rule of procedure in existence at that time which, according to Miller's interpretation, might bar one spouse from testifying on behalf of the other. If only one of the victims was going to be able to give an account of that dreadful night, he wanted it to be Robert — once again because of the sympathy factor. Mary Lou engendered a varying array of emotions in both men and women, but sympathy was not one of them. Strong and spirited people hardly ever induce that dubious affection.

The courtroom itself was bulging with people. In the aisles, around the walls, even on the steps leading up to the judge's bench, onlookers strained to see every move and hear every word. Outside the room, the corridors were lined with persons craning their necks and moving quickly to secure a place inside when an opening occurred.

Every party to the contest looked their part. Robert was stooped, seemingly frightened. Mary Lou was erect and proud, immaculately and fashionably dressed with a stylish choker supporting her dazzling good looks. The defendant farm boys uncomfortably corsetted in suits and ties, faces scrubbed and hair uncharacteristically parted, looked on with varying degrees of attention. Some appeared to be bored while others exhibited great interest which even bordered on delight. None looked worried or apprehensive.

On opposite sides of the divide were brothers — Robert and John Hollowell. Occasionally their eyes would meet and quickly retreat. In the throng of onlookers sitting nearby, the third son Arch, a loving and devoted brother to them both, suffered inside. Desperately he had strained to hold the family together. He had attempted to mediate between the two and, once the lawsuit was filed, had approached Robert beseeching him to drop the matter. "If you keep on," he had warned, "you will draw your brothers to the halter." But now he undoubtedly knew as he watched the drama of that courtroom unfold that the family cause was hopelessly lost.

In retrospect, Miller made two tactical mistakes in the trial. First, he allowed Mary Lou to override his better judgment in the acceptance of one juror to hear the case. His name was W.A. Gresham from the town of Kuttawa which was situated right in the middle of the Night Rider territory. During questioning by Miller as to his qualifications to sit as a venireman, Gresham appeared nervous and ill at ease, seeming to be uncomfortable with the voir dire. But Mary Lou insisted that he be retained as one of the twelve determining their fate. She and Robert had

known the man for many years and considered him a loyal friend
of the family. Mary Lou had many strong points. Sizing people up
and selecting jurors were not among them.

The other error that the plantiff's attorney may have made was
in allowing Mary Lou to testify in Robert's behalf. Granted, it was
a onesided case at best as far as the number of witnesses was
concerned, with the Hollowells matched up against all of the
defendants and their deponents. To Miller's surprise, when Judge
Walter Evans ruled that Mary Lou would be allowed to testify for
Robert giving a different interpretation to the Kentucky rule, it
would have taken a cyclone striking the courthouse full side to
keep the impetuous beauty off the stand.

But it opened the door.

After she had dramatically testified, along with Price and Robert, of the brutal assault upon them that spring night about a year
past, the attorneys for the defendants began their attack upon her
character. Had she not taken the stand, the rules of evidence
would probably have precluded their doing so.

Numerous so called "disinterested witnesses" joined the defendants in testifying that, to their knowledge, the reputation of Mary
Lou Hollowell within the community where she lived was bad. Not
only did they muster this counter offensive intending to discredit
the veracity of the female plantiff but also to cast her in the dim
light of being a base woman, possibly deserving the good licking
she received.

In addition, each of the defendants denied their involvement in
the raid and produced an alibi witness to account for their whereabouts during those fateful hours. From this common approach
came the sarcastic labeling of the Night Rider defense as "a mask,
a lash, and an alibi."

Miller submitted that such amazing recall by the Night Riders
account of their exact locations during those wee morning hours
was made even more ludicrous by those witnesses — hard working
farmers by day — who were awake at that time to account for
their whereabouts. It was unbelievable, also, the persuasive advocate would point out in argument, that so many of these people
had lived near the Hollowell farm and had not heard the noise of
the perpetrators. It was as if a small army of marauders had simply
dropped out of the sky to inflict bloody havoc and then just as
quickly had been swallowed up and erased from the face of the
earth.

In their rebuttal evidence, the plantiffs were able to provide four incredibly courageous witnesses who attested to Mary Lou Hollowell's character as being excellent.

One very crucial question of fact which arose during the trial has never been settled completely. The defendants presented evidence that Robert Hollowell had made numerous statements after the raid that he was not able to identify any of the culprits because they were all masked. Yet at the trial, both Robert and Mary Lou swore that they were without disguise.

After days of testimony, the question was finally in the hands of the jurors as they filed out of the courtroom to begin their deliberation.

As the hours wore on, the buoyant spirits and confident faces of the defendants began to fade. A sense of foreboding fell upon the waiting horde of participants and their sympathizers.

The jury finally returned to the courtroom, hopelessly hung. A mistrial was declared by Judge Evans and a second trial set for May 11.

Of the two men who had stood firmly and adamantly on the side of the Night Rider defendants, one was W.A. Gresham, the "loyal friend" of the Hollowell family.

The near miss of the plantiffs was no doubt rather unsettling to the militant members. Fortunately for them, the dreadful anticipation of the second trial would not be hanging over their heads for long since it was less than a month away.

But those few weeks between the first Hollowell trial and the second would be determining.

It must never be forgotten that the greater number of Night Rider membership was composed of substantial, even highly respected, citizens of society. The high regard afforded men like David Amoss, Guy Dunning and Sam Cash was typical of the guerilla organization. John Kelly, for instance, a highly thought of trial lawyer of the day, was reportedly an active member in the Hopkinsville raid.

Yet, like all organizations, the Silent Brigade also had its weak links. There were within its ranks the borderline citizens who from their youth had been on the shady side of life. Some were downright moral degenerates who saw in the Night Rider mask and torch a chance to exhibit the lawlessness that had always been simmering just beneath the irregular surface of their character.

It was upon these vulnerable and unsteady spirits that the opponents of the Night Riders sought to prey, looking for the key to unlock the seemingly invincible vault of secrecy which encased the militant fraternity.

They found such a man in Sanford Hall of Lyon County.

On May 5, 1908, Governor Willson, who had been correspond-
ing regularly with John Miller concerning the Hollowell trial,
forwarded to the attorney a most illuminating and, at the time,
most electrifying letter which he had received from a waivering
member of the "mask, lash, and alibi" club.

While some of the declarations made within that epistle were
highly suspect, it definitely contained many elements of truth.

What was more important, this lengthy and informative letter
signed merely by a cryptic "S.R." divulged for the first time that
there were people within the fraternity who were willing to
"switch" to the other side and tell all. Adequate protection from
retribution was, of course, a condition to such a dangerous turna-
bout.

The letter to the Governor related a peck of information.

First, it stated that Denny Smith, Commonwealth Attorney of
Calloway, Christian, Lyon and Trigg counties, was a Night Rider
— assisting them in the courts at every opportunity.

Secondly, W.A. Gresham of Lyon County and one of the two to
hang the jury in the "Paducah case" was a Night Rider also. He
had taken the oath only ten days before the Hollowell trial and had
sworn to hang the jury until "hell freezes over."

Thirdly, Steve Choate, the hired hand of Mary Lou who allegedly, along with Ned Pettit, had scraped the plant beds of her
neighbors, was also a member of the Silent Brigade. His whole
involvement, according to the letter, had been a ploy to have Mary
Lou indicted and the lodges of the Night Rider organization had
collected money for the upkeep of Choate's family while he was in
prison.

And there was much more in this revealing chronicle which
corroborated what the general public pretty well knew but was
unable to prove, especially as to the strong and aggressive leadership of David Amoss.

When all of the pieces are put together now in retrospect, it
appears to be little doubt that "S.R." was in fact Sanford Hall.

On May 11, the second trying of the "Paducah case" began.
This time the highly skillful and perceptive John Miller did not
make the same mistakes. A jury of twelve men was obtained who
resided well out of range of the Black Patch influence, including
six members from Louisville. The rest were from that general area
and central Kentucky.

To the astonishment and disappointment of the attorneys for the defendants, Miller did not put Mary Lou on the stand. This blocked them completely from introducing any evidence as to her character. Only frail, harmless, and highly believable Robert and tender aged Price told of the harrowing experience they had been through.

And then came the testimonial stick of dynamite.

As their only other witness, they called Sanford Hall.

Although Hall the Night Rider had not been directly involved in the violent visit to the Hollowell home, he pried open the creaking door as he had done in his letter to Governor Willson, allowing the world to look for the first time into the inner workings of the Night Riders. He also proceeded, as indicated by his letter, to tell of admissions made to him by some of the defendants concerning their involvement in the assault upon Robert and Mary Lou.

To top it off and to throw salt into the festering wounds of the defendants and their supporters who listened incredulously in the packed courtroom, he related how the "Paducah case" had induced lodge meetings to map out trial strategy, including fabricated alibis.

Hall's testimony closed out the Hollowells' case with dramatic flare.

Compared to the plaintiffs', quick moving and convincing case, the defendants' tedious repetition of their alibi defense seemed stale and rehearsed.

Judge Evans in his final charge to the jury commented, as federal judges were allowed to do, upon the evidence. Relating to the exacting recollection of the defendants and their witnesses as to the night in question, he said, "Such memory is remarkable and beyond my powers."

Within just a very few minutes of those words it was all over. The jury deliberated briefly and then returned an award to Robert Hollowell for thirty-five thousand dollars in damages against the Night Rider defendants.

The stunned courtroom quietly and peacefully exited. The soldiers stepped in to protect the victorious plaintiffs and the now despised traitor, Sanford Hall.

The defendants' attorneys boasted loudly that the case would be appealed and won; but, after the passion of the courtroom fight had cooled somewhat, the legal minds concluded they had better strike a deal. So they went to the plaintiffs with hat in hand seeking some type of settlement.

Numerous influential people of Caldwell County, having no direct interest in the lawsuit, approached Miller beseeching him not to pursue the cases of Mary Lou and Price. The community was already torn asunder, they opined, and could not withstand any more. Also Robert Hollowell was still not recovered emotionally from the injury sustained in the Night Rider outrage and had been badly shaken by the terrible ordeal and tension of the trial. He did not relish a lengthy appeal or protractive litigation that was bound to occur over the collection of what was considered in those days a monumental award. With all pressures coming to bear, a settlement was finally reached whereby the Hollowells were awarded fifteen thousand dollars. The defendants appeal was not pursued, and the two actions still not litigated, those of Mary Lou and Price, were dismissed.

The Paducah verdict reverberated throughout the dark tobacco region like the crackling echo of a long rifle shot. Reaction was mixed but profound. After a short while, the shocks within the camps of the Association and Night Rider partisans turned to bitter acceptance. Lodge meetings were once again urgently called.

This time their somber proceedings pondered ways to assist their ill-stricken brethren in paying off the judgment. Every member was once again assessed and the defendants themselves had to come up with the difference. It was told with a bit of sardonic humor that one Night Rider defendant meeting another on the streets of Princeton would note that they had not seen each other in some time and, asking where his friend had been keeping himself, would be answered, "Worming tobacco for Mary Lou."

On the very day that the second Hollowell trial had begun on May 11, another judicial proceeding was taking place on the banks of the Cumberland River at Eddyville about thirty miles southeast of Paducah.

While Sanford Hall awaited nervously his time to testify in federal court, he was, perhaps unknown to him, the center of attention of the Lyon County Grand Jury. On that day, he was indicted on four different counts of bootlegging. Hall's trial was set for the following term.

Later that summer of 1908, on August 27, the Commonwealth of Kentucky, through its Night Rider Commonwealth Attorney Denny Smith, announced it was ready for the prosecution of Sanford Hall.

Hall did not show.

Smith moved that his bond be forfeited and a bench warrant be forthwith issued for this fugitive traitor. Up to the bench stepped the unrelenting Night Rider foe, County attorney Walter Krone, who had first taken Sanford Hall's earthshaking Night Rider confession back on May 1. From within his vest pocket, Krone pulled a legal document and smugly presented it to the Circuit Judge, J.T. Hanberry.

It was a pardon for Sanford Hall from the Governor of Kentucky.

The judge promptly dismissed the indictments and the County Attorney serenely walked away under the bewildered stare of the Commonwealth Attorney.

Now it all falls into place.

The weak link, through which the veil of secrecy had been torn asunder, had been discovered and exploited.

Sanford Hall was a man of questionable marital habits and had at last come under the gun of the law. Krone had him dead on four indictments of bootlegging. And there was talk of forgery and hog theft charges. Hall, the rattled and quaking accused, was ready to do some horse trading.

His letter to Governor Willson bearing his soul and asking for protection was dated April 30, 1908. His conference with Krone and the confession came on May 1 — the very next day. No doubt Krone was quick to advise John Miller of the developments. Together the deal was struck — his turning state's evidence against the Night Riders in exchange for a pardon to the Lyon County charges.

It was becoming convincingly clear that David Amoss and his high ranking confidants were not the only ones in this battle of wits who were abundantly blessed with gray matter.

Chapter Twelve

The fears of General Amoss were well founded.

For those Night Riders who might have been superstitious or, as was quite common in those days, placed special meaning and portentous messages in the signs of nature, the Hollowell verdict in 1908 followed fast upon a very unusual event. Just a few days prior to that second trial in the merry month of May, a freakish and surprising snowfall had blanketed west Kentucky.

By the time the next snow fell the following winter, the handwriting would be on the wall.

A quiver of hope now mingled with the warm anticipation of revenge which moved through the hearts and souls of Night Rider victims following the Hollowell victory.

Beaten little Henry Bennett, now living in Jeffersonville, Indiana, recouped some of his abrasive manner and filed suit against David Amoss and one hundred and fifty-five other men in Federal District Court. His request was for one hundred thousand dollars. There was a partial settlement and the suit was dismissed after his death on October 20, 1910.

C.W. Rucker of Eddyville became a plaintiff from the hillbilly sanctuary of Metropolis, Illinois, and sued Amoss and three hundred and twenty-seven others, including citizens of both Kentucky and Tennessee, for his beating on the night of the Eddyville raid. This case was settled as to some defendants, but not Amoss. At his trial on November 22, 1910, Rucker was awarded ten thousand dollars against the Night Rider leader and one other man. Interestingly enough, Amoss did not even attend that trial. He was in bed suffering from a back injury he had sustained when he fell off the roof of the Wallonia Christian Church where he had been donating his labors a few days before.

There were numerous other civil suits placing a ruinous financial drain upon the Association and the Silent Brigade. Mary Lou Hollowell had conjured the demon out of the Aladdin lamp and no amount of fuming, storming, lashing or night riding could get it back in again.

The defendants of Lyon County alone were saddled with a nine thousand dollar lump sum obligation from all the suits. Needless to say, this was substantial and prohibitive in those days.

An interesting and significant footnote of the Lyon County judgments has survived down through the years. It illustrates the elevated stature and esteem that many of the hooded outlaws held within their communities. The taxpayers of that county, through its fiscal court, contributed the grand sum of two thousand dollars towards satisfying the civil judgments.

Some of the lawsuits filed in the aftermath of the Paducah case would wallow around in the courts for many years afterwards.

With the unleashing of the civil judgments, a sense of paranoia swept through the Black Patch. Farmers began looking for ways to hide their meager assets from potential plaintiffs. Lawyers paid visits to the many Night Rider lodges advising the errant members of the Silent Brigade on how this could be done. Needless to say, the legal business in many smutty windowed law offices throughout the area picked up in those uncertain days. One of the most common steps taken was to deed the farm over to the wife. Thus, there was a rush to vest the lady of the house with holdings that had been passed down through male hands for years.

If the lawsuit of the Hollowells and the active litigation that followed did not put a stop to the night riding, it, at the very least, broke the spirit of this militant group.

Other factors also began to fall upon the rural communities of Kentucky and Tennessee in those months of 1908 and 1909 which bore equal weight with those civil suits.

The troops of Doc Amoss no longer enjoyed the universal popularity they had had in their earlier days. As the tobacco prices reached their previous levels, many active members lost interest and the general public no longer saw the armed and hooded horsemen as romantic Robin Hoods.

Excessive violence by the Night Riders and other outlaw groups tarnished the erstwhile noble purposes of the Night Riders. With reports of atrocities at Birmingham, Hickman and elsewhere, it was becoming harder and harder to tell the good guys from the bad. Decent upstanding people who had supported and many times were active members of the Silent Brigade were now becoming convinced, that the movement had gotten out of hand.

And there were other more profound changes afoot.

The farmers' energetic friend A.O. Stanley had scored in Congress.

In 1908, the newly elected President William Howard Taft called the United States Congress into special session to take up the tariff issue. Stanley saw this as an opportunity to catch the agrarian mood of both the country and the legislative body to attempt to repeal the onerous tobacco tax. He was able to get enough Republican assistance to successfully pass the abolition of the six cents tax on tobacco natural leaf which the farmer had been collared with since 1872. This great legislative stroke which would become known as the "Stanley Bill" lowered the price of tobacco products at the store to the consumer thus increasing the demand and bolstering the market for the farmer. The ardor running in the Night Rider veins, based upon the suspicion and even fear that the elevated prices of tobacco were temporary and superficial, slowly ebbed away. It is a solid, irrefutable fact of human nature that the hunter is no longer welcome in the city once the wolves have been beaten back from the gates.

And, significantly, if the Night Riders were having their troubles in court, so was James B. Duke.

On November 7, 1908, after many months of proof taking and high-powered legal volleying, the New York Court of Appeals handed down the momentous ruling which declared that the American Tobacco Company had a virtual monopoly on the domestic and foreign tobacco trade and was in violation of the federal Sherman Anti-Trust Law. The court, through a rambling and somewhat apologetic opinion, directed that the Duke conglomerate be busted asunder.

To no one's surprise, the battery of Duke lawyers quickly appealed the decision to the United States Supreme Court and the historic edict was stayed until the process could be finished. While the final outcome of this continuous and crucial litigation would be in doubt for almost three more years, the handwriting seemed to be on the wall for the Duke monopoly as well.

In any event, the news was greeted warmly by the Association and its members. The optimism about the long range economic forecast helped to offset somewhat the smarting pocketbooks left in the wake of the "Paducah case."

If persons and organizations do not change with the times, the times will change them. This was happening to the Night Riders during those cloudy months of 1909 and 1910. The clandestine army had been put together by an ingenious leader to fight an enemy it could no longer find.

At the beginning of 1910, dark tobacco prices for the farmer in the Black Patch were up as high as twelve cents a pound — far cry from the penurious rate of three cents at the time of that first Guthrie meeting in 1904. The vilified and cursed Duke Trust which had been responsible for the drastically low income of the farmers was, by 1909, under the gun itself by the federal prosecution and was quickly running out of time. The oppressive tobacco tax which the Association and its members had railed against so long and hard was now repealed and no more. In short, all the causes of the turbulent years of discord in the tobacco district were gone.

And there is no doubt about it. The state militia, as unpopular as they may have been at first, had proven to be quite effective against the Night Rider groups. In patrolling the backroads and the cities in those last weeks of 1908, they interceded unsuspecting Black Patch riders on numerous occasions, disarmed them and sent them on their way. Lodges of the Silent Brigade could no longer meet in country schoolhouses without being interrupted by uniformed soldiers. In short, the military presence successfully intimidated and discouraged the Night Riders. By Christmas of 1908, their success had been so marked that most of the militia had been withdrawn from the towns within the tobacco areas with the exception of a small group in Eddyville that remained until March 20, 1909.

The Dark Fired Tobacco District Planters' Protection Association and the Night Riders were no longer jostling at windmills. They were jostling at the wind.

So the great clock of time began to toll the final hour of the Night Rider movement.

Their outings and activities became sporadic, infrequent and almost totally localized in 1909. Some of the lodges continued to meet. But unlike the electrically charged gatherings of the past where grand designs were laid, they now wrangled ignominiously among themselves over the inglorious task of raising cash to pay off money judgments against their brethren. Understandably, interest was waning and to even put together a productive meeting was an arduous chore for the local captain. If you want to kill an organization, levy assessments. Once again, it's not the principle, it's the money.

The leadership of the Silent Brigade watched as its once active membership of over ten thousand men now came sputtering to a halt. They were, in short, stacking arms and striking tents.

The parent Association itself was also going through stormy times. Adversity and oppression seem to solidify. Euphoria of success soon fades into fragmentation. During the years of its formation, the Planters' Protection Association had steadily increased the volume of tobacco it handled and was flush with success. However, in 1908, dissension arose among its own members concerning the manner in which their tobacco was being sold. The difference is explained best by James O. Nall in his book, **The Tobacco Night Rider:**

> Many members wanted to sell their tobacco on the loose leaf auction floors which was prohibited by the Association's rules. The Association could control the crop and prices only by pricing and selling by sample and requests for other methods were rejected although petitions were signed by members and delivered directly to Mr. Ewing.

Ewing then fell under extreme criticism by members of his own Association and even a lawsuit was filed in McCracken County against the organization, attempting to throw it into receivership and requesting that all members be allowed to sell their tobacco to whomever they pleased.

It was a strange and ironic twist to the whole affair.

The crisis was finally abated when Ewing decided to let the dissatisfied members withdraw from the Association. By that time wounds had been opened and the leadership of the Association was broken apart in bitter resentment. Leaders like Charles Fort, Joel Fort, Guy Dunning and others were labeled as traitors by Ewing. Dunning was fired from his position as inspector for the Association.

Over six thousand members withdrew from the Association due to this rift, and the previously revered Felix Ewing was now held in contempt by many members. After extensive wrangling, the Association finally survived but was battered and much weakened. Its headquarters was moved from Guthrie to Clarksville, Tennessee, in 1910, and the membership had dropped to fifteen thousand or less. The golden days of the noble order were gone.

With all of his brillance, daring and character, it seemed that the chink in the armor of David Amoss was his inability to retreat gracefully or even to recognize when his troops had won. Posterity would no doubt have regarded the Black Patch War in a much clearer light had it been finished with a flourish and a clarion declaration of victory by the masked riders. Had the magnetic little commander — who of course never publicly admitted his leadership position with the Night Riders — called a general session of the many lodges and finally and decisively announced that the struggle had been won and that the war had been fought to a final and glorious conclusion, then their success would have been more clearly defined for history. Amoss should have eloquently appealed to them as did the regional tobacco publication, **THE BLACK PATCH JOURNAL.** In 1911, it published the call to disband: "Rider, turn the reigns of your horse's head homeward and there dwell in peace."

Although it was a secret fraternity, there were ways for their voices to be made public, even across the front pages of the local newspapers. In fact, many editors were either members themselves or strong supporters. The printed media could have easily done its job. At the urging of Amoss and others, the front pages could have placed a winning crescendo on the Night Rider battles by declaring to the general public a V-day for their movement.

There were no grand parades or celebrations. There was no clear cut end to the Black Patch War. It, like old soldiers, simply faded away.

To fully understand the existing chaos and confusion of those closing days, we must turn our attention to the leader of the Silent Brigade.

After the Hopkinsville raid in December of 1907, Amoss had been a constantly harassed and beleaguered man. The hillbillies and the state militia recognized the Cobb physician as the genius behind the highly trained and effective underground army. To neutralize or even eliminate him would be a bold stroke towards putting an end to the whole bothersome outfit.

Of course, until the prying loose of the Night Rider secrets from Sanford Hall in May of 1908, there was little blame with which Doc Amoss could be saddled. It was common knowledge that he was the Commanding General of the entire Black Patch of Night Riders. Proving it, however, was another matter.

So the opponents of Amoss and his militant followers set about the painstaking chore of dogging his tracks in an attempt to build a case against him.

It was known by all that the leader of the assault on Hopkinsville had been wounded, reportedly in the head. State Detective

Warden Hale was disbursed by the militia to stake out the house of Amoss in Cobb and observe if the country doctor did, in fact, appear to have any wounds.

It was a tedious and time consuming chore for Hale. After the raid, Amoss had almost vanished from sight, hiding himself in his home by day and going out to make his calls in the darkness of night.

Finally, the patience and diligence of the detective paid off.

One afternoon he observed, from his hiding place in the woods next to the Amoss home, a lone rider approach the back of the house and furtively move up to the back door and knock. In a few moments, Amoss emerged from the doorway and went with the rider to the barn.

The doctor wore a bandage around his head.

The visitor and the injured leader went into the barn, and Hale sneaked around to the clapboard siding to see if he could hear their conversation. Their voices were lowered but the hidden eavesdropper could still make out the meaning of their meeting. The visitor warned Amoss that a group of hillbillies two hundred strong were planning to attack his home that night and take him out and hang him. At first, Amoss was incredulous but, at the insistence of the messenger, he was finally persuaded. Silently, Amoss began whittling vigorously at a sliver of wood. Then he advised the newcomer to go out and solicit a gathering of the nearest lodges of the Silent Brigade to his defense.

Later that night, the State Detective observed about five hundred Night Riders bearing arms of all descriptions coming together under the leadership of David Amoss and moving to Tandy's Crossroads, an interesection of country roads not far from Cobb. There they waited throughout the night for the hillbillies to arrive. If they were looking for a fight, they were sorely disappointed because the morning sun finally broke over the hills without any sign of trouble.

These types of reports continued to badger Amoss. Death threats from throughout the Black Patch became common. One day the little commander received word from Princeton that a member of the militia had boarded the train for Cobb under direction to kill the Night Rider leader on sight. It was also reported that the militia was about to move in and arrest him. This rumor gained substance when a detachment of soldiers was moved into Cobb and pitched their encampment upon the railroad right-of-way not far from the Amoss home.

Dr. Amoss decided it was time to make himself scarce.

In the early months of 1908, Amoss became a leader in exile. No one knows exactly when he left, but it soon became apparent to the stalking soldiers that he was no longer residing at his home in Cobb. Where he was during the greater part of 1908 and the first few months of 1909 is still, to a large degree, a mystery. Reportedly, when the soldiers were about to pounce upon him, he went to Arkansas for a while. This, however, is in no way substantiated.

One thing is certain.

Amoss led the Night Rider activity throughout that last year and directed his troops while apparently hidden out at the homes of various friends throughout the area.

Process servers pursuant to the civil suits searched for him in vain. Later he gave a limited account of his whereabouts. According to Amoss, he had left home about the 1st of June, 1908, because he feared for his life. Only one time — for two weeks in October — did he return home. That apparently was brought about by the serious illness and death of his mother-in-law.

Families took him in and sheltered him from the searching soldiers who by and large weren't too enthusiastic about arresting the folk hero anyway. Many of the soldiers who were from other parts of the state would not even recognize him on sight. This is evidenced by the reported incident that the physician himself was questioned by a militia man while riding on a train one day if he was acquainted with Dr. David Amoss.

As it generally occurred with cases of the hunted, the middle aged country doctor, popular enough as he was, gained deeper empathy of the people because of his underdog role.

Adding to the growing mystique of his clandestine wanderings, Doc Amoss reportedly remained faithful to his professional obligations, unexpectedly checking in with his "confined" maternity patients, assuring them that he was close by and would be there when "it was time."

Several inflated and inaccurate accounts have passed down through the years concerning those months of rambling by David Amoss.

One has it that he lived in a cave that was made livable by friends and neighbors. This may have been true in part. There were probably several temporary hiding places such as attics, cellars, lofts and even caves where Amoss could hide when the homes in which he might be staying were being paid a soldierly visit. But with his bountiful supply of aides and relatives and the lukewarm pursuit of the militia, it is unlikely that he resided permanently and literally underground. Besides, his wife Carrie accompanied him on his wanderings most of the time and the dark soil environs of cavernous living would not have been easily endured by her.

Perhaps the most popular account is a story that Amoss moved through the military pickets periodically in Cobb to and from his home for visits with his family while disguised as a woman. This is an interesting and captivating report but probably untrue.

Such distortions are entirely unnecessary. The truth is impressive enough. For this man — a leader of a band of masked raiders responsible for the destruction of thousands of dollars worth of property and the infliction of terror and pain upon hundreds of law abiding citizens — was loved, guarded, harbored and protected within his own community among the finest people of that day. And, for all of his unlawful pursuits, Amoss still maintained an almost routine affection for the sick and afflicted.

Finally, by April 1909, with quiet settling in on the western front and the troops gone home, Dr. Amoss surfaced.

Returning to his white bungalow in Cobb, he promptly went about his business as if nothing had ever happened. Of course, he was busy fending off and settling most of the lawsuits filed against him. There were at least six such actions then pending with more to come.

Amoss had always been a man of modest means. Medicine offered a living but not affluence in those days — at least not in Cobb. Numerous times during his career he had borrowed money to help his family along. By no means was he able to come up with the kind of cash required by judicial settlements and verdicts against him. The fact that he survived with his assets intact is proof positive that the Association and its members somehow came to his financial aid.

While fifty-three year old Doc Amoss was trying to put his life back on track, a plan was being concocted in nearby Christian County to do him in.

There were many in Hopkinsville, including mayor-editor Charles Meacham, who were still simmering over the humiliation placed upon them by the Silent Brigade of Dr. Amoss and Guy Dunning. The dramatic, devastating Hopkinsville raid still rankled.

Of all the civil lawsuits bouncing around the area, "Hoptown" could not lay claim to any until February, 1911. That month the widow of John C. Latham sued Dr. Amoss and two hundred and fifty-six other citizens of Christian, Lyon, Caldwell, Trigg and Calloway Counties for fifty thousand dollars in damages stemming from the destruction of the Latham warehouse during the Hopkinsville raid. The case was assigned to the Federal District Court in Owensboro and was destined to drag along sluggishly for years.

It galled the Hopkinsville victims of the Night Rider transgressions that the commander of the Silent Brigade was now springing about freely on his professional rounds in Cobb, seemingly undeterred by all the litigation swarming around him. If the Association was picking up the tab for the financial penalties imposed upon Amoss, there was one ticket that even Felix Ewing could not fix — the penitentiary.

In March of 1910, Dr. Amoss, Guy Dunning, B. Malone, John Robinson and Irving Glass were all indicted by the Christian County Grand Jury for "willfully and feloniously confederating, conspiring and banding together for the purpose of molesting, injuring and destroying property of other persons" in the early morning hours of December 7, 1907, and more especially the destruction of the Latham factory.

The penalty carried from one to five years in the penitentiary and a fine of up to ten thousand dollars.

One must wonder now, as no doubt many did then, how Night Rider friend, Commonwealth Attorney Denny Smith, could let such a draconian measure be taken against his friends. Of course, theoretically, grand juries are independent investigating judicial bodies capable of thinking and acting for themselves — the prosecutor be damned. Granted, there were such things as "runaway" grand juries — those that totally disregarded all advice and cajoling of the state's attorney.

But as a practical matter, indictments which are born from grand jury deliberation without aid and encouragement from the prosecutor were, and are, about as rare as the offspring of a monk.

More closely to the truth as to the reason for the change in the attitude of Smith was the politics of the day. At the time of the indictments, the romance and popularity of the hooded tobacco riders had waned considerably. Over two years had passed and times were good. Life had returned to normal and people had forgotten the misery, destitution, and want which had afflicted the tobacco farmer only a few short years before and which had given impetus to the uprising.

A few prevailing facts are worth noting if we are searching for a motive in the Denny Smith turnaround.

The political powers in Christian County wanted the scalp of David Amoss. And 1911, just one year away, was an election year. Denny Smith was considering a statewide race of his own.

In any case, the dramatic criminal charge that fell upon the heads of the Night Rider leaders that spring of 1910 was a rumbling roar of thunder at a time when most had assumed the sky was clear of clouds.

If indictment #88 in the Christian Circuit Court had seemed to be a parting shot in the dark by the state against the Night Riders, there was no denying that the prosecution had done its job well.

Sanford Hall, the undoing ex-Night Rider of the Hollowell case, would again be on hand to point the accusing finger — this time at Doc Amoss. For the first time, however, he would be joined by other turncoats, namely: Milton Oliver, Arthur Cooper, Carl Cooper, and Tennessean Robert Warfield. All the men had to be closely guarded once it became known that they would turn evidence against their former confederates. Hall, of course, had been a marked man since he first dealt out with the other side in the "Paducah case" of the Hollowells.

Oliver, of the Lamasco community in Lyon County, had at first believed that he did not need protection.

He would soon change his mind.

After testifying before the Christian County Grand Jury against Amoss and company in March of 1910, he returned home to his farm. At first Oliver went about his business without any trouble. Then one evening in May, as he was standing in his yard peering up into the sky in an attempt to spot Halley's Comet, he was startled by a noise just a few feet away. Then, from the adjoining field, he was shot down by the blast of a shotgun. Oliver survived this serious wound, but immediately thereafter a detachment of from five to eighteen militia men were assigned to his farm in order to provide round-the-clock protection. The armed soldiers accompanied Oliver everywhere he went, including stringing along with him as he worked his tobacco patch.

As the trial date approached, the opposing legal teams began to gather. Attorneys for the prosecution were composed of Smith, County Attorney John Duffy, and a distinguished trial lawyer from Bowling Green, Kentucky, James Sims, who came into the case as a special prosecutor. Apparently there was still some lingering distrust of the loyalties of Denny Smith, and Sims had been employed to keep the case on track.

Interestingly enough, just a few weeks prior to the trial date Commonwealth Attorney Denny Smith publicly announced his candidacy for Attorney General of the state of Kentucky.

The group of five defendants was represented by a like number of lawyers with Charles H. Bush, a highly respected and adept barrister from Hopkinsville as chief counsel for Amoss.

Both sides announced boldly to the press that they had "left no stones unturned" and were eager to proceed.

As if to set the tone for the contest and perhaps to even persuade public opinion, Governor Willson boldly proclaimed on March 4, 1911, just two days before the trial was to begin, his renewed offer of a five hundred dollar reward for information leading to the arrest and conviction of any Night Rider involved in the Hopkinsville raid.

On that first weekend of March in 1911, the town of Hopkinsville, Kentucky, began to take on an aura of excitement and anticipation. Lawyers and witnesses began to arrive by train. Sanford Hall and Milton Oliver arrived on Saturday night accompanied by details of militia men who were wearing civilian clothing.

Tall and impressive, Guy Dunning had spent most of the previous week in the city and Amoss, like two of his accusers, arrived on Saturday.

All of the players were preparing for the great drama which was about to unfold. Like stage stars, most of them were easily recognized and identified by the gawking citizens of the town. Amoss, of course, was the center of attention.

The Christian County courthouse was the same then as it is today — a stately and substantial edifice of justice sitting high upon a hill facing Main Street. If the old structure could have talked, it would have been the only witness needed. On the night in question, the command position for most of the evening had been set up on this high ground with the re-grouping point only a couple of blocks down the hill at Ninth Street.

Talk it couldn't.

But it would provide the forum for those who could.

In those early months of 1911, Buck Duke was also in court. But his case was a long way from the Christian Circuit.

The United States Supreme Court would determine in only a matter of weeks whether the gigantic American Tobacco Company — as the farmers of Kentucky and Tennessee knew it — would long endure.

If the spring snowfall of 1908 had portended bad things for the farmers in the Hollowell suit, James Duke may have received a bad omen also when his lawyers argued the monopoly case before the highest court in the land. His attorney became intolerably ill during his oration to this august body and had to be replaced during the middle of his argument by a less prepared barrister.

But the resilient tobacco tycoon did not allow the legal ordeal in which he was enveloped to keep him from enjoying the good life. This North Carolina Tarheel was a tough soul.

He and his lovely Nanaline were now living in their new luxuriant mansion on the corner of Fifth Avenue and 78th Street in New York City. This magnificent marble structure, designed by one of the leading architects of the day, exemplified the immense wealth of the tobacco tycoon.

The home possessed the refined and elegant taste of Nanaline. It was graced with furniture of French design and valuable works of art hung from its high walls. Meticulously sculptured statuettes flanked the grand staircase in the foyer just inside the doorway.

Buck and Mrs. Duke enjoyed the splendor of this Manhattan home but were by no means confined to it. The couple shuffled between there and the Duke estate in New Jersey while summering a great deal at their scenic oceanside abode in Newport, Rhode Island. And, of course, the affluent pair also traveled to Europe on occasion in grand style. Buck even took one of his prized automobiles with him overseas.

He never stayed in one place very long. His restless spirit and business demands carried him back and forth to North Carolina as well as to other parts of the country in his luxurious train car.

Married life had changed James B. Duke a great deal. In his younger, aggressive years he had possessed an aversion to frivolous spending or any form of leisure — unless his work could be deemed recreational in some form. His parsimony had even extended to walking great distances along the streets of New York in pursuing his business plans so as to save the fare of public transportation. "Walk while you're young," he would say, "so that you can ride when you're old." Not only had he been austere with his own habits but also strongly discouraged social activities among his employees.

But the soft touch of Nanaline Holt had changed all of that to a large degree.

He readily, even eagerly, grew into a lavish lifestyle.

He loved expensive cars and purchased a fleet of them. Unable to discard his lifelong hankering for Southern cooking, he had transported to his Northern homes such culinary delights as freshly ground cornmeal, chickens, hams and even turnips from North Carolina.

His private railroad car was never without an abundant supply of champagne and cigars. In fact, Buck himself was never to be found without his smoke. So enthralled was he by this form of tobacco use that he sent his friend, J.P. Morgan, two thousand of the best Havana cigars that money could buy.

Duke also began to dress better in his happier married days. Nanaline was not one to hold back on the purchase of extraordinarily expensive clothes and precious stones for herself. Evidently, this indulgence rubbed off on Buck.

His exquisite Georgia better half also lent a touch of class to this previously unpolished entrepreneur. They rented a box at the Metropolitan Opera House for alternate Thursday evenings during the opera season. Whether the Durham native actually shared his wife's love for such rich culture is not known. But he began to move in such circles with ease and confidence. He prided himself upon his exorbitant taste in automobiles, collecting them like toys. At one time he possessed as many as four Rolls Royces in his own personal fleet.

If anyone begrudged the tremendous wealth of James Duke, no one could doubt that he knew how to enjoy it.

Brother Ben also shared the work and the fruits of their labor with Buck. But Ben was less intense, more easy going.

Never in the best of health, this older brother still managed to live an industrious life. He and his wife Sarah had two children and much of his leisure time was devoted to them and his subsequent grandchildren.

By 1911, Ben Duke and wife had become neighbors with his brother Buck on Fifth Avenue in New York — a neighborhood which, at that time, was known as "Millionaires Row."

But Buck and Ben were never close — at least as brothers go. In their joint business ventures, they worked together in complete harmony and mutual respect, but there was very little affection exhibited between the two.

Benjamin Duke was also the unofficial philanthropist of the Duke empire. After his father's death he became even more active in disbursing large sums of money to numerous types of charitable causes — hospitals, schools, orphanages, and churches. He was constantly gouging Buck for donations and, to the younger brother's credit, he usually obliged.

Benjamin, like his father, was also a devout Methodist and spent a great deal of time and money in church related activities. Buck again was quite different.

Although raised by the pious Wash Duke, he must have spent his time in the Sunday morning services conjuring up business schemes. By his own admission late in life, he didn't even know the difference between a Methodist and a Presbyterian.

But his indifference to the fine points of organized religion did not diminish his admiration for men who excelled in any field — including the ministry.

No lesser than Billy Sunday, the great evangelist, received the personal attention of the tobacco king. This, be reminded, was at a time when the evils of smoke were lumped in by the fundamentalists of the day with the sins of alcohol. The meeting of these two master spirits occurred in Charlotte where Duke went to hear Sunday preach. So impressed was he with the peppery proselytizer that he invited him home for a visit.

During their conversation, Duke inquired of Sunday why he became so animated and theatrical in his sermons. The gist of the preacher's answer was that if he didn't put on a show no one would come to hear his sermons.

This reply amused Duke, no doubt appreciating the keen business angle of this approach.

So enamored was Duke by the pulpit master that he gave him a thousand dollars before his leaving.

Billy Sunday's religious crusades exposed him to a varied company and carried him into the far flung nooks and crannies of America.

He was especially effective throughout the rural South. It was a familiar tool of Sunday's oratorical skills to constantly refer dramatically and with great stirring affect in his sermons to his lost and evil grandmother, relating that she had now passed on to eternal torment and damnation.

On one of Sunday's barn storming tours, he reportedly lighted in west Kentucky where he preached at a large tent revival. The fiery persuader was launched into one of his famous deliveries, gyrating around the platform, sweat pouring down his face, his voice literally screaming out the message of fear and redemption. His terrified and overwhelmed congregation was completely under his spell.

Suddenly, a note was passed from the back of the gathering to a rural doctor sitting in the crowd. It was an emergency call from a seriously ill patient.

Dr. David Amoss arose from his seat and headed for the exit. Sunday, apparently incensed that anyone would have the nerve to get up and abruptly leave one of his sermons, pointed to the retreating physician and exhorted, "There goes a man to hell right there!"

Visibly annoyed at the pious condemnation by this formidable evangelist, but not in the least intimidated, Amoss turned in the sawdust trail, "That's right." he chortled, "Do you want me to take a message to your grandmother?" He then left the meeting amidst the roaring laughter of what had been a most damned and quivering congregation as Sunday tried without success to recapture the forlorn and desperate mood.

As far as is known, Billy Sunday was the only man that both James B. Duke and David Amoss personally encountered.

Most assuredly, Sunday remembered both for very different reasons.

Chapter Thirteen

Early on the morning of March 6, 1911, the Christian County Circuit Courtroom began to fill. By nine o'clock that morning, when Judge J.T. Hanberry gaveled the proceedings to order, the slanting floor of the spectator section was completely packed all the way up to the railing. People lined the walls and shouldered in for standing space.

The air was highly charged as if all concerned were aware that this was the ninth inning of an era and that, within the days to follow, David Amoss, the Night Rider leader, would either strike out for the penitentiary or head safely home once and for all.

All eyes turned to the back entrance of the courtroom as David Amoss, surrounded by lawyers and followed by his wife Carrie and daughter Harvey, moved into the courtroom and took his seat at the counsel table. Dunning and the others joined him. The country physician would remain the object of attention from that moment on.

Now fifty-five years of age, he was stoutly, if stockily, built with a ruddy complexion and steel blue eyes. His abundant head of hair was now almost completely gray and his sandy mustache was full and well trimmed. General Amoss was immaculately dressed in a dark gray suit with turned down collar and what was called in that day, a "four in hand tie." His movements were smooth and calm and his demeanor completely composed and self-assured. If he was tired and battered by the hectic ordeals of the past seven years, he did not show it. A writer for the Socialist paper, THE APPEAL TO REASON, described the Cobb physician graphically when he said, "There is nothing frivolous or superficial about Dr. Amoss. Always he is cool and self-possessed and has said nothing between hell and heaven could scare or intimidate him. In the Black Patch he was regarded as the Eugene Debs of the Farmers Union movement."

The initial order of business in the proceedings that first morning was a motion to sever the defendants for separate trials.

The motion was sustained and the Commonwealth went into conference to determine which to elect for the first trial. Not a soul in the courtroom was surprised when David Amoss was chosen as the defendant to be tested.

For the remainder of the day, the litigants went about the tedious job of picking a jury. Although it had been more than three years since the Night Rider raid, details were still fresh in the memories of the local people. Many prospective jurors had opinions as to the guilt or innocence of the defendant. Lawyers for both sides carefully questioned those who were called. Some were Night Rider supporters and had to be ferreted out by the searching and probing questions of the prosecutor, Denny Smith. Others acidly opposed the members of the Brigade. Typically, it was proven by the defendant's attorney through the submission of an affidavit that one of the candidates for the jury had said publicly, "Every damn Night Rider ought to be killed."

On and on the process continued until weary Judge Hanberry called a halt for the day. So many of the names had been exhausted that the sheriff was ordered to resupply the jury wheel for the following morning.

Finally, well into the afternoon of the second day, a jury of twelve men was accepted by both sides to determine the fate of David Amoss.

The defense had to be happy with the selection. The jury was composed of eleven farmers and one carpenter.

The chosen twelve settled in along with the attentive spectators to hear the evidence. But first there was legal technical sparring as to whether the other defendants should be allowed to stay in the courtroom insomuch as they were not to be tried at that time and might well be called as witnesses. The prosecution wanted them out of the courtroom. Judge Hanberry wrestled over this issue and finally ruled that Dunning, Glass, Nichols, Malone and Robinson could all remain.

Every head in the large room bent forward and ears strained to catch every word as Commonwealth Attorney Smith presented his opening statement. As expected, he recapped the events of the night of December 6, and the early morning hours of December 7, 1907, to include the massive destruction and terrorizing assault upon the city of Hopkinsville by the Night Riders. Then he assured the twelve somber jurors within the box that the guilt of

David Amoss of Cobb, Kentucky, would be established beyond a reasonable doubt as to his being the leader of that raid and also the entire militant movement.

A low mumble passed through the crowd as Smith returned to his seat. The buzzing quickly subsided into a tomblike silence, however, as Charles H. Bush slowly rose to convey to the jury and the world for the first time what the defense of Dr. Amoss would be. It didn't take the gathering long to recognize an old familiar theme. If Smith in his opening statement had presented the lash and the torch, then Bush provided the alibi. He contended that his evidence would show that David Amoss was not even present in Hopkinsville on that ill fated evening but was at the bedside of sick patients in Cobb and Wallonia. Bush further assured the jury that he would prove the bad reputation of many of the prosecution witnesses while establishing that of Doc Amoss as being good.

Many a former Night Rider seated behind the rail shot knowing glances at each other as Bush concluded his offer of proof.

With both sides now having shown their cards, the second day of trial came to a close.

Much of the beginning testimony presented in the state's case was old stuff.

Through numerous witnesses who had observed or experienced violations by the Night Riders, the whole violent and unruly escapade was relived. Hardly a person in the courtroom, to include the pencil toting reporters from the large city papers of Louisville and Nashville, was not aware down to the very last detail of the nature of those depredations. The masked horsemen numbering in the hundreds, their reckless and incessant shooting up of the town and their precision type movements were all recounted as Doc Amoss looked on without the slightest hint of emotion.

W.T. Tandy testified as to the fiery destruction of his tobacco warehouse even though it was not part of the indictment. Evidence of the Latham warehouse going up in smoke was related by numerous witnesses including Fire Chief E.H. Hester who told of being restrained by the invaders from taking out the fire wagons.

Accounts were given by the local policemen captured by the raiders and by the telephone operators who were also abducted.

The story that was given by the prosecution's case was listened to attentively by the crowded gallery. Such information had been told and retold many times with regularity since that fateful night.

Out of all the eyewitnesses to the crime, not one single person could positively identify David Amoss as even being present, let alone as being the leader of the onslaught.

A couple of testifiers came close.

Tom Greer, a citizen observer of the uproar, related that it appeared to him that the group was following the direction and orders of a man riding in a buggy. Another said he saw two men unmasked in a buggy, one a rather heavy man with a brown mustache and the other a slender fellow. For those members of the Silent Brigade who had been there and who were now listening to the trial, it was easy to recognize right away that the winesses had seen Amoss and Guy Dunning in the command buggy that night.

Lindsay Mitchell became the most dramatic witness for the state in the early going. He told in graphic detail of the frightening visit made to his home by the hooded outlaws and of the beating he received. For the craning necks of all to see, Mitchell then pulled away his shirt and pointed to the scars from his wounds.

A gathering sense of tension and excitement ran through the audience as the trial ground through its third day. For the word was out that the Commonwealth was nearing the presentation of its key witnesses — the Night Rider traitors — who would testify under heavy security to the guilt of their erstwhile leader.

Midway through the afternoon, as one witness was excused from the box and left the courtroom, the prosecutors huddled at their table in a serious discussion. Then a low roar broke out in the courtroom as Denny Smith stood up and announced, "The Commonwealth calls its next witness, Milton Oliver."

The reaction by the crowd subsided as quickly as it arose when the fifty year old Lyon Countian, now sporting a mustache for partial disguise, moved into the courtroom with plain clothes guardsmen at his side. Slowly he took the oath and settled in the witness stand. The stillness which had attended previous testimony now seemed like a clatter compared to the breathless quiet which settled in over the throng.

Slowly and with the twangy drawl of a true western Kentuckian, Oliver laid it all out.

He had joined the Silent Brigade in 1906 and had known David Amoss for about five years, having met him at the Cedar Grove Schoolhouse during a Night Rider lodge meeting. Amoss, according to the witness, had visited various lodges throughout the Black Patch periodically, teaching his followers the tricks of the trade.

Smith then led the ex-Night Rider up to the Hopkinsville raid.

His testimony told of the gathering places on the night in question — naming the main points of congregation of Wallonia,

Nabb Schoolhouse and Cedar Grove.

The group of marauders, some three to four hundred men strong, moved toward Hopkinsville on horseback and in assorted horse drawn vehicles. Guy Dunning had taken part in the whipping of Lindsay Mitchell while Amoss had directed the shooting, burning and general havoc from his vantage point in a buggy.

Then the wary witness related a relatively insignificant but fascinating piece of information. Throughout the testimony of citizens who had been in town that night and who had observed the invading horde, there was constant mention of a signal which was continually being given by the leader of the group. Some said it sounded like a whistle while others called it a horn.

According to Oliver, it was neither.

Amoss had the amazing ability of producing a loud shrill sound by blowing into the barrel of his pistol — bottle style. This was the device used to signal his troops.

In spite of strong opposition by the defense team, Oliver then proceeded to relate matters about David Amoss which had transpired after the Hopkinsville raid. Amoss had met within the Night Rider lodges just prior to the Hollowell trial in Paducah and had suggested different methods to be used in defending that action. One tactic was simply to swear falsely. Oliver now testified that he had done just that as a defendant in that case when he took the stand and denied any connection with the secret fraternity of hooded horsemen.

Finally, the wounded informer told of the signals and gestures passed among members of the militant farmers which made it almost an impossibility for them to be successfully prosecuted in state court. One signal was that the sympathizing attorney would look at a juror and put one hand to his collar. The Night Rider juror would reply by making the same motion.

At this juncture, no doubt, minds were racing at the prosecuting table to recollect if any of the twelve poker faced men now listening to the evidence had shown any signs of an itching collar.

At five o'clock that afternoon on March 8, 1911, Oliver was finally excused from the witness stand and court was adjourned amidst the exciting rumblings of the crowd.

He had held up well.

The first witness the following morning was a familiar, if unwelcome, face to the camp followers of the Night Riders.

Sanford Hall was a weary and battered man.

Since drawing blood in the Hollowell case, he had laid low,

presumably in either Paducah or Louisville, living upon the dole of state money. It was a miserable life.

A few weeks after his Hollowell testimony, Hall narrowly escaped being blasted into eternity by a homemade bomb sent to him in the mail. The package was received at the Paducah Post Office but, since he had no regular address and did not call for the box, it simply remained in the possession of the postmaster. It was then moved around in storage for a couple of months. Finally the package was opened by the postmaster and found to contain sticks of dynamite, several of which were attached to the underside of the lid and labeled "pull." Fortunately, the postmaster was smart enough not to follow the directions or both he and the post office building would have been blown to pieces.

Then in September of that same year, several hundred Night Riders made a voyage to Louisville by train to search out and destroy the despised turncoat. The ill willed farmers walked the streets and called upon the house where Hall supposedly lived. The fugitive, however, must have been living a charmed, if frightened, life for he managed to evade them.

Unable to lay their hands upon Hall, some frustrated Night Rider killed his brother, Herbert, instead. On the morning of June 7, 1908, while heading across the field to work near his home in Lamasco, Herbert Hall was murdered from ambush by a shotgun blast.

But Sanford Hall had survived as a circuit riding witness for the plaintiffs of Night Rider suits. He began his testimony now by stating that he had been absent from the Hopkinsville raid because of his sick father. But he gave the jury plenty of other testimonial nuggets to digest.

He had joined the Night Riders at a secret meeting in a Trigg County barn and had seen Dr. Amoss at Cedar Grove on numerous occasions. He especially remembered a meeting there after the successful Hopkinsville raid. Amoss had praised his men at that time by saying, "We did a pretty good job, boys. It was pretty well managed. Keep up the good work."

Then Sanford Hall told about the death of George Gray and the poignant efforts by the Night Rider members in collecting money for the funeral expenses of the dead boy.

Hall did not fare as well on cross examination as did Oliver. The defense lawyer Bush wove the responses of the witness into a pattern which gave the jury the distinct impression they were listening to a shady character. The prosecution objected strenuously when Hall was asked by the defense lawyer whether he had been indicted by the Lyon County Grand jury for forgery and hog stealing. Judge Hanberry upheld the objection and did not allow the witness to answer. But the seed had been planted in the minds of the jury and the credibility of Sanford Hall was limping badly when he left the witness stand.

The youngest of the turncoats was Arthur Cooper of Trigg County. His testimony was perhaps the most astounding of all. Convincingly, he proceeded to drop bombs of sensational evidence upon the ears of all who were present.

First — despite the fact that he had never actually taken the Night Rider oath — he had been a paid "recruiter" for their cause for about eight months, going out to other counties to set up lodges and assist them in their initial organization. He was paid for this service in cash by Guy Dunning.

He also related that plans had been made by the Night Riders to kill Judge A.J.G. Wells of Calloway County and that Clan McKool, the person wounded in the Hopkinsville getaway, was the trigger man appointed to do the job.

Cooper testified that he was under orders in the Hopkinsville attack to stay close to Amoss and Dunning to learn how the raid was directed. This valuable "on the job training" was supposed to be put to use in his leading a similar assault on Murray. A close vantage point put Cooper within ten feet of the defendant when he was shot. Before receiving the wound to his head, Amoss, along with Dunning, had personally directed the torching of the Latham warehouse. Then the Commander-in-Chief had turned the remainder of the raid over to Dunning with the instruction, "Take it and go ahead and make good work of it." At that time the leader was evacuated out of town to seek medical help.

The Trigg County farm boy then set the courtroom to buzzing by naming some prominent local lawyers as Night Riders and stated that John Kelly, lawyer for the co-defendants of Amoss, was even involved in the Hopkinsville raid.

It was brought out on cross examination that Cooper's brother, Axiom, had been killed by Night Riders at a Lamasco barbeque the previous July and that it was only after that tragedy that the witness had come forth to confess all. It was further drawn out by the prodding counselor Bush that John Kelly, now an accused accomplice to the crime at hand, had successfully defended the persons charged with killing Axiom Cooper. But the one time recruiter for the Night Riders persisted in denying that he had concocted any of his testimony because of his brother's death at the hands of Amoss' army.

By and large, Cooper, like Oliver before him, held up well on cross examination and left the stand with his credibility pretty much intact.

Cooper's nephew, Carl, followed him and corroborated substantially the testimony of his uncle. Carl Cooper admitted being in the Hopkinsville raid. In addition to describing the leading role of Dr. Amoss, he also pointed a finger at lawyers John Kelly and John King, both of Cadiz, as playing active parts in the attack. The witness further stated that he and his uncle only decided to turn state's evidence after Axiom Cooper had been gunned down at the Lamasco picnic. Furthermore, he admitted on cross examination that they had not made allegations against attorney John Kelly until he had become the defense lawyer for the slayers of his kinsman in the Lyon County trial.

Rounding out the number of confessed Night Rider witnesses was Robert Warfield of Clarksville, Tennessee.

Warfield was undoubtedly the least notorious of the prosecuting attesters and easily the most credible. Later on that same year, his testimony would help obtain the only verdict against the Night Riders in Tennessee when he testified in federal court in Nashville for Thomas Menees against twenty-five prominent men of Robertson and Montgomery Counties.

The Tennessean was the only one the jury could comfortably accept as not being a co-conspirator in the Hopkinsville affair. At the end of the trial, this would be of great legal significance.

Warfield, a mechanic and farmer, was of a respected family in Robertson County. A long string of character witnesses called by the prosecutor would subsequently prove this in spite of the feeble efforts by the defense to show otherwise.

Through his deliberate and solid professing, not only did he reveal incriminating evidence against Amoss as to the charge at hand but also gave the straining listeners their first real look at the unofficial and denied link between the Dark Tobacco Planters' Protection Association and the little General's Silent Brigade.

Night Rider meetings had at first been held in Guthrie, the birthplace of the Association, on each Saturday night with Amoss leading the organization and recognized as the Commander-in-Chief in both Kentucky and Tennessee.

This clandestine group was, to use Warfield's own phrase, "a private order, a wheel within a wheel, a branch of the Association." Both he and his late father who was an Association tobacco grader were Night Riders but had become members without knowing what they were really getting into. They had joined when summoned to Guthrie to what they had been told was an executive committee meeting of the Association, only to find that it was really a secret organizational meeting of the Silent Brigade. The Night Riders had a regular meeting place in the poolroom up over Buck's Grocery Store.

The Robertson Countian then went on to describe remarks made by Amoss a few months after the Hopkinsville raid at a Night Rider meeting in Guthrie. His former commanding officer, now sitting stoically to Warfield's right, had described the Hopkinsville raid and reported that one of his own men had accidentally shot him, requiring that his lieutenant, Guy Dunning, take charge while he sought medical attention. Amoss had expressed dissatisfaction with the work of some of his men on that night, complaining of their failure to obey orders in cutting the telephone cable. Amoss had further blamed the killing of Night Rider George Gray on the failure of his troops to obey his order to maintain a vigilant rear guard.

Amoss had concluded those incriminating remarks, the witness went on to say, by lightly referring to his efforts to conceal his own wound. On the very next day after the raid, the physician had visited his patients with a cap pulled down low on his head to cover the evidence and had explained to inquisitive friends that he had a "bad headache."

On cross examination, the able and experienced defense lawyer, Charles Bush, did what every good attorney does when confronted with a truthful and impressive witness. He asked very few questions and got him off the stand as fast as possible.

From there on out the case for the prosecution was made up of relatively inconsequential bits and pieces, filling in some of the missing details of the raid itself.

The Commonwealth's last evidence was a melancholy report by Jim Gray, the father of the Night Rider George Gray who was shot and killed in the blazing getaway. He sadly told how three masked men had brought the body of his son home and had simply dropped him off and left.

With that somber testimony, the state closed its case against David A. Amoss at 11:55 a.m. on March 10, 1911.

As in all sensational criminal trials, the announcement by the state that it had finished its proof was received by a low mumble in the courtroom. Tension relaxed momentarily with the realization that the prosecution had shown all that it had.

But quickly the aura of anticipation began to rise once again as all eyes moved to the defense side of the chamber. There the neatly dressed and composed family doctor conferred with his lawyers.

Attorneys for both sides were no doubt sizing up the case.

The Commonwealth had to feel confident.

Although some of their witnesses, such as Sanford Hall, may have faltered somewhat in either their testimony or demeanor, by and large their evidence had held up strongly. Even though the motives of the Night Rider traitors may have been brought under suspicion, there was a ring of truth which sounded through the rough edges. After all, why would the state go out of its way to fabricate a case against such a seemingly innocuous individual as the diminutive Doc Amoss of Cobb, Kentucky?

The overflowing crowd was hushed when David Amoss rose from his seat and moved to the witness stand. Raising his right hand, he took the oath to tell the truth.

In the perfect courtroom silence, he began his testimony, speaking plainly, slowly and directly to the jury.

Responding to the questions of advocate Bush, he truthfully related his age and occupation.

Then he proceeded to lie.

Never had he been a Night Rider, he said, and most certainly had never been present, let alone the leading participant, in the Hopkinsville raid of December, 1907. Instead, the doctor stated, he had been in Cobb on that evening taking care of sick people.

In essence, his testimony told of the following scenario.

Amoss ate a late supper at home on that crucial night in question and had no sooner finished when he was called to the home of his neighbor, W.H. White, whose wife was seriously ill with pneumonia. At about nine o'clock that evening he returned home and went to bed.

Between eleven and eleven-thirty, he was rousted from his sleep by the son of J.H. White, asking him to travel five miles away to Wallonia and attend to his sick sister. This he reportedly did, arriving at the White household at approximately one o'clock in the morning. There he was met by Dr. W.C. Haydon and the two country physicians conferred over the ailing child.

Amoss went on to state that he had remained in Wallonia for about an hour and arrived back at his home in Cobb around three o'clock.

As he crossed the railroad on his return trip into Cobb, he had passed in front of Sizemore Store where he saw Lee Sizemore on the upper porch of the building and Walter Wadlington standing on the ground. They called his attention to a light in the east which they were discussing and conjecturing that it must be a great fire in the city of Hopkinsville some twenty miles away. Amoss proceeded directly home where he immediately retired. His wife, daughter and a girlfriend of his daughter were sleeping in other rooms. His son, Harold, was away at college.

Amoss stated that the first time he had even heard about the raid was later that morning when the early train had brought the news to town.

The balance of his direct testimony, interrupted by the noon recess, was a series of denials of the allegations made by the main prosecution witness.

Never, said Amoss, had he even been in the Cedar Grove Schoolhouse nor had he told anyone that he was the General of the Night Riders. Point by point through the solicitation of his attorney, the defendant repudiated all of the incriminating part of the state's case. Some of the witnesses, he contended, such as the Coopers, he had never even laid eyes on before the trial.

Never had he met with anyone to discuss the Hopkinsville raid.

Never had he met with anyone to talk about the assassination of Judge Wells of Murray.

Never had he met with anyone at Guthrie to discuss Night Rider procedure.

Never had he made any attempt in any gathering to collect money for George Gray's family.

Never had he told anyone, to include a gathering at Nabb Schoolhouse, to swear to anything in the Paducah Hollowell suit in order to clear the defendants.

Never had he been involved in any way, form, or fashion in the Night Rider movement.

Finally, at about three o'clock on Friday afternoon — the fifth day of the trial — defense attorney Bush passed the witness.

Once again, the electric tenseness of the courtroom relaxed briefly into low whispering and talking as the attorney for the defendant took his seat and all eyes shifted to special prosecutor, James Sims, who began the cross examination.

For hours, concluding at ten-thirty the following morning, David Amoss was plied with questions covering every detail of his testimony. Under heavy grilling from the able Bowling Green lawyer, Amoss remained resolute and calm, taking his time to carefully think through every question before answering. Only a very few times did the witness show any signs of nervousness.

It was a classic courtroom matchup between the razor sharp mind of an accomplished and probing cross examiner and a brilliantly tough minded witness who undoubtedly was being anything but honest.

Two professionals, one of law and one of medicine, were meeting on the counselor's own turf and going at it — not in a ferocious or argumentative manner — but in an intellectual death grapple, slow, methodical and toe to toe.

The mixed gallery of rough hewn country folk and slickly polished big city reporters looked on with a common fascination.

These two great combatants, like two strong boxers, countered each other, exchanging blow for blow.

Sims established through the doctor's own admission, that on December 4, 1907, only two days before the Hopkinsville raid, Amoss had made a special trip to meet with the executive committee of the Association in Guthrie.

What was the purpose of that meeting?

It was never satisfactorily answered by the witness, though he made a feeble attempt to do so.

The definite impression left upon everybody in the courtroom was that the train ride to Guthrie by Amoss on the eve of the assault was for the purpose of providing the Association leadership with a secret briefing of the planned attack. It also corroborated the testimony of Robert Warfield concerning the close Night Rider connection to the Association.

But the defendant scorched the prodding prosecutor good when it appeared that Amoss was about to be inescapably trapped.

This line of questioning concerned his testimony of the two White visits the night before the raid. Sims came at this particular matter in a roundabout way by questioning Amoss about his actions of the morning following the Hopkinsville attack. The witness had stated that he had walked across the field once again to check on Mrs. White who was ill with pneumonia.

QUESTION: What time was it when you got home?

ANSWER: I suppose it was twenty minutes after ten or half past ten.

QUESTION: What did you do then?

ANSWER: To my best recollection, I posted up my books.

QUESTION: Do you keep books in which you record the visits

to your patients?

ANSWER: I keep a ledger.

Here Sims totally underestimated the savy of this formidable tale bearer. Suspecting that Amoss would not have the ledger with him and more especially the entries of that evening before, he proceeded to ask him about the whereabouts of the book. Amoss promptly responded by saying that he had the books with him there in court.

Fearing what evils might lurk within those bound records, Sims quickly left the subject.

But it was too late.

On re-direct examination later by his own attorney, Amoss would smartly exhibit to the jury the ledger book, including the entries on the White accounts with dates which fully substantiated his testimony. The attempts by Sims to insinuate that the entries had been added later fell flat.

In regard to the head wound Amoss allegedly received at Hopkinsville, the defendant emphatically denied ever being shot in his life. In fact, he insisted that he would be perfectly willing to submit to a physical examination by the all male jury — in private chambers, of course, he hastened to add. This brought on smiles and giggles from the crowd which was by now composed of a large number of women who found the virile and self-assured little country doctor sexually appealing in spite of his fifty-four years.

Back and forth they parried over the full scale of his testimony. Finally, at mid-morning on Saturday, the encounter came to a close as the Honorable James Sims advised the court that he had no further questions of David A. Amoss.

For all practical purposes, the trial was over when the defendant returned to his chair.

Either the jury believed him or they believed the string of turncoat witnesses — there really was no middle ground. As a reporter who was covering the trial for the **BOWLING GREEN MESSENGER** stated with no great stroke of genius, "It may be set down as a safe proposition that somebody has lied in the Amoss Night Rider trial down in Hopkinsville."

But the case groaned on into its second week with the defense calling witness after witness, mostly Night Riders, to either attack the character of the prosecution witnesses or vouch for the character or whereabouts of David Amoss on the night in question.

A lot of time was spent corroborating the physician's visit to the bedside of the pneumonia patient, Mrs. W.H. White, during that first week in December. Of course, much of this was simply a smoke screen, since no one doubted that the good Doc Amoss was ably doubling as a devoted country doctor as well as General of the Silent Brigade. It would have been an easy matter for him to have been attending to the critical patient at approximately the expressed times and still have been wearing his mask and leading the raid on Hopkinsville a few hours later.

Two defense witnesses, however, proved rather crucial.

One was Vernon White, the man who supposedly summoned Amoss to his father's house in Wallonia to attend to his sick sister. The other was his father, J.H. White. They both accounted for times that could not have squared with Amoss being guilty of the charge against him. For both men stated that Amoss was at their house between midnight and two o'clock. In other words, they were the two vital alibi witnesses who, if believed, would clear the popular physician.

The truth of the matter, however, was that both men were not with Dr. Amoss at the bedside of their ailing family member on the night of December 6, 1907. They were both with Amoss in Hopkinsville.

Many years later when told of what her husband and father-in-law had testified to in the Hopkinsville trial, the wife of Vernon White recoiled in astonishment: "Why there's not a bit of truth to that," she exclaimed. "They were all in Hopkinsville with Dr. Amoss."

Much time was spent by the defense in refuting the allegations made by Arthur and Carl Cooper that Attorney John Kelly was in the Hopkinsville fracas.

This caused the proceedings to bog down into a seemingly collateral matter as the scene shifted to a hunting camp in a remote area of Trigg County. That was where Kelly had supposedly been on the night of December 6, 1907, with a group of other men. Several members of that party, including the Negro cook, were called to support Kelly's alibi.

By the middle of the second week, the jury was worn down with the myriad of testimony pouring out from the witness stand, some of which was undoubtedly perceived as being unimportant. By and large, after the defendant's crucial testimony, the defense had spent the rest of its case bolstering the alibi theory and attacking the character and stories of the witnesses for the prosecution.

Their attempts to cast doubt upon the veracity of Robert Warfield backfired, however. For, on rebuttal, the state sent no less

than fourteen witnesses to the stand attesting to the good reputation of the Tennessean.

Finally, just before noon on Wednesday, March 15, all of the
evidence came to a sputtering and anticlimatic conclusion.

Most of the observers would agree that all of the scoring on both
sides had come in the early inning. It had been, as old timers like to
say, a swearing contest. Hidden under all the conflicting reports
was a tantalizing paradox which most likely went unnoticed at the
time. The state of Kentucky had to rely upon some questionable
characters to carry its case. But for the most part, they told the
truth.

The defense side unquestionably won the battle of reputations
and sent some of the most respected citizens of the community to
the stand. For the most part, they totally ignored their testimonial
oath and lied.

In retrospect, this aberration of values might appear puzzling.
Admirers of David Amoss who may have romanticized his role as
the gallant and brillant General of the Silent Brigade surely had to
strain in swallowing his seemingly total disregard for truth and his
trampling of the witness oath underfoot.

But closer study of that most unusual situation leaves David
Amoss and his perjured confederates in a much better light.

Their dilemma was staged in a time when what a person spoke
was basically the sum total of their character. Business, social, and
even political statements were taken at face value. An oath was
almost superfluous. A man's word was his bond — sworn or
unsworn. Contracts were kept, marriages preserved, and debts
paid solely because it was said that it would be so. But when oaths
were taken, they were total — unwavering and permanently fixed.
A swearing was a swearing, whether at the altar, on a witness
stand, or upon bended knees in some heavily guarded and dimly lit
country schoolhouse.

The Night Rider oath was simple, direct and without hesitation
or reservation:

> I furthermore promise and swear that I will never reveal
> or cause to be revealed by word or act to any person or
> persons any of the transactions of this order in the lodge-
> room or out of the lodgeroom unless, after due trial and
> examination I find them or him just and legally entitled to
> the same and not then unless I believe the business and
> welfare of the order will be benefited by such information
> given.

So it was an easy choice actually for these riders of the night to make. The deep and unrelenting loyalty and pledge to their secret fraternity made the courtroom promise a mere formality. It was, in effect, a hollow recitation devoid of any moral significance.

There were heavier and more spiritual considerations at work also. The commitment by David Amoss to the cause of the Silent Brigade had been induced by the misery, poverty, and hardship of his own people. He had attended them in sickness, closing forever the eyes of their dead, and shared with them the merriment of birth. It was for their cause that he had fought. To that order and its obligations, and no other, would he remain true — petty sacraments of the establishment notwithstanding.

One thing can be safely and perhaps sadly surmised. The defendants lost much less in their falsehoods than did the Night Rider turncoats in their declarations of truth.

Yet, regardless of how fallible the proof, the law abideth forever. And the learned judge, J.T. Hanberry, answered the bell and wasted no time in proceeding to charge the jury immediately after both sides had announced finished. "If you should believe from the evidence in this case beyond a reasonable doubt," he enunciated clearly to the twelve serious men in the box,

> "that in this county and before the finding of the indict-
> ment here, the defendant, Dr. D.A. Amoss, did willfully
> and feloniously conspire and confederate with his co-de-
> fendants, J.B. Malone, Guy Dunning, Newton Nichols,
> John Robinson, and Irving Glass ... for the purpose of
> molesting, injuring, or destroying property of other per-
> sons ... and pursuant to the common designs thereof, set
> fore to, burn, molest, injure and destroy the tobacco ware-
> houses of John C. Latham in the city of Hopkinsville ...
> you will find the defendant Dr. D.A. Amoss guilty as
> charged in the indictment and fix his punishment at con-
> finement in the state penitentiary for not less than one
> year nor more than fifteen years, in your discretion."

The court proceeded to instruct on five other points of law relative to the case, one of which was of particular significance. It dealt with what has been long called the "accomplice rule." Basically, it admonished the jury that if they believed that witnesses for the prosecution, namely Milton Oliver, Sanford Hall, Arthur Cooper and Carl Cooper, had conspired with the defendant, Dr.

D.A. Amoss, in carrying out the raid upon Hopkinsville and the destruction of the Latham warehouse, then Amoss could not be convicted unless their testimony was corroborated by other evidence in the case which tended to connect him with the crime charged. Here the practically unchallenged testimony of Robert Warfield as to his own observations of Amoss' involvement in the Night Rider movement, to include his admissions as to his participation in the Hopkinsville raid, took on monumental importance. It was all of the corroboration that was technically needed.

Each side was given six hours to sum up their case. And even though the prosecution of David Amoss was severed from the other defendants for purpose of trial, their counselors remained in the courtroom to assist Charles Bush. Though they did not actively participate, all of the lawyers of the defendants were permitted to divide up the time for the summation. The state's speeches were to be given by County Attorney John Duffy, James Sims, S.Y. Trimble, and Commonwealth Attorney, Denny Smith.

To good trial lawyers of the day, and these were all above average, closing argument was showtime. Throughout the long and tedious proceedings, they had been crafty technicians, marshalling evidence, routing strategy, and taking witnesses apart on cross examination. But summing up to the jury was the time for drama, eloquence, and emotional fervor. It was an art form and splendid entertainment. The skills of an advocate in the courtroom were appreciated only by the seasoned onlookers who had an understanding of some of the subtleties of law and procedure. But in those days, at least, everyone enjoyed a good speech.

In anticipation of these final hours of oration, the courtroom was packed to the limit, people filling the aisles and as many as three hundred people standing, filling every available space.

No less than the old Night Rider himself, Defense Attorney John Kelly led off as the first barrister to sum up the case.

He tore into the lawyers for the prosecution as pawns of the tobacco buyers engaged in an effort to break up the farmer's Association. He was sternly rebuked by Judge Hanberry. After awhile, he came back around to the same accusation at which time he was threatened with contempt.

The audience was getting a sparking good show.

Kelly went on to speak about fifty minutes, stating that he had been a life long friend of David Amoss and had been in his Sunday School class. His friend, Kelly said, had induced him to stand by his side in that hour of tribulation.

County Attorney John Duffy took the floor next and not only answered Kelly's accusations but made a scathing denunciation of the Night Riders. The eloquent prosecutor claimed that if night riding was to prevail, then it was time to "tear down churches and courthouses and homes."

He pled for the establishment of the supremacy of the law, "a law which would guarantee to every citizen the right to raise what he pleased, sell it how he pleased, and the protection of his home and perpetuation of peace and happiness."

It was indeed, by all accounts, a fine piece of speaking.

Back and forth the attorneys took their time flailing in the air, pointing to the defendant or to the prosecutors, lifting their voices high in a dramatic crescendo and then dropping to a bare whisper which even the jurors bent forward to hear.

To that large audience, including a group of college girls, it was theatrics at its best.

Into the evening hours they went and, in spite of the coldness of the late winter night, over two hundred people had to be turned away at the courthouse door for lack of space. James Sims, the special prosecutor, orated for an hour and a half, ridiculing the alibi defense by saying that it should be spelled "a-lied-by." He said that the alibi was the defense of criminals of high rank, of bank presidents, embezzlers, and "gallant and gentlemanly Night Riders." He made a final plea to render equal justice to all classes and conditions of people and for a conviction for the sake of the homes of the country and the maintenance of law and order.

THE HOPKINSVILLE NEW ERA reported the widespread interest in the goings on in the next day's newspaper by saying, "Prayer meetings, the moving picture show, and the opera house had rather slim attendance for most of the people who ventured out from home in the face of the winter wind which raged went to the courthouse to hear Judge James Sims of Bowling Green speak for the prosecution in the trial of Dr. Amoss."

The following day the speeches continued on into the afternoon when Charles Bush, attorney for Dr. Amoss, closed the arguments for the defense in a speech of over two hours duration. He pointed to the good character of David Amoss and contended that the state was only looking for a scapegoat for the embarrassment of the Hopkinsville attack and his client had been selected. Then he bore in on the law which stated that Dr. Amoss could not be convicted on the testimony of accomplices and claimed that the state had failed to properly support the stories of the confessed

Night Riders.

Lastly and to the enduring attention of the large gathering, Commonwealth Attorney Denny Smith gave the final argument of the trial. In it he made some rather peculiar statements. He alluded to Governor Willson as being a "crazy governor," but completely correct in his handling of the Black Patch lawlessness. And, as if to defend himself for past Night Rider sympathies, he declared that he had always done his "full duty without fear or favor."

At five o'clock on the evening of March 17, 1911, the case went to the jury.

The first order of business for the jury was supper. They immediately returned to their hotel where they had been sequestered for the past ten days and partook of their last meal together.

Then they returned to the jury room at the courthouse and began their deliberation.

As was customary for that time, the defendant, Dr. Amoss, was turned over and placed in the custody of the jailer and ordered to confinement. He was not placed in a cell, however, but was allowed to remain in the hallway to await the decision of the jury.

The judge and the lawyers left the courthouse, expecting a long wait. A sizable portion of the large crowd also dwindled away into the night. At approximately ten minutes past eight o'clock, only forty minutes after they had begun their deliberation, there was a loud and abrupt knocking from within on the jury room door.

The twelve men had a verdict.

Immediately word spread and the courtroom began to rapidly fill with spectators. Judge Hanberry was telephoned as to the development and in short time appeared back on the bench. The prosecuting team stood waiting by their counsel table as Dr. Amoss arrived in the courtroom joined by his wife and a number of relatives. John Kelly was the only one of the defense lawyers present. The jury filed into the jury box with all eyes present riveted upon them.

"Have you reached a verdict?" inquired Judge Hanberry.

"We have, your honor," responded foreman, John H. Williams, holding a slip of paper in his hands.

"You will pass the verdict to the bailiff," instructed the court, and in turn it was handed to the deputy clerk sitting at the bench with the judge.

Before the verdict was read, Judge Hanberry stationed a sheriff and his deputy in front of the bench and warned the audience that whatever the verdict was, there would be absolutely no demonstration of any kind tolerated within the courtroom. After that strong admonition by the court, the clerk was directed to read the verdict.

Time hung suspended within the paralyzing silence of the courtroom for what could have only been a split second but seemed much longer.

"We the jury find the defendant, Dr. D.A. Amoss not guilty as charged in the indictment. John H. Williams, one of the jurors."

It was over.

Taking Judge Hanberry as a man of his word, the crowd remained silent and still.

The judge then expressed appreciation to the jury for their time. Next he discharged them.

Kelly immediately jumped to his feet and thanked them for their verdict.

The elated defendant hastened over to the box and quietly shook hands gratefully with each juror. The crowd then began to shuffle out of the courtroom in a most orderly and almost reverent manner, obviously satisfied with the work of the jury.

Then, in the first display of emotion, the family, friends, and relatives of Doc Amoss converged upon him and tearfully embraced the country doctor.

As the crowd slowly emptied the old courthouse it buzzed with the excitement, and dispersed into wagons, carriages, and motor cars.

The prosecution witnesses had already begun their exodus out of town under guard. Back in the courtroom, now almost empty, the lawyers exchanged customary handshakes and reminisced briefly upon the sensational trial in which they had just participated. It wasn't long until they too were gone and the courtroom was left completely barren of human life. The lights were turned out and darkness engulfed the large cavernous chamber.

A strange and even tomblike quietness settled in on the empty chamber perched high above the clamor of downtown Hopkinsville.

Row upon row of empty seats, fought over and filled only hours before, were now deserted in the darkening gloom. Vacant tables and chairs within the railing were now torn asunder, frozen in their random positions by the ringing verdict which seemed even now to reverberate throughout the stillness.

The trample of feet, the occasional outburst of the crowd, and the heavy rapping of the gavel echoed still — like the lingering echoes of a lone rifle shot in the night.

And the ghostly images — the chiseled sternness of the judge, the stoic strength of a defendant, and the uneasy glances of frightened witnesses — all remained captured within the stillness of this large hall.

A courtroom is a hallowed place — the temple of justice. An empty and deserted courtroom is a graveyard of lost causes. Thousands of feet have trampled across these soiled floors on the way to prison, and worse. There are no winners. The losers lose and the others are only avenged for past wrongs. Each verdict carries vindication to some but remorse to others. Victors, at best, simply draw even.

So within this somber and time worn arena of human tragedy was laid to rest the Night Rider movement.

Chapter Fourteen

There was peace over the land.

But some lives would remain tormented throughout their earthly stay.

Sanford Hall and his fellow informers were marked and endangered men for the rest of their days. After his years of testifying against the Night Riders in numerous courts throughout Kentucky and Tennessee, Hall left the Black Patch for good. It is believed he made his permanent home in Louisville where he was able to gain anonymity within the bowels of the large city. Some reported that Hall received a large financial indemnity from the Night Rider enemies for his dangerous role.

Whatever happened to the rest of the so called traitors is unknown. They simply left the country and were eventually dismissed from the minds of the people.

Commonwealth Attorney Denny Smith apparently found that the Amoss acquittal substantially impaired his chances of election in his statewide race. Within a few weeks of the trial, he quietly withdrew from his bid for Attorney General. The following year in 1916, however, he successfully ran for re-election as Commonwealth Attorney and concluded an eighteen year tenure when he stepped down in 1922. He moved from Cadiz to Hopkinsville in 1927 where he set up his private law practice and, in 1929, he was elected to the state legislature as state representative. That was his last stop, however, along the political road. He passed away in 1934.

Lyon County Attorney Walter Krone has remained the most underrated and unsung hero of the Night Rider opponents. It may well have been Krone, more than any other person, whose ingenuity, shrewdness and courage led to the numerous courtroom setbacks for members of the Silent Brigade and their eventual demise. But Krone could not endure to the bitter end. By the time of the Amoss trial, he was residing in Metropolis, Illinois. On the night of March 29, 1908, a dozen Night Riders had called on him and warned him to dismiss the charges he had pending against them in that county or die. He chose to appease both his conscience and his physical well being by moving to Illinois. There he became quite prominent and was elected city judge. As far as it is known, that is where he died never returning to Kentucky.

Henry Bennett lived less than three years after his brutal beating. Heartened by the Hollowell success story, he filed suit against a string of Night Riders, including Amoss. But Bennett's lawyer made a bad mistake. He had given in to Bennett's urging and listed a prominent lawyer and former state senator as one of the defendants. The Night Riders then used a little legal maneuvering of their own. Bennett and his lawyer were promptly sued for malicious prosecution by the reputable accused. This suit was filed in the friendly confines of the state circuit court in Lyon County. All kinds of interesting and potentially dramatic developments around these two cases were cast about on stormy seas. They all went to the bottom, however, with Bennett's death on October 20, 1910. He had previously obtained a partial settlement of over six thousand dollars. Boone Bush was the only Night Rider successfully prosecuted and convicted criminally for the injury imparted upon Henry Bennett. He received a one year sentence in the penitentiary.

The criminal indictment against Guy Dunning and his co-defendants in Christian County was dismissed soon after the Amoss acquittal. Dunning continued as one of the leading farmers in the Wallonia area until his health failed and he had to sell his land. He moved to Princeton where he operated a furniture store until his death on May 23, 1925.

The "Moses of the Black Patch," Felix Ewing, in spite of his nervous condition, outlived the Dark Tobacco Planters' Protection Association by a good margin. Beginning in 1909, the loose leaf auction sales became the method of buying and prices continued to climb.

In May of 1911, the United States Supreme Court put the Duke Trust to rest once and for all by upholding the lower court decisions and directing that the giant tobacco conglomerate be dismantled. Buck Duke was able to artfully comply with the court directive without any financial drain upon his own personal resources. Unlike Amoss, the North Carolina tycoon had mastered the art of retreat. In any regard, with the death of the strangling monopoly, the primary aim of the Association had been obtained and it had simply outlived its time. There were a few attempts to revive the old warhorse, more out of sentimentality than need, but it finally expired for good in 1915.

This well laid organization, despite the prophets of doom who had looked on since its beginning, had lasted over eleven years and was a victim only of its own success. **THE CADIZ RECORD** afforded it a final tribute: "It made the fight and won. It humbled the greatest trust in America. It protected every man in the Black Patch alike. It weathered the storms of eleven years, four of which in bitterness and meanness can never be equalled."

Tragically Felix Ewing would die a bankrupt man years later in Nashville, Tennessee.

Appropriately enough, the most fiery and resilient battler of them all outlived everybody. After their harrowing ordeal, Mary Lou Hollowell, along with Robert and Price, relocated in Livingston County near the small village of Pinckneyville where they bought a farm with their "Night Rider money."

Robert died in 1925 without ever returning to Caldwell County to see his elderly mother or other relatives. Mary Lou continued as both a beautiful and sturdy woman who, along with Price, remained on the farm until she grew quite old. Price married for a short time but was soon divorced. The brief marriage was no doubt sabotaged by his overbearing and intrusive mother.

When both Mary Lou and Price became too old to handle the farm, they moved a few miles north to Salem. People there still remember her well. She was a good cook, a friendly if blunt spoken neighbor, a meticulous housekeeper, well dressed and very attractive for such late years. Occasionally she would visit old friends in Princeton and attend funerals there. But the trips were infrequent and brief for she was still very distrustful of the people there.

Through her later years, Mary Lou remained spirited and unabashed. Once in Salem, she insisted on purchasing from a neighbor a narrow fifteen foot strip of property adjoining her boundary. The neighbor refused to sell. She then threatened to set a privy on her property line between her house and his attractive dwelling. He relented and sold her the land, becoming the last of a long string of manly victims.

On April 25, 1965, the effervescent spirit of Mary Lou Hollowell finally succumed and she died in a Paducah resthome at the age of ninety-five.

Her son, Price, lived only ten years after his mother's death. He is buried, along with Mary Lou and Robert, in the little Pinckney-ville cemetery.

Price died a man of substantial means, leaving a large endowment to the Livingston County Hospital. His last will and testament also bore a provision of some interest. He specifically directed that under no circumstances were any of his Hollowell kin to have any part of his estate. It was the final wishes of a searing and unforgettable memory etched into the mind of a horrified thirteen year old boy.

The street scene of tiny Cobb, Kentucky, in that spring of 1911 was picture book U.S.A.. Buggies and clattering wagons mingled with the coughing and sputtering of an occasional motor car. Lean farmers moved about the stores as trains whistled and steamed into the depot with daily regularity. Large picturesque farm houses set nestled upon well kept lawns underneath the huge sugar maples.

Even the country doctor was present, moving about his daily calls in his buggy, greeting ladies with the tip of his hat when he called for his mail at the post office.

Seemingly, everything had returned to normal for David Amoss.

By and large it was true. But there was still the occasional threat which caused him to keep his trusted pistol near his side at all times. Not long after the trial, his health began to slip. He suffered from chronic heartburn and a persistent cough developed in his throat. Mildly irritating at first, it gradually grew deeper and more painful as the months turned into years. Consultations with his good friend, Dr. W.C. Haydon in Wallonia, along with his own treatment, proved unsuccessful. Finally, he began to spit up blood.

Doggedly, the former commander of troops kept making his rounds, unwilling to give in to this tumor growing in his throat. On August 25, 1915, he inked in a payment to Kolb Brothers Drug Company of Paducah, Kentucky for his last order of pharmaceuticals and closed his old worn ledger book for good. Arrangements were made for a trip to Boston, Massachusetts, where the growth was removed. But Amoss responded poorly to the surgery and was transported to the Rockefeller Sanitarium in New York City where he continued to fade.

As the golden autumn days of October turned toward the drabness of winter, Doc Amoss lapsed into semi-consciousness.

Once again, he sat in the open summer night whittling away as he talked politics and tobacco with Guy Dunning.

He strolled along the narrow and spring infested lanes of Cobb, Kentucky, with his pretty fiancee, Carrie Lindsay. He cleared away nature's bandage from the miniature face of a squalling baby boy and placed the infant into the tanned and muscled arms of a beaming father.

Once again, the smell of burning tobacco pierced his nostrils and bright flames danced and flickered off his masked face.

He heard again from his corner spot on the winter hearth the heroic tales of Stonewall Jackson, Nathan Bedford Forrest, and Lee.

Then, on November 3, 1915, he died, just a few city blocks from the splendid home of James B. Duke.

When Amoss had left Cobb for the last time, he openly and without self pity proclaimed to his friends and relatives that he would be dead within seventy days. His last medical prognosis was right on the mark.

His body arrived back home in Cobb by train just as darkness was gathering on the evening of November 11. It was taken to his home where it remained until eleven o'clock the next morning.

The funeral was attended by hundreds of people from all walks of life and of every age. Craggy and calloused tobacco farmers clad in overalls and clean shirts walked past the open casket to extend their last farewells. Fathers held children up in their arms so that they might take a last memorable glance at the legendary figure.

Former soldiers of the Silent Brigade, including Guy Dunning, came in bountiful numbers to bid a final salute to their fallen leader.

The Hopkinsville newspaper — the headlines of which Amoss had often helped make — bantered the old Night Rider's demise. It spoke of the large gathering and grand funeral. In conclusion it reported, "The cortege from the church to the cemetery was unusually long."

The Wallonia Masonic Lodge acted as an escort of honor and conducted the traditional rites at the gravesite in the rural Millwood Cemetery. "Man judges not of man," the ritual goes, "it whose infinite and tender mercy passeth all compensation, whose goodness endureth forever, has called out brethren hence. Let him judge."

So mote it be.

Duke University is intimidating.

Flourishing like a shangrala amidst the dark pine woods of Durham, North Carolina, its gothic structures of stone arches, turrets, and tall dormers are reminiscent of ancient European centers of learning. Its inner campus connects through a complex maze of quads and beautifully kept lawns, punctuated by the majestic Duke Chapel — which is really not a chapel at all but a cathedral whose two hundred and ten foot high tower reaches into the sky and houses a fifty bell carillon at the top.

The history of this university is as impressive as its architecture.

It all began with Trinity College, born in Randolph County, North Carolina, in 1838, as a very strict Methodist school. The little college survived many setbacks along the way, including the devastating effects of the Civil War. It was gasping for its last breath when, in 1892, it was literally rescued, picked up and moved to an old abandoned race track in Durham by none other than Washington Duke, himself a devout Methodist. An initial gift of thousands of dollars by the tobacco benefactor shoved the college a long way down the road to recovery.

As the Duke family was becoming unfathomably rich by their growing tobacco monopoly, Trinity College became an obsession with father Wash and son Ben.

Buck could, in the early going at least, have cared less.

Trinity College was not the only charitable recipient of the good will of these two men. While Buck tended strictly to business, his father and brother devoted large amounts of money to all kinds of philanthropic causes in North Carolina, including orphans and struggling young ministers. Buck would relent occasionally to the solicitation of his brother Ben, but by and large he practiced his expressed belief that he could get better interest for his money than could God.

In any respect, Trinity College at Durham became more or less underwritten by the Duke family.

This brought no small amount of consternation among the fundamentalist supporters of the school. They deplored the use of tobacco as sinful. For their religious institution to be supported by money coming from the sale of this satanic weed was for many a hard matter to square with their spiritual convictions. Also, when the price of tobacco fell for the tobacco grower and as the Duke fortunes rose, many of the farmers saw the enormous grants given to Trinity College as spillover "blood money" soaked out of their impoverished hides.

But the school administration knew a good thing when they saw it and, while no doubt sensitive to the criticism of their fine Christian neighbors, they also recognized that religious schools do not always have the luxury of choosing their donors. Once again, it wasn't the principle, it was the money.

In 1902, Ben Duke, along with his father, finally persuaded his brother Buck to turn loose of some of his money to build a library on campus. But, over the years, it was Ben who gave not only his money but his valuable time and administrative talents to assist the resurgence of the Methodist guild.

In 1922, James B. Duke, himself then sixty-six years of age, began to do what most men of great wealth do as they grow older. He began to think of a monument to himself. He explained to a reporter for a Raleigh, North Carolina newspaper, "I want to leave something in the state that five hundred years from now people can look upon and say that 'Duke did that.' "

The president of Trinity College, William Preston Few, got wind of these sentiments and proceeded to court Buck Duke's immortal longings.

In December of 1924, less than a year before the time of his death, Buck Duke paid Trinity College six million dollars to change its name to Duke University. Included in the deal was an enormous indenture through which millions more of this money would be funneled for the construction of a new campus and a perpetual endowment to fund the continual existence of the university.

It was a monumental stroke. This "Duke Trust," unlike the one which had taken food from the mouths of lean and hungry dirt farmers some twenty years before, now provided huge sums of money for the construction and maintenance of Duke University as well as other charitable causes such as hospitals, orphanages and churches. The Duke Endowment, like all his other great schemes, was one of enormous impact. It placed him in a class with Rockefeller and Carnegie, other giant American philanthropists.

So the new Duke University was being built on an eight thousand acre tract a mile or so west of the old Trinity campus when James B. Duke died in New York on October 25, 1925.

The rise of Duke University to a place of academic preeminence in a relatively short time was due in large to the tremendous talents brought there by the endowment monies. From the very beginning, it laid a solid foundation, not only for its attractive buildings, but for its scholarly achievements as well.

The best minds of the day in law, medicine, the sciences, and administration were attracted not only by the high pay scales, but also by the excitement and challenge of constructing a completely new university from the ground up.

So it thrives today, having already attained in a relatively short time, the distinction of being one of the finest educational institutions in the world.

One must walk the campus today, not only to feel its intellectual heartbeat, but also to touch its history.

The cathedral, or chapel, extends far above the skyline of the other structures and draws the visitor to its doors. In front of its towering spires anchored solidly to a marble base is a large bronze statue of James B. Duke. He stands there with his left hand lifted slightly, holding the faithful cigar as he peers out with a certain intensity down the manicured mall of his domain. Some students can tell you in an articulate and informed manner the story of this man. Many others, to include those from upper classes who pass at his feet daily, do not even know who he was.

In other words, it's an all American campus.

Standing just inside the large heavy doors and looking west through the dim light of the vaulted nave, one might well be in Canterbury or Westminister. It is not unusual to find there — at the end of the middle aisle in front of the chancel — a casually dressed, string ensemble of student musicians rehearsing a piece from Haydn. The mellow sounds from the cello and violins add a touch of warmth to the cold, cavernous confines.

Moving down the left side past the supporting columns, one passes under the beautifully colored stained glass windows which depict biblical figures and stories. Nestled into a transept at the rear of this great structure is the smaller memorial chapel set off from the rest of the sanctuary. There against the massive stone of the south wall are the crypts of Washington, Ben and James B. Duke. End on end, the elaborately sculptured vaults dominate the chamber. Each base emulates a bier, on top of which is a slightly enlarged stone replica of the reposing resident sleeping inside, to include serenely folded hands resting in front.

It's intimidating.

One is drawn to the tomb of Buck Duke. Standing there before it under the canopy of the grand cathedral with winter night slowly falling against the chromatic windows, it is difficult not to reflect.

From this grand and slightly ostentatious resting place fit for royalty, the mind wanders to another more humble grave site many miles away.

Nearby, in the university library's archives, are stacks of manuscripts containing volumes of the yellowed accounts and letters of Buck Duke. In a regular and casual fashion, they reveal the collection and dispensation of incomprehensible millions. Thousands of dollars not to a single automobile, but to a fleet of the newest models. Precious stones, European tours, private and plush train cars, mansions, and a fairyland farm are just token items on a fantastic inventory of wealth.

But there are other books as well, only two in fact, again many miles away that tell a different story. They encompass the total income of a country doctor's medical career. In faded ink and on crumbling paper, they reflect accounts never paid and frantic calls in the dead of night which were rewarded by eggs, milk or ham. Life giving services — birthings and death bed struggles — some no more than the price of a taxi fare on Duke's Fifth Avenue. Other accounts are marked paid without explanations and some settled simply out of respect as long as four years after the doctor's death. A lifetime of professional giving totaling hardly enough income to cancel the postmortem debts.

Then the spirit begins to move.

Not merely the essence of Duke or Amoss, but the soul of America as well.

Two struggling men, born within a year of each other, in a republic posed upon the brink of disintegration. Both deeply influenced, though in different ways, by the Civil War which raged about them during their formative years.

Men of great strengths — within each is found a scintilla of this country's greatness.

Their lives represent both the irrepressible drive of those who accumulate wealth and the inner toughness of the very humble who keep it in line.

One possessed the ability to build, dominate, hoard, intimidate and, at last, to give. The other from a profession of giving learned how to lead, intimidate and even destroy.

Both men possessed of clashing ideals as to what this democracy was intended. Each being both right and wrong. Each man carried by his passion to the extreme, breaking the law in pursuing what he thought was the American dream.

The lives of these two men also give testimony to the resiliency and depth of a free country that can absorb the abuses and wealth and the violent reaction to it. In lesser lands, governments have collapsed with bloody revolutions and total anarchy. In America, it has all been just a step along the way.

Continuing the tour of the grounds, one leaves the memorial and moves out into the falling dusk. To the left of the cathedral across the main grassy quad is the entranceway to the Duke School of Medicine. The Davidson Building possesses a magnificent stone facade with a doorway positioned between two castle-like turrets which extend far above the roof line. It is medieval, even tranquil, in appearance.

But that is a great deception.

Once inside this fortress, one is thrust into a beehive of activity. Color coded and brightly lit hallways lead through the initial stages of the Duke University Medical Center. Plush administrative offices lead off from both sides of the corridors as busy people in white scurry hurriedly along their way.

Meandering through the maze, one moves through a large set of glass doors where the rambling complex of modern buildings are connected by sidewalks and paved alleys. This magnificent center of the healing arts is so vast and sprawling that a new rail transit system is in use. The trams sweep by packed with teachers and students.

It's intimidating.

The Mudd Research Building, situated in the middle of the medical college, is a modern structure of chrome, glass, and winding stairways. In this library one can find interesting information, not only about medicine but the history of Duke University as well. There is, for instance, tucked away on an upper floor shelf, the work of Dr. James F. Gifford, Jr. entitled, "The Evolution of a Medical center: A History of Medicine at Duke University." It makes for interesting and informative reading. It tells of the aggressive and high powered recruiting drive that went on by that first Duke University administration in packaging the best professionals possible for the new medical school.

In his waning days, James B. Duke had shown a keen interest for a viable and productive medical facility at his university. It was emphasized by a special bequest of six million dollars in his will to that end. The first dean of that college, Wilbert Cornell Davidson, went to work pursuing the best talents available for the most crucial appointment of Professor of Medicine.

After much searching, he found his man and the name leaps

from the pages of Gifford's chronicle.

The appointee was an infectious disease specialist with two degrees from Harvard University. Prior to being a professor at the prestigious John Hopkins University Medical School in Baltimore, he had served ten years at the Rockefeller Institute for Medical Research. There Davidson's choice had been a member of an elite research team which had discovered the cause of infantile paralysis.

At one time he had been a professor of medicine at Peiping Union Medical College in China and served as chairman of the Fairfifle County Medical advisory Board in Connecticut.

His impressive professional pedigree included being consultant to numerous prestigious hospitals in the northeast and holding an honorary degree of Doctor of Science from George Washington University in Washington, D.C..

The specialist was certified by the American Board of Internal Medicine and was a member of the Association of American Physicans, the American Society of Clinical Investigation, the American Clinical and Climatological Association, and the American Society of Experimental Pathology.

The credentials ran on and on.

John Hopkins University, disappointed at the prospect of losing such talent, nevertheless sent a ringing endorsement to his application for the new position at Duke.

When the selection of this leading specialist was officially announced, congratulations poured in to the fledgling Duke administration from the most renowned medical authorities of the day. It was, in short, recognized by all as a grand catch for the new school.

The new Professor of Medicine took hold immediately with a fervent zeal for the job. Davidson asked for his assistance in planning and equipping the new hospital. The former John Hopkins professor warmed to the idea of Durham possibly building a city infectious hospital next to Duke University where additional research and treatment of his speciality could be carried on. Fleshing out the medical school's professional staff, setting salaries, and settling on ways to spend the ample Duke monies became part of his job.

On July 19, 1930, just two days before the grand opening of what was destined to become one of the supreme medical facilities in the world, a group picture was taken of its elite first team. The combined administrative staffs of the schools of medicine, nursing and dietetics as well as that of the Duke Hospital posed upon the steps of the gothic entranceway to the new medical school. It was obviously a proud and dynamic assemblage of professionals.

Squinting in the sunshine at the extreme right on the second row was the prestigious first Professor of Medicine at Duke University. He appears slight and immaculately dressed.

He was a Kentuckian.

He was from a long family line of physicians.

He was Dr. Harold L. Amoss, son of the Night Rider leader.

Cavaet

The story of the Night Riders of Kentucky and Tennessee is a difficult one to tell. Secrecy shrouded the inner workings of their organization. Identities were highly protected. While the newspapers and magazines gave fairly good coverage of the events as they occurred, much about that era has come down by word of mouth. Consequently, more than one version of certain significant events has developed. In handling this, any writer must pick and choose as to which account is the most plausible. Hopefully, this narration of the Night Rider saga is as accurate as mortal efforts will allow.

Acknowledgments And Bibliography

PEOPLE: This book could not have been written without the assistance of many people.

First and foremost has been Professor William Turner of the University of Kentucky, Hopkinsville Community College, Hopkinsville Kentucky. Bill Turner, an outstanding teacher and a premier historian of western Kentucky, has spent a considerable amount of time in advising, gathering information, collecting and assembling valuable photographs for this publication, and generally serving as a close confidant and abettor to this effort. He deserves much more credit than time and space will allow in these pages.

Rick Gregory of Springfield, Tennessee, without question the most knowledgeable person alive today concerning the Night Rider activities of that state, has provided valuable information as well as a guided tour of the picturesque and historic Robertson County.

George Everette, Extension Specialist in tobacco for the Western Kentucky Research and Education Center, College of Agriculture, University of Kentucky, Princeton, Kentucky, deserves very special recognition. Mr. Everette, who knows as much about dark fired tobacco as anyone around, has taken his valuable time to be the agricultural consultant for this book as well as providing photographs and research material.

Bits and pieces of important information have been assimilated from numerous other people. The late David Porter, nephew of Dr. David Amoss, and his sister, Eloise Jacobs, have both lent a tremendous amount of valuable biographical material on the charismatic leader of the Night Riders.

A special recognition is paid to members of a group of Kentucky history students from the Black Patch area who through their research papers, tape recorded interviews, and other miscellaneous sources have compiled a great deal of the research for this book. They include: J.J. Badalich, Judy Banister, Bonnie B. Brown, Wanda DeName, Madge Holland, Dwight E. Lawrence, Judith T. McCalister, Bob McKnight, Brenda Gail Morse, J.L. Oldham, Maurean Owen, Ginger Powell, Sandra Peek Tabor, Charlene Towery, Teresa Lou Tyler, and Susan L. Wood.

Other persons who have contributed are as follows: Keith Heim, Librarian, Special Collections, Murray State University, Murray, Kentucky; Frances Utley, Eddyville, Kentucky; Sadie Belle Owen, Kuttawa, Kentucky; Odell Walker, Princeton, Kentucky; Mary Grace Pettit, Librarian, George Coon Library, Princeton, Kentucky; Gladys Carner, Princeton, Kentucky; Mrs. W.C. Haydon, Princeton, Kentucky; Sulia Henry, Hopkinsville, Kentucky; Ronnie Morris, Adams, Tennessee; David Whalin, Washington, D.C.; **THE HERALD LEDGER** and its owners, C.L. and Frances Baccus, Eddyville, Kentucky; Thomas W. Pruett, Princeton, Kentucky; Dr. Elizabeth Locke, The Duke Endowment, Charlotte, North Carolina; Mr. Thad Sparks, Duke University, Durham, North Carolina; Carolyn Sims and Kathy Stone, Lyon County Public Library, Eddyville, Kentucky; Gary Luhr, Editor of THE RURAL KENTUCKIAN, Louisville, Kentucky; Willard Moore, Hopkinsville, Kentucky; Dr. Ed Settle, Princeton, Kentucky; Dr. Charles Bussey, Western Kentucky State University, Bowling Green, Kentucky; Sam Steger, Princeton, Kentucky; Mrs. Ray Wilson, Cadiz, Kentucky; David Moore, Denver, Colorado; Mr. and Mrs. D.C. Trull, Charlotte, North Carolina; George Lee, Eddyville, Kentucky; Walt Apperson, Murray, Kentucky.

Many people assisted in this effort who asked to remain anonymous. To those valuable sources much appreciation is given.

PUBLICATIONS:
Without question, the greatest work done on the Night Rider era in Kentucky and Tennessee is the book of James O. Nall, **The Tobacco Night Riders of Kentucky and Tennessee; 1905-1909** by The Standard Press, Louisville, Kentucky (1939). Mr. Nall wrote the book at a time when there was little written material available and he blazed the trail which made the work of future historians much easier.

Other publications, either quoted or relied upon in this work, are as follows:

Kroll, Harry Harrison. **Riders in the Night.** Philadelphia: University of Pennsylvania Press, 1965.

Durden, Robert F. **The Dukes of Durham 1865-1929.** Durham: Duke University Press, 1975.

Miller, John G. **The Black Patch War.** Chapel Hill: University of North Carolina Press, 1936.

Jenkins, John Wilber. **James B. Duke — Master Builder.** New York: George H. Doran Company, 1927.

Gregory, Rick. "Robertson County and the Black Patch War, 1904-1909." **Tennessee Historical Quarterly.**

Winkler, John K. **Tobacco Tycoon: The Story of James Buchanan Duke.** New York: Random House, 1942.

Gifford, Jr., Dr. James F. **The Evolution of a Medical Center; A History of Medicine at Duke University to 1941.** Durham: Duke University Press, 1972.

Ramage, Thomas W. "Augusta Owsley Stanley — Early Twentieth century Democrat." Doctoral Dissertation, University of Kentucky, 1961.

Cash, W.J. "Buck Duke's University." **American Mercury,** September, 1933. **New York Times,** December 8, 1908.

Copeland, J.C. "Settlement of Court Case Ended Violence of the Night Riders." **Sun Democrat,** July 17, 1974.

The Princeton Record Herald. March 15, 1911.

Evening Post. October 4, 1910, Louisville, Kentucky.

Cincinnati Inquirer. December 6, 1908, Princeton, Kentucky.

The Charlotte Daily Observer. December 8, 1907, Charlotte, North Carolina.

Jennings, Dorothy and Kirby. **The Story of Calloway County, 1822-1976.** Murray, Kentucky: Murray Democrat Publishing Company, 1978.

Daily Kentucky New Era. November 11, 1915; November 12, 1915; April 11, 1911; March 4, 1911; March 6, 1911.

The Princeton Leader. November 12, 1906, Princeton, Kentucky.

Warren, Robert Penn. **Night Riders.** Random House Publishing Company, 1939.

Axton, W.F. **Tobacco in Kentucky.** Lexington, Kentucky: University Press of Kentucky, 1975.

The Daily Kentucky New Era. March 4-6, 7, 8, 9, 10, 1911, March 11, March 13-18, 1911, April 11, 1911. Hopkinsville, Kentucky.

Coppock, Paul R. "Tobacco Growers in the Smokey War Against the Trust." **The Commercial Appeal,** July 4, 1976.

Louisville Courier Journal. December 8, 1907, pp. 1, 3-4.

Beach, H.L. "The Great Tobacco War." **Saturday Evening Post,** August 3, 1907.

Manuscript Department of the University Archives, William R. Perkins Library, Duke University. Letters, documents.